Future of War
and
Future of Battlespace

Future of War
and
Future of Battlespace

Cpt. Prem Singh

Prashant Publishing House
DELHI - 110094 (INDIA)

PRASHANT PUBLISHING HOUSE
C-34, 28 Foota Road, Gali No. 3
West Karawal Nagar, Delhi-110094
Phone : 9810396373, 22963970

Future of War and Future of Battlespace

First Published : 2008

ISBN : 978-81-906344-1-0

PRINTED IN INDIA

Published by Mr. R. K. Jha M/s. Prashant Publishing House, Delhi and Printed at H.S. Offset Press, Delhi.

Preface

Around the world, nation-states are hard pressed to meet the needs and demands of their population, whether for development or security. Again, the glare of the Information Age is a factor. Outside of North Korea, regimes have little success at preventing their populations from learning about conditions in others parts of the world, as well as the excesses and shortcomings of their rulers. The time is past when misery was considered normal and natural by its victims. The result is global disillusionment and frustration. A wide range of nonstate organizations are stepping into this void, providing everything from coherent ideologies that explain the source of the frustration and plan to alleviate it to more concrete goods like security.

The information revolution and other factors like the expansion of the global market in arms serve to empower nonstate groups. In fact, one of the defining features of the information revolution is that the diffusion of knowledge and the multiple sources of information that it has brought tend to give small, versatile, and adaptive organizations a comparative advantage over large, ponderous, bureaucratic ones. This is most evident in the business world, but the same tendency holds for organizations that provide security and a sense of shared meaning and purpose-states are finding nonstate organizations to be more competitive and, in some cases, more threatening than ever before.

The present book tries to explore all these topics and problems in an easy and comprehensive manner, undersigned is confident enough that readers will enjoy and grasp the matter of the text. Your valuable suggestions are welcome.

—*Editor*

CONTENTS

Preface

1. Introduction 1

2. Recent Events and their Significance 28

3. Historical Perspectives on Future War 60

4. Military Theory and the Future of War 75

5. Future of Arms Control 134

6 . The Future of War and Peace 199

7. Pakistan's Nuclear Future 209

8. Post-Cold War Military Conflicts 223

Bibliography 314

Index 317

1
INTRODUCTION

Military organizations are, by their very nature, resistant to change. This is, in no small part, due to the fact that the cost of error is exceedingly high. Change, particularly change that may affect the relationships among organizations and between commanders and their subordinates, presents significant risks and generates considerable concern.

The explosion of information technologies has set in motion a virtual tidal wave of change that is in the process of profoundly affecting organizations and individuals in multiple dimensions. The military is no exception. At the very beginning of the information age, technological advances made it possible to provide more complete, more accurate, and more timely information to decision makers. As the costs of processing and communications power tumbled, it became cost-effective for organizations to adopt and utilize information technologies in more and more situations.

Military organizations have traditionally provided information to forces in three ways: commands, intelligence, and doctrine. Commands serve to define the specific task at hand. Intelligence provides information about the environment in which the task is to be carried out. Doctrine provides the "rules of the game" or standard operating procedures. Doctrine, unlike commands and intelligence, is not provided in real time, but serves to shape the culture and mind sets of the individuals involved. Thus, information has, until recently, been inseparable from commanders, command structures, and command systems. Each of these three ways of communicating information about what is expected of subordinate organizations and individuals has evolved over time to be mutually supportive of an overall command concept or approach matched to the nature of the conflict and the capabilities of the forces. The success of military operations depends to a large extent upon the ability to coordinate activities to achieve synchronized operations. Ensuring that individuals behave as intended or as expected in the face of uncertainty ("the fog of war") and under stress is a key to achieving coordinated activities. The selective dissemination of information has been used as a tool to define and shape the environment in which soldiers operate to ensure conforming behaviour.

The military is now on the road to becoming an information age organization. The transformation involved is fraught with both risks and opportunities because it will affect the nature of the information provided as well as the manner in which it is provided.

BACKGROUND AND PURPOSE

The C4I for the Warrior (C4IFTW) concept that currently guides the military's adoption of information technologies involves the provision of vastly increased access to information at all echelons. The full implications and consequences of achieving the stated goals and objectives of C4IFTW will, of course, not be clear for years to come. The analysis reported upon herein was initiated as a result of concerns expressed by the Chairman of the Joint Chiefs of Staff regarding the unintended consequences of providing too much access to information.

Implicit in the concerns being expressed by the Chairman and others throughout the Department of Defense (DoD) are uncertainties about the impact of separating information flows from the command structure and the effects of almost unlimited amounts of information upon decision making. Questions remain regarding exactly how much information should be provided to each echelon. For example, how does the pro- vision of information relate to a unit's mobility and lethality? The appropriate command concepts for an information-rich battlefield have, as yet, not been determined even at the most basic level. Concerns have been raised regarding the potential adverse effects of increased visibility into operations at all levels, including potential for information overload, second guessing, micro-management, stifling of initiatives, and distraction.

A separate but related set of concerns involves the manner in which our potential adversaries adopt and utilize these technologies and the capabilities that result. A final set of concerns involves our ability to protect information and information assets and to deal with failures of and degradations in the systems that provide information to decision makers, shooters, and others with crucial roles.

The purpose of this analysis is to identify a strategy for introducing and using information age technologies that accomplishes two things: first, the identification and avoidance of adverse unintended consequences associated with the introduction and utilization of information technologies; and second, the ability to recognize and capitalize on unexpected opportunities.

Given that our potential adversaries have access to virtually the same information technologies that we have, the margin for victory will be the degree to which we manage our transformation into the information age. Our ability to integrate a wide variety of systems into a true system of systems will depend not only upon our technical skills but also upon how well we adapt our doctrine, organizations, and culture to take advantage of the opportunities that technology affords.

OBSERVATIONS

In the search for a solution to the problem of adverse unintended consequences inherent in the adoption of information technologies, care must be taken to define an approach that is enabling rather than limiting. Some argue that the problems and risks associated with change can be addressed simply by avoiding significant changes. Others advocate that changes be introduced slowly and systematically, thoroughly testing proposed alterations until the probability of error is acceptably low. In many circum-stances, these very conservative approaches may be appropriate. In this case, they are not.

We are not in a position to take the apparently safe and comfortable road to the introduction of change. The environment in which we must operate is being transformed in a number of critical dimensions; consequently, business as usual (the default decision) carries with it significant adverse consequences of its own. Thus, "doing nothing" is neither conservative nor safe.

The low cost of obtaining information age technologies will help potential adversaries improve their military capabilities as they learn to leverage these technologies effectively. Thus, inaction will lead down a path that exposes us to new and improved adversary capabilities that we may not be able to counter effectively without change. In addition, in an era in which budgetary pressures will continue, a failure to take advantage of opportunities to improve cost effectiveness translates into less capability.

The pace of the advances in information technologies and their adoption make it imperative that our approach to change must be capable of keeping pace or it is doomed to failure from the start. Further, we must recognize that there are two kinds of risks associated with the selection of an approach to change. In addition to the widely recognized risks associated with adverse consequences, there are the risks associated with failure to recognize and capitalize on unexpected opportunities to do things more effectively and efficiently. Thus, risk management becomes the name of the game.

Since we cannot stop, slow down, or control the information explosion or totally prevent unintended consequences, we must design a strategy for introducing information technologies that a) identifies and anticipates negative repercussions and enables us to avoid those repercussions or minimize their impacts, b) recognizes and takes advantage of unexpected opportunities, and c) balances the risks associated with the failure to achieve these two objectives. This strategy must also be capable of facilitating change fast enough to keep pace with exogenous forces impacting technologies and technologies' adoption by potential adversaries. A technology insertion strategy designed to fully leverage information technologies requires alterations in our concepts of operation, doctrine, organizations, and force structure. Associated changes in logistics, education, and training will also be required. Without these changes, we will only obtain incremental improvements in effectiveness and efficiency while foreclosing opportunities for the order of magnitude improvements necessary to maintain the winning edge.

After analyzing the pros and cons of following the path specified by C4IFTW, it is clear that the potential benefits of information technology far outweigh the potential costs associated with unintended consequences. The specific concerns raised regarding the deleterious effects of excessive information access can be addressed.

However, a cautionary note needs to be struck. The above conclusion is predicated upon the adoption of an effective technology insertion strategy. Without the adoption of a comprehensive and systematic process for introducing and using these technologies, their positive potential will not be realized and the probability of adverse impacts will increase to unacceptable levels.

Business as usual is truly a prescription for disaster. It is recommended that leadership at all levels clearly articulate the need to move out smartly on the transformation to an information age military, a military that embraces rather than resists the changes permitting the full leverage of opportunities afforded by information age technologies. It is further recommended that appropriate investment strategies be developed and supported at the highest levels.

The technological insertion approach proposed here, based upon mission capability packages, stresses that all types of changes required to fully exploit emerging technologies and to manage the consequent risks must be developed as a coherent group. Any new mission capability package also needs to be tested and refined before widespread adoption will be appropriate. Therefore, it is recommended that a joint mission be selected to serve as a prototype to examine the nature of the changes necessitated by the information age and to test the mission capability package approach for developing concepts and implementing change. Success requires innovative ideas. It is recommended that leaders across the board encourage the development and strengthening of centres of innovation within their organizations.

INFORMATION TECHNOLOGY IMPACTS ON THE WARFIGHTER

Impacts on the Warfighter

Information technologies, for the purposes of this analysis, include collection, processing, display, and communications technologies. Processing technologies include data fusion and analysis as well as support for decision making, such as knowledge-based expert systems.

Advances in these technologies have resulted in an enormous amount of near real-time information being potentially available to individuals anywhere at anytime. The "intelligence" level of systems and our confidence in their ability has also increased dramatically to the point where life and death decisions are now routinely being made automatically by computers, albeit with some degree of human supervision.

Even at this early point in the information age, the battlefield is awash with vastly increased amounts and improved quality of information. The dynamics of information dissemination have changed considerably in the latter half of this century, from flowing primarily through command structures to the point where significant amounts of information are obtained outside of the command hierarchy. Thus, what was once a predominantly highly constrained and vertical information flow has evolved into a mix of vertical and horizontal flows. Naturally, the amount, quality, and dynamics of information dissemination have begun to impact the ways decisions are allocated (delegation) and the manner in which those decisions are made.

Thus, advances in information technologies provide us with significant opportunities both to improve our ability to command and control our forces and to add to and/or improve our force capabilities.

Our information-related vulnerabilities have also increased. Increased reliance on high-tech systems for information collection, interpretation, processing, analysis, communication, and display has made failures in these systems more disruptive. The ubiquitous nature of these technologies provides our potential adversaries with capabilities that help them understand how to attack our information assets and give them the tools to do so. Our command and control systems can no longer be evaluated on the basis of measures of merit (MOMs) related solely to the production of quality information in a timely manner. It is now important to consider such attributes as availability, integrity, and authenticity of the information, its ease of use, and its value-added for decision making.

Command and control has long been a recognized force multiplier, and improvements in information technologies offer tremendous opportunities to perfect existing approaches and explore new ones. Quicker, better decisions will allow us to operate more effectively within the enemy's decision cycle, providing us with an opportunity to control engagements. Improvements in information technologies also enhance the capabilities of our weapons, providing them with increased standoff capability and accuracy.

But the opportunities that new and improved weapons and command and control offer cannot be successfully exploited unless we make appropriate changes to our concepts of operations, doctrine, and organizational structures and provide the required personnel education, training, and programs of exercises.

This is not to imply that we must wait for improvements in technology to actually occur before considering new approaches to command and control, concepts of operation, doctrine, or organizational arrangements. Quite the contrary, if we wait, the inertia associated with developing and implementing these changes will permanently keep us behind the technological power curve. Nor does this imply that changes in command and control or force capabilities must necessarily precede alterations to concepts of operation or doctrine.

In reality, these elements (e.g. concept of operations, doctrine, technology, etc.) constitute a package that, taken as a whole, provides real operational capability that can be applied in a specific mission. A mission-specific perspective is important because no organizational structure or approach to command and control is going to be well suited for the range of likely missions, missions as diverse as an MRC and peace-keeping. New MOMs will be required which must also be mission-related. For example, classic measures, such as taking and holding territory, are not relevant in some mission contexts.

NATURE OF FUTURE WAR

Future war can be envisioned as consisting of three general classes of activities. First, there is the perfection of traditional combat. Second, there is the evolution of what have been called non-traditional missions, a very mixed bag of activities including humanitarian assistance, SOLIC operations, counter-drug operations, peace operations, and counter-proliferation. Third, there is the birth of a form of war unique to the information age.

Information technology not only will change the nature of what we know today as war and operations other than war, but also will spawn a new set of activities that will become familiar to future generations as constituting "warfare" in the 21st century. Today, we might have some difficulty in viewing this set of activities as "war" or as the concern or responsibility of DoD. Current planning and budgeting approaches find it difficult to address these aspects of the future, since they are not extensions of existing military missions and responsibilities.

However, in each of these three cases, information technologies will shape the battlespace and define the possibilities.

FUTURE "TRADITIONAL" COMBAT

The future conventional battlespace will be neither contiguous nor orderly. Tempo will be extraordinarily high by today's standards. Given expected improvements in weapons and command and control, if a target can be seen it will be destroyed. Therefore, survival will depend upon organic defensive capability, suppression, and stealth.

Concepts of operation will centre around massing fires rather than forces. Command and control concepts will involve dynamic tradeoffs between ensuring that Rules of Engagement (ROEs) are followed, prioritizing targets, and minimizing the time required to pass information from sensor to shooter.

Commanders will have more direct influence on shaping the battlespace and influencing the initial conditions of the engagement. Staffs will be significantly reduced as organizational structures flatten. Most commands will be automatically disseminated and incorporated in decision aids. Many decisions will be fully automated. Virtually all information will be distributed horizontally.

In short, many significant changes will need to be made to respond to the challenges of the information age. With this much change foreseen down the road, care must be exercised to ensure success.

EVOLUTION OF NON-TRADITIONAL MISSIONS

Since the end of the Cold War, the nation has looked to DoD not only to reduce overall spending, but also to undertake a more diverse set of roles, both at home and around the globe. The unique capabilities developed by the U.S. military to meet the global challenge posed by the Soviet Union and maintained to protect U.S. interests around the world are seen as national assets that can be employed beyond their traditional combat and combat service support roles.

Global air and sea lift are important for disaster relief, crisis intervention, humanitarian assistance, and support to peace operations. Similarly, the secure global communications capacity of the U.S. military is a crucial asset in a wide range of situations.

The capability of the military to surge from its training bases and to react rapidly when dangerous situations arise far exceeds the capacities of most civilian agencies, for whom surge capacity is a slow and cumbersome process and crisis response is an alien practice. These unique capabilities, combined with the absence of an urgent, direct military threat, have caused the nation to expect greater involvement by DoD in non-traditional missions, such as humanitarian assistance, maintaining law and order when local and state authorities cannot, disaster relief, and countering drug smuggling and the proliferation of weapons of mass destruction.

The international environment has also changed in ways that make non-traditional missions more likely and more diverse. The absence of a single military threat and the need for international legitimacy when force is threatened or used have made coalition operations the norm rather than the exception. International organizations, particularly the United Nations, have become increasingly assertive and have pressed a vision of global interests in peace and cooperation. As the only remaining global superpower, the United States is expected to respond whenever international peace and harmony are threatened and the nations of the world feel action is needed. This has been interpreted to mean that the U.S. must lead when the peace is threatened, international crimes are committed, or human tragedy looms.

The growing internationalism is undercut by parochial clashes and conflicts. Freed from the smothering constraints of communist governments, national movements in Eastern Europe and the former USSR have proven willing to challenge the peace to seek independence. Clans and tribes in Africa have reasserted their interests, sometimes violently. Asia is the site of arms races and uncertain relations between nations. Domestic and international struggles for the long-term control of the Middle East oil wealth and the worldwide resurgence of fundamentalist Islam add to the dangerous international situation. Drug traffickers present a frustrating cross-border challenge. Recent attention has also focused on conflicts arising from environmental issues, particularly disputes over water rights, ocean areas, and transboundary air pollution.

Perhaps most important, media coverage and recent successes have led to very high expectations about the performance of the U.S. military. Minimum casualties among both com-bat forces and civilians is widely perceived as an important and achievable goal. At the same time, the military is expected to be effective by accomplishing missions precisely and quickly. Finally, all this is expected within the context of declining budgets.

WARFARE IN THE INFORMATION ARENA

As the global society enters the information age, military operations inevitably have been impacted and transformed. Satellite communications, video conferencing, battlefield facsimile machines, digital communications systems, personal computers, the Global Positioning System, and dozens of other transforming tools are already commonplace. Moreover, DoD has gone from being the driving force in information technology to being a specialty user with a new reliance on commercial-off-the-shelf (COTS) technology in order to acquire and field cost-effective systems. The widespread proliferation of this technology, as well as the increased reliance on COTS, has contributed to a significant increase in our vulnerablity.

The implications of warfare in the information arena are enormous. First, national homelands are not sanctuaries. They can be attacked directly, and potentially anonymously, by foreign powers, criminal organizations, or non-national actors such as ethnic groups, renegade corporations, or zealots of almost any persuasion. Traditional military weapons cannot be inter-posed between the information warfare threat and society.

Second, even where traditional combat conditions exist (hostile military forces face one another in a terrain-defined battlespace), kinetic weapons are only part of the arsenal available to the adversaries. Indeed, electronic espionage and sabotage, psychological warfare attacks delivered via mass media, digital deception, and hacker attacks on the adversaries' command and control systems will be used to neutralize most traditional forces and allow concentration of fire and decisive force at the crucial time and place in the battlespace.

However, warfare in this information age will require enormously complex planning and coordination, very near real time and total situation awareness, decision support systems that filter and fuse information very rapidly and perform simple plan extensions and revisions almost automatically, and massive database and information exchange capabilities to track both friendly and enemy situations as well as rehearse and forecast battlespace dynamics. This rapidly evolving situation means that the U.S. military must be able to perform the following three fundamental information warfare missions: (1) protect its own information systems, (2) attack and influence the information systems of its adversaries, and (3) leverage U.S. information to gain decisive advantage in a battlespace where national security is threatened.

CONCERNS AND REMEDIES

C4IFTW will bring about a series of changes that will profoundly affect both the nature of information available to the warfighter and how this information will be disseminated. Concerns arise regarding the impacts that these changes will have on the decision process and upon decision makers. Other concerns involve new or increased vulnerabilities associated with information age systems and processes. Finally, a set of concerns centres on our ability to design and acquire systems given the information age realities of increased reliance on COTS hard-ware and software and the ever-shrinking technology life cycle.

Non-essential information swamping critical information becomes a major issue for C4IFTW. The sheer volume of information received could frustrate the ability to quickly identify critical information for the decision at hand. To avoid situations in which more information than can be processed is presented, decisions must be made about what information is really needed, what is nice to have, what is irrelevant, and what is potentially distracting or confusing.

The requirement for information clearly depends upon both the mission and the situation. Unless individuals are given an opportunity to think through what they really need, requirements for information will always be inflated. Furthermore, this cannot be a "paper" exercise. Individuals with appropriate military experience must be placed in realistic situations and must be allowed to experiment with different amounts and types of information. The lessons learned from these experiments can be used as inputs to requirements and design analyses.

While refining information-related requirements in a more systematic manner will certainly help, it will not be sufficient to avoid the effects of information overload. Better education and training, devoted to information processing under stress and in environments characterized by uncertainty, are needed to develop the necessary skills to handle these information-rich situations. System designs must track these "information domains."

Finally, practice is key to perfecting and maintaining the skills necessary to function in an information-intensive environment. Therefore, exercises, "on the job" training, and continuing professional education need to be added to complete the necessary set of "remedies" associated with increases in the amounts of information that will be provided.

Sophisticated presentations can also obscure vital information and/or mask poor quality or incomplete data. Designing presentations that illuminate issues and facilitate decision making involves tradeoffs and choices between "raw" or unprocessed data and information that contains a mixture of "fact" and inference. Often fusion algorithms or decision aids "fill in the blanks" and provide users with inferences from available data. In some cases, valuable information is lost in the process. The remedies to address this concern include those discussed above as well as the development of better visualization techniques enabling individuals to better understand the nature of the underlying data for a given presentation.

Uncertainty regarding the quality of the information being presented or its integrity could lead to a lack of confidence that inhibits use of information or intelligence systems. Decision makers clearly need confidence in the reliability, currency and accuracy of data in order to act on it. In the information age, the integrity and authenticity of the data are important as well and should be considered as additional MOMs for information. In addition to the remedies discussed above, effective defensive IW protection measures and decision aids need to be developed that can permit decision makers to rely on the authenticity and integrity of the data. Presentation techniques that convey the quality of the underlying data are an important issue in their own right.

DYNAMICS OF DISSEMINATION

Not only is the amount of information available dramatically increasing as the information age unfolds, our ability to widely disseminate this information is keeping pace. As information sources proliferate, individuals are increasingly receiving inputs from multiple sources in a less than coordinated manner. This asynchronous arrival of information has been found to confuse and distract decision makers. Studies have also shown that the weight individuals place upon information may be related to the order in which that information is received. This is potentially dangerous because it can lead to differences in individuals' perceptions of a situation.

The C4IFTW concept virtually assures that individuals will be receiving different information in different sequences. To avoid the potential pitfalls associated with this phenomena, education and training are needed to heighten awareness of these issues and help individuals assimilate new data into their "information domains." Doctrine is needed to ensure that behaviour is consistent across the organization. Display techniques are required to facilitate information collection and analysis. Decision aids are needed to help synthesize and fuse information on a continuing basis.

As with other concerns discussed previously, practice is a key element in ensuring that individuals develop and maintain proficiencies in dealing with this potentially confusing phenomenon.

Given the thrust of defense initiatives, particularly DISA's Global Grid and the Army's efforts to digitize the battlefield, there will be an enormous increase in the amount of information moving through communication pipes. With the C4IFTW vision of a mix of information "push" and "pull" with an emphasis on "pull," inability to anticipate or control requests for information could result in system degradation, particularly in times of great stress. In these situations, vital as well as non-vital information flow may be affected. To avoid this potentially crippling scenario, appropriate policy, doctrine, and procedures regarding the use of information retrieval mechanisms need to be developed and instituted. Again, education, training, and practice are required to raise awareness of the problem and to develop the skills needed to operate in a "degraded" information environment. Network tools are also needed to provide warnings when the limits of the distribution system are being approached and to help bring the situation under control. Finally, the design of our information distribution infrastructure needs to maximize robustness. The only certainty is that systems will not be used exactly as intended or under precisely the conditions assumed in their design, development, and testing.

DECISION MAKING

The linkages between information quality, distribution, communications patterns, and decision making are complex and diverse. A review of organization theory, group dynamics, information theory, and past research on command and control offers key insights into these linkages and how they function.

First, when information is freely available, role overlap tends to be commonplace. Superiors tend to micromanage, particularly when the stakes are high; there are no higher stakes than combat. Subordinates, however, when provided with the larger picture historically available only to senior commanders, are also likely to second guess decisions made at higher levels and (in richly connected systems) have the information required to undertake initiatives their superiors may find inappropriate. Avoiding this set of counterproductive behaviours and management practices requires doctrine, appropriate organizational structures, self-discipline, and training.

Second, decision making in an information rich environment increasingly means media attention. The pressures of a "fish bowl" environment affect performance in a variety of often adverse ways. Tendencies to overreact, to act quickly, to appear decisive despite limited information, or to "posture" for the media can only be overcome through realistic training and experience.

When decision making becomes a collective process, which tends to occur when several principals have easy access to one another in a situation they all consider important, decisions tend to converge on options that meet group consensus. This "collective wisdom" has been demonstrated in both theoretical and empirical analyses to tend strongly toward risk averse options or poorly thought out "group-think" alternatives. The "brilliant" alternative or innovative approach foreseen by one individual is unlikely to survive this deliberative process. The potential strength of this collective process, which has excelled at solving complex problems such as those at operational and strategic combat levels, can only be achieved by an open approach to command and control decision making and a doctrine that stresses individual innovation and leadership at all levels.

Fully-connected systems also reduce the need for detailed action coordination by commanders because they make available information that would have to be requested from other elements in a classic military information structure. For example, rather than having to request information about the availability of transportation assets or ammunition needed for a combat operation, a line commander will be able to check stock levels directly through the information grid. This can lead to insufficient or ineffective coordination because subject matter experts are not consulted or because more than one command makes plans to use the same asset but none has a clear commitment of asset availability. Industry experience with richly connected systems has shown that collaborative planning and decision aids (which automatically perform coordination tasks and/or pass information between nodes in decision-making structures) are needed to avoid these problems. In addition, "red team" procedures to cross-check decisions can help to ensure adequate, timely coordination.

As generations of military commanders who have become accustomed to the availability of high density and high quality data about the battlefield mature and move into senior command positions, the expectation of near perfect information and the willingness to delay decisions in the expectation of better information will grow. However, the very rapid pace of future battles, as well as the imperatives of turning inside adversary decision loops, will punish procrastination and inaction severely.

The commander who waits for near perfect information will be defeated by one who acts on "good enough" information. Doctrine and effective training for commanders must instill the judgement required to differentiate between sufficient and necessary or desirable information.

Because of the increased pace of battle and the high lethality expected in future battlespace, more and more decisions will be assigned to expert systems. This will include not only "sensor to shooter" linkages where the identification, assignment, and killing of targets must be so rapid that unaided human decision making cannot keep pace; but also other complex domains characterized by rapid developments in logistics planning, air tasking order development, and medivac helicopter routing. However, development, testing, and training are inadequate to ensure confidence in these systems. Testing is particularly important. Technology demonstrations are a good, cost effective way to gain user feedback and to develop positive attitudes toward these systems, but operational testing in realistic field conditions is also necessary to avoid systems failure or lack of use in the field. Failure during early field experience will poison attitudes which can only be overcome slowly and at great expense; thus, care must be taken to involve users early on in the design process.

Finally, by their very nature as automatons, computer systems have no inherent ability to recognize their own limitations. When applied in inappropriate circumstances, they will produce answers which may be "logical" but quite incorrect. The entire process, from concept through design, testing, and doctrine development, must include a recognition of this inherent problem. Ultimately, humans must make sound decisions about when and under what circumstances to rely on automated systems.

VULNERABILITIES

As the sophistication of the military information systems support structure grows over time, the inherent vulnerabilities will become more important. Planning and doctrine can minimize these vulnerabilities, but they cannot be safely ignored.

First, all military equipment is in danger of capture. Even rear areas are raided to capture or destroy vital elements of important systems. Hence, steps must be taken to prevent equipment loss, to ensure that losses are known, and to frustrate enemy exploitation of captured systems. Unique keys that identify and authorize users on particular systems, devices that report current locations on key hardware items via satellite, authentication procedures, and security codes will be important defensive systems. Doctrine and training necessary to ensure their proper use will also be necessary.

Moreover, DoD's increasing reliance on COTS hardware and software increases vulnerabilities by making military systems familiar to sophisticated adversaries and by exposing them to soft- ware developers and technicians who are not subject to security regulations. Hence, design and acquisition procedures need to consider security and minimize exposure. Indeed, some systems may be too sensitive to rely on COTS designs or procurements.

As the information "grid" is readily available in the battlespace, the system's vulnerabilities will increase because: (a) the number of valid users with access to the system rises, magnifying the "insider" threat; (b) the number of nodes and connection points grows, providing adversaries with more opportunities to penetrate the system from the outside; and if a compromise does occur, the perpetrator will have access to more information than would have been available in the past.

Indeed, as this system grows and becomes more fully interconnected, the mere task of noticing a penetration or penetration attempt becomes extremely difficult. Often system problems cannot be readily diagnosed as "natural" or the product of information warfare attacks. Even a single penetration can be extremely damaging, particularly in a richly connected information system. Obviously, some data (such as concepts of operations, planning documents, and orders) are extremely sensitive. A well-crafted "worm" or computer virus can spread literally with the speed of light once inside a complex system. Moreover, knowing that databases have been penetrated and may be corrupted can be expected to greatly inhibit decisive and effective decision making. New types of defensive decision aids will be needed to detect, assess, and counter such attacks.

C2 DESIGN AND ACQUISITION

Because the inventory of information systems will inevitably continue to undergo rapid development and replacement, the design and acquisition arenas become crucial in the defense against many vulnerabilities and represent an opportunity for proactive postures to prevent or limit exposure.

As they focus on definitive, exhaustive testing against technical, often arcane, specifications, traditional test and evaluation procedures have developed a bad reputation in the operational community, where they are viewed as often preventing the adoption of a "good enough" system. Technology demonstrations have emerged as a way of exposing new systems to operators and operational conditions without having to address arcane testing standards. Reliance on demonstrations alone can be equally unhealthy because it encourages adoption of systems that have not really been tested at all. A more robust, integrated, and operationally oriented process of user assessment, as well as realistic applications (including baselines and benchmarks to ensure new systems add measurable capability) are needed.

DoD's increasing reliance on COTS is having an almost unnoticed deleterious impact on the U.S. Government's in-house capability to maintain the expertise required to adapt COTS systems and create capabilities not needed by the commercial sector.

The engineering base required to meet military standards is an essential element of COTS reliance strategy. A coherent program designed to maintain and exercise this capacity is needed. At least part of this program could be devoted to the post deployment support of information systems. In many cases, these systems will need to be revised in order to maintain interoperability with new systems, a process that necessitates the linkage of COTS systems with military requirements. This means not only building linkages between systems, but also having the capacity to "reengineer" the systems and the processes the systems support.

Because C2 systems are never complete and will be continuously undergoing transitions, the ability to maintain mission capability while upgrading or integrating systems remains crucial. This capability requires planning and creativity. The Army's concept of selecting one unit as a "living test bed" for new ideas and equipment and fielding only what is successful in the chosen environment represents one approach to this problem. Other approaches, such as parallel operation of new and old systems during a test period, may be attractive in some circumstances.

Finally, COTS reliance in military systems is very different from relying on commercial systems. Plans for DoD to rely on commercial satellite communications systems must recognize that other clients can make demands on these systems and may limit DoD's access to them in times of crisis. Moreover, commercial services are not always designed for graceful degradation or fully backed up in the event of system failure. Hence, basic "availability" will be an issue when relying on commercial systems, particularly in times of crisis, and needs to be addressed (a) when contractual arrangements are made and (b) when contingency planning is done for crises.

STRATEGY FOR TECHNOLOGY INSERTION AND UTILIZATION

Some remedies can be built into the processes of technology insertion and utilization. Indeed, these remedies represent a crucial line of defense against unintended consequences. The Mission Capability Package (MCP) approach, which permits analysis of each system in the context of the military mission(s) to be supported and encompasses the full range of tools by which problems can be addressed or managed (from technical requirements to training), is the key to success.

Reviewing the extensive lists of concerns identified and the relevant remedies, five action areas emerge:

1) professional military education and training;
2) doctrine, concepts of operation, and command arrangements;
3) technical requirements to perform missions;

4) system design; and

5) organizational issues.

In addition, acquisition reform, particularly transformation of test and evaluation from an arcane process to a robust, holistic, and functionally-oriented process, is essential.

Not all remedies are off the shelf. Basic research, applied research, and programs of development will be needed in some areas. For example, defensive decision aids may require basic research.

Similarly, decision maker behaviour under stress is well understood in the abstract, but may need applied research in a military context before sound design practices can be specified for information presentation and decision support. The tools for realistic training, simulations, and virtual reality programs may need to be developed, although the technologies for them already exist.

Because the unintended consequences of adopting information age technologies are

1) virtually ubiquitous,
2) complex enough to require more than one type of remedy, and
3) involve actions among various organizations that need to be closely linked or coordinated in order to be effective, the orchestration of appropriate remedies into a coherent solution approach is crucial.

To be successful, the approach must allow, even force, those responsible for conceptualizing, designing, developing, and implementing information age technologies to recognize potential unintended consequences and relevant remedies, and to integrate these remedies into existing structures and processes while facilitating the required changes to those structures and processes. This is a tall order.

The stakes here are very high. The major source of adverse unintended consequences is a lack of coherence or a conflict among the different elements of an existing MCP resulting from uncoordinated changes in MCP components. For example, when an organization is provided information that was previously unavailable,

that organization may take advantage of the opportunity for improvement and perform a task differently. This change in behaviour could create a conflict in the way the organization relates to other organizations if other adjustments (e.g. doctrine) are not made.

Thus, a major advantage of using the MCP approach is that the approach facilitates the early identification of potential conflicts within proposed MCP concepts and provides a mechanism for testing coordinated sets of changes designed to achieve or maintain MCP coherence.

MISSION CAPABILITY PACKAGES

The MCP approach begins with a clearly defined mission or set of missions and seeks to define a) what is required to meet the mission(s) successfully and b) how those requirements may differ from the current force structure, command and control arrangements, organizations, doctrine, and technologies.

Solutions, or initial MCP concepts, are developed in the concept development phase based on prior research, lessons learned, and expert judgement. Their strength lies in their thorough-ness and coherence, from a clear mission statement to organizational and force structure, doctrinal approach, and technology needs.

The MCP approach calls for exposing the MCP concept to review and critique by the operational community and domain experts early and often in order to refine and improve the concept. This review may take the form of demonstrations, experiments, exercises, simulations, modeling, or expert criticism.

What matters is that, as the concept matures, the process becomes increasingly focused and that required refinements are incorporated into the MCP. As consensus and supporting evidence emerge, the refinement process is transformed into a development process characterized by a "build a little, test a little" philosophy. Finally, the MCP moves into its implementation phase.

This implementation phase is also comprehensive in nature. Systems may be built, but not in isolation. Doctrine development, command reorganization, relevant professional military education and training, as well as the technical systems themselves, are all specified.

This process has the comprehensiveness, coherence, and orientation necessary to transform ideas and technologies into real operational capability while avoiding adverse unintended consequences. Hence, MCPs are the recommended approach to ensure effective remedies and to minimize risk.

RECOMMENDATIONS

This section deals with the specific initiatives and actions that can be under-taken to ensure that the Department of Defense avoids, mitigates, and manages the unintended consequences of adopting information age technologies.

There are a number of opportunities for DoD leadership in this arena. These include providing vision to ensure the community understands the problem and the required types of solutions, articulating particular operational needs, influencing the investments in information systems and their implementation, using joint doctrine to reap the benefits of new technologies while guarding against inherent problems, establishing professional military education and training requirements, and providing an operational perspective on research priorities and the test and evaluation process.

VISION

The vision needed includes a determination to harness and leverage information technologies as an essential part of the requirement to maintain the military strength of the United States in the global arena and to protect against asymmetric vulnerabilities arising from foreign exploitation of information technologies. More-over, this vision should stress the need to tailor systems to missions and to focus attention on mission capability packages as the vehicle for addressing this problem.

REQUIREMENTS AND INVESTMENT

Three types of requirements can be identified: operational, technical, and budgetary. Warfighters can and should help shape the requirements for information systems and influence DoD's investments in these by playing an active role in the MCP process.

The technical and operational communities need to work much more closely together to develop new MCP concepts and to refine these concepts. Given the set of inertias involved in some components of an MCP, these concepts need to be incubated and nurtured long before the technology reaches the marketplace.

Defense planners and budgeteers need to think more in terms of MCPs than in terms of individual programs, using MCPs to link programmatic activities needed to implement or maintain an MCP. This would help ensure that all of the necessary components are adequately funded and properly synchronized, thus eliminating one significant cause for an MCP's lack of completeness or coherence.

JOINT DOCTRINE

The doctrine community should be involved at the beginning of the process. When the nature and distribution of information changes, radically new ways of doing business and complications in the old ways of doing business emerge.

In many cases, new or modified doctrine can ease or simplify these changes. Changes in doctrine are often essential if the benefits of new information systems are to be realized and inconsistencies between capacity and doctrine avoided. Involving the doctrine community early will also facilitate the key process of "embedding" doctrine in new systems.

Doctrine is being written or changed when decisions are made about who will automatically receive some class of information, who has the work stations from which a database can be updated, or who is able to access and use some class of data. This process needs to be consciously and carefully monitored. Unless the doctrine community is involved, technical personnel responding to technical criteria and standards will be, in effect, making doctrine. If, however, the doctrine community is involved, new systems being fielded will contain and help support current doctrine.

Finally, the movement toward on-line doctrine delivery systems should be supported and rein-forced. The process of doctrine development tends to be slow and cumbersome, in many ways because of the number of people and organizations involved.

Automation of the doctrine development and review process will enable simultaneous review at many locations, ease the process of updating or modifying drafts, and enable almost instantaneous distribution of new doctrine publications. Field units could also reduce the paper they maintain if they had global access to publications they use infrequently.

JOINT PME AND TRAINING

Professional Military Education (PME) must serve as a change agent for the military grappling with the information age. Raising awareness of the threat, opportunities, and vulnerabilities inherent in the changes underway can best be done through the PME structure.

If a "teaching hospital" model is adopted so that this new information is conveyed in the context of "real world" experience and actions, the impact can be direct and effective. While some progress has been made toward bringing PME into the information age, the process needs to be accelerated. This involves changes in the curriculum so that students become current in information technologies (including their advantages, vulnerabilities, limits, and applications) as these impact and are likely to impact military affairs; developing methods of teaching that enable (and require) PME students to become computer literate and knowledgeable of how to obtain information electronically; and developing connectivity within and between PME institutions as well as between these institutions and the simulation and training centres with which they have natural synergy.

Training is perhaps the arena of military affairs where information technology has already had its most profound effect, but also remains an arena where much more can and should be done. Educated military professionals are ready to train on information systems, but these systems must be mastered and their practical limits learned in the more realistic training environment. Moreover, improvements in virtual reality technologies and connectivity provide options for diverse mission rehearsal and training at a fraction of the cost of field exercises. Defining when and where these lower cost training opportunities exist and taking advantage of them must remain a priority. The most cost effective systems will be those that possess embedded training packages and provide near real time feedback, easing the comprehension and retention of lessons learned.

RESEARCH AND T&E

There is a need for more operationally-oriented command and control research, research that focuses on exploring command concepts and approaches rather than on the technologies that support them.

Another significant contribution can be made to reducing costs, accelerating schedules, and improving the quality of new information systems if the operational, technical, and test and evaluation communities can come together to develop a new approach to T&E. What is needed is an approach that is less "arm's length" and adversarial and is more supportive of an evolutionary design and acquisition strategy. Currently, the T&E community tends to focus on easily measurable technical standards while avoiding the more difficult task of assessing the operational capabilities and impacts of new systems or their defenses against unintended consequences. Tests are typically pass/fail rather than designed to provide constructive feedback. This approach is more in keeping with traditional acquisition practices than with the evolutionary acquisition processes, adopted more than a decade ago, that have been proven essential in the command and control arena.

CONCLUSIONS

A wide range of potential important unintended consequences were identified in the analysis, some representing vulnerabilities, others opportunities that can be exploited if understood, and others that will require or enable new ways of doing business. While these consequences represent challenges, they are changes that cannot and should be neither avoided nor taken lightly. More importantly, those consequences identified can be managed if a coherent, holistic approach, such as the Mission Capability Package, is adopted and pursued energetically. While systems designers can bypass some problems, the real solutions tend to cluster around PME, training, and doctrine. Success will also require some new knowledge, so both basic and applied research will be needed. Acquisition and T&E reform will also be required if this process is to be fully successful. Senior DoD management can positively impact the prevention and management of these conflicts by developing and articulating a vision and by demonstrating the importance of these issues through personal involvement and leadership. Mission Capability Packages that ensure linkage between the information systems, the missions for which they are relevant, the needs of the commanders in the field, the force structure, doctrine, training, and education represent the optimal coherent approach.

2

RECENT EVENTS AND THEIR SIGNIFICANCE

Although the events of September 11th signified the end of the short-lived post-Cold War era, they did not necessarily render obsclete U.S. inter-agency, future war analysis and planning. Rather, future war concepts require adaptation to the strategic environment. In order to link Army Transformation to security environment trends with specific focus on the "Objective Force" timeframe, this report's conceptual framework assesses the nature of the emerging security environment, the modes of future armed conflict, the Objective Force characteristic requirements to remain strategically decisive, an Objective Force conceptualization for the emerging security environment, and the enduring relevance of the U.S. Army.

Two conclusions emerge from this report: first, the marked decline of large-scale state-on-state warfare and the rise of ambiguous, protracted, indecisive conflict in complex environments; second, because the collective international community will seek to harness American military hegemony, the United States should adopt a broad spectrum strategy based on partnership and shared risks for long-term national interests.

The future security environment will be characterized by minor conflicts due to the influence of the following interconnected trends: WMD proliferation, globalization ("Golden Straightjacket"), the glare of the information age, U.S. conventional military dominance, the positive and negative effects of rapid change on states, and the rapid diffusion of knowledge and technology.

Largely marginalized by the Cold War, smaller conflicts have assumed greater attention since the fall of the Berlin Wall, and with the inevitable fall of rogue states like Iraq and North Korea, major conflicts will become extremely rare as a result of the aforementioned trends. WMD proliferation will constrain states from conventional war because of the increased risks and decreased benefits. To ensure the nuclear threshold is not crossed, states will engage in quick incursions with limited objectives. The increasing globalization of economies will restrain aggression because of the immediate, negative impact on an aggressor's economy. The glare of the Information Age means that any use of force will gain instantaneous world attention and if aggression is involved, will result in the immediate severance of the aggressor's external capital flows and markets. Few regimes can survive economic stagnation.

The sheer dominance of the U.S. conventional military will serve to deter most aggressors, and despite theoretical uses of asymmetric methods—anti-access strategies, terrorism, or weapons of mass destruction—to thwart U.S. intervention, aggressors will have to pause and weigh the associated risks. The continued period of decolonization will entail the struggle for resources and power, the opposition to globalization by failing states or non-state actors will result in a backlash against change, and the traditional competition for resources among poorer nations will continue unabated. Ordinarily, the machinations of non-state actors would be of small consequence, but for the greater availability of knowledge and technology. With greater access to WMD, funding and situational awareness, and unconstrained by norms, rules, and laws, non-state entities pose a serious threat to even the United States.

Unlike traditional adversaries, these non-state entities seek victory by avoiding defeat. Protracted conflict, ethical, political, and legal ambiguity, and operating within population centres make them particularly virulent.

Three big strategic shifts demand a reshaping of American strategy. First, future adversaries will be much more savvy regarding U.S. capabilities and triggers for intervention. The era of the "stupid" enemy is over. Second, precision operations are crucial to avoiding the unintended and second order of military effects. Victories which inadvertently alienate, destabilize, or impoverish neighbouring states or regions (those not directly involved in the conflict) will prove counterproductive and debilitating in the long term. Third, the armed forces will most likely be employed to restore and sustain stability rather than to defeat a discernible enemy. Internal conflicts will be more prevalent, which if left unchecked, could grow or become intolerable to the international community. Hence, the security concerns will focus on staunching a conflict early, which will be characterized as protracted, complex, and ambiguous.

The future battlefield/battlespace expands the concept of armed conflict by placing the operational aspects within a broader context to include political, economic, social, ecological, demographic, legal, normative, diplomatic, and technological. Adversaries will employ complexity, ambiguity, and asymmetry to prevent, deter, and complicate outside intervention, and should that fail, avoid rapid, decisive operations. Adversaries will use any device (information warfare, the unlegalist paradigm tendencies, provocation attacks, and human shields) to fetter U.S. military power.

The four distinct but interrelated dominant strategic battlespaces are direct interstate war, nonstate war, intrastate war, and indirect interstate war. Direct interstate war is the traditional and conventional, but is declining in frequency. Nonstate war involves criminal and terrorist actors that thrive among various host states (knowingly or unknowingly) and use information technology for funding, intelligence, and internal communication, command and control. The Al Qaida terrorist network is an example. Indirect interstate war entails aggression by a state through proxies. Serbia's support of the Bosnian and Krajina Serbs is illustrative. Intrastate war involves a conflict between a state and a nonstate actor, such as an insurgents or separatists, or a conflict between two or more nonstate entities. Of the four strategic battlespaces, indirect interstate and intrastate wars will be the most prevalent.

U.S. landpower is vital to operations within the strategic battlespaces. The United States prefers to fight rapid, decisive operations, but must also be adept at protracted, complex, and asymmetric warfare. Without this robust, flexible landpower, the U.S. military would be like a medieval knight or a battleship—very proficient at a narrow range of military tasks.

The Army role in future war transcends traditional warfighting. Although it is integral to defeating an adversary as part of the Joint Force, it must also help consolidate success by providing security and support to partners, other government agencies, and nongovernment agencies in the aftermath. Furthermore, the Army must render stabilization for a challenged state or uncontrolled region. History instructs that success entails military victory followed by a committed peace.

The Objective Force supports the Army's role in future war by providing strategic speed, full scale decisiveness, broad band precision, success in protracted, asymmetric, ambiguous, and complex conflicts, the ability to operate in a coalition, and rapid conceptual and organizational adaptation. As the Objective Force continues to mature, the Army must not lose sight of the need for adaptability and flexibility that modularity of the armed forces brings to the strategic battlespace. Transformation must continuously develop new operational and strategic concepts, educate soldiers and officers to implement them, and develop organizations and technologies to ensure they function.

To ensure dominance, Transformation must adopt two parallel tracks: one aimed at direct interstate war, and the other aimed at indirect interstate and intrastate war. Both tracks are naturally mutually supporting but require mutual cognizance to prevent tunnel vision. The conceptual design of the Objective Force must permit maximum effectiveness in protracted, ambiguous, complex, and asymmetric conflicts. The three components of the Objective Force would be Strike Forces, Special Forces, and Support Forces. Together, they permit the Army to respond to the full spectrum of conflicts and crises with robust capabilities and without eviscerating standing units as occurs currently.

The Army serves a vital role to the Joint Team. It is the most versatile, permitting the United States to respond to every strategic battlespace without causing substantial unintended consequences and political fallout. In short, the Army will be extremely effective at the type of armed conflict that will dominate the global security environment in the coming decade as Transformation continues.

THE STRATEGIC ROLE OF AMERICAN LANDPOWER

Many American strategists, military leaders, and politicians concluded that all previous thinking about the new security environment and future war became obsolete on September 11, 2001. No one could deny that the attacks were seminal events, driving the last nail into the coffin of the "Post-Cold War" era. But it is important to avoid overreaction by placing the attacks into a broader historical context. The world was not created anew on September 11.

All of the analysis and planning for future war that had been undertaken by the Army, the Department of Defense (DoD), and the other Services was not rendered archaic but needs adjustment and refinement.

To continue to serve the Nation's interests, the Army's capabilities, organizations, and operational concepts must reflect the realities of the global security system and the forms of armed conflict that will occur in it. This report is intended to provide a conceptual framework for linking Army Transformation and trends in the security environment. Concentrating on what might be called the "Objective Force" time frame—the years 2015 and beyond— it will assess the nature of the emerging security environment, the modes of future armed conflict, the strategically decisive characteristics that the Objective Force will need, a broad structure for the Objective Force that reflects the emerging security environment, and the enduring strategic relevance of the U.S. Army.

The report will not, however, examine the full gamut of security challenges that the United States will face in coming decades. Important topics such as nuclear force posture, national missile defense, cyberwar, the role of the Army in homeland defense, force sizing, and technology requirements must be left for later. The focus, instead, will be on the role of American landpower and the Army in armed conflict abroad. In the broadest sense, this report seeks to both make suggestions about the shape and capabilities of the Objective Force, and to explain why that force will play a vital strategic role in the emerging security environment.

Most of the analysis in this report is at the *military strategic level*. During the past 5 years several seminal futures studies have been conducted at the grand strategic level, seeking to understand the emerging global security environment. Recent examples include the 2001 *Quadrennial Defense Review* and the reports of the U.S. Commission on National Security/21st Century. At the same time the Army, particularly TRADOC, has undertaken extensive analysis and experimentation to understand the operational level of future war. This report will not replicate either of those efforts but will, instead, link operational concepts and capabilities with trends in the security environment. The primary analytical tool will be *strategic battlespaces*. A strategic battlespace is a mode of war in which the operational and technological aspects of armed conflict are placed within their broader political, economic, social, ecological, demographic, legal, normative, diplomatic, and technological contexts. By using strategic battlespaces as a heuristic device, Objective Force requirements can be derived from discernible trends in the global security environment. In addition, this report will update the assessment of the global security environment in the *Quadrennial Defense Review* and the reports of the U.S. Commission on National Security/21st Century to consider the effect that the September 11th attacks might have on American strategy and future armed conflict.

To do this, the report will answer to five key questions:

1. What will be the shape and characteristics of the future international security environment?
2. What will be the characteristics of the future battlefield/ battlespace?
3. What are the potential or probable roles and missions of the Army?
4. How should the Objective Force contribute to the successful execution of those roles and missions?
5. Why an Army?

The ultimate goal is to build a consensus within the Army on these questions, to use it to shape the Transformation process, and to explain the vital contribution of landpower and the Army to the wider strategic community.

Two broad conclusions lie at the heart of this report. First, a range of factors will make large-scale, state-on-state war rare or even obsolete. Put simply, the costs and risks of traditional, cross-border armed aggression will mount to the point that most states will not consider it. This trend is reinforced each time the United States trounces an opponent decisively. At the same time, ambiguous, protracted, nondecisive armed conflict in complex environments, often involving nonstate participants, is likely to become even more common and strategically significant now that an enemy tiny in size can generate massive effects. All of this suggests that the United States in general and the Army in particular should assure that Transformation leads to an Objective Force suitable for this type of warfare.

Second, as the memory of the Cold War continues to fade, a natural tendency of the international system will be to balance, contain, or counter American power, often using international law or diplomatic maneuvers. The way that the United States exercises its power will determine the extent and intensity of such attempts. A strategy based on partnership and shared risk rather than imposition of force from afar will maximize the degree to which other states accept America's leadership. Landpower must be a central component of such a strategy.

THE EMERGING GLOBAL SECURITY ENVIRONMENT

The global security environment includes multiple types of armed conflict. An effective strategy identifies the most strategically significant type or types and allocates the most resources—people, effort, money—to them. For nearly 400 years, large-scale conventional war has been the most strategically significant form of armed conflict. It was never the most common, but the level of effort and quantity of resources it required, along with the immense danger and cost of defeat, kept it preeminent. The world's great powers thus focused their strategy on this type of war and treated other modes of armed conflict as secondary or "lesser included" problems.

This norm began to change with the creation of nuclear weapons. In the decade following World War II, strategists recognized that "limited wars" would be a major concern since major war between a nuclear-armed West and a nuclear-armed East could literally obliterate the human species. But even though nuclear weapons made full-scale war between the superpowers extraordinarily dangerous and unlikely, the fact that the Soviet Union retained a massive, offensively-configured conventional capability forced the United States to focus on it. Other types of armed conflict, particularly rural leftist insurgency, were more common, but less important. Limited warfare doctrine languished after the U.S. involvement in Vietnam turned out disastrously. Tacitly, the U.S. military vowed not to become embroiled in such messy conflicts again.

By the 1990s the chances of conventional aggression from Russia faded as its military disintegrated and Moscow became dependent on Western aid, trade, and market access. Leftist insurgencies still sputtered on around the world, but with the major sponsors of revolution dropping that policy, multinational peacekeeping becoming more effective, Third World states undertaking political reform, and counterinsurgency becoming more successful, "people's war" was moot outside a handful of places like Nepal, Colombia, and Algeria. As a result, the U.S. military lost interest in counterinsurgency by the end of the 20th century.

Yet even as superpower war and rural insurgency faded, two new forms of armed conflict were on the ascent. The most dangerous was what became known as major theatre war—conventional armed aggression against a neighbouring nation by a Soviet- or Chinese-equipped "rogue state." Iraq and North Korea were, of course, the classic rogue states since they possessed substantial military capability and were ruled by dictatorial regimes little concerned with the pariah status that aggression brought. The second form of armed conflict was internal war along sectarian, ethnic, or religious lines, most in the territory of the former European colonial empires. This was by far the most common form of armed conflict in the 1990s. While some "small wars" of this type lurched along without attracting outside intervention (for instance, Sudan and Ngorno-Karabakh), humanitarian disasters in Somalia, Northern Iraq, Rwanda, and Bosnia galvanized the will of the world community, particularly the United States, to intervene. Luckily, U.S. military forces optimized for major theatre war proved effective at small wars, at least when used in combination with peacekeepers from other nations.

The Iraqi problem certainly demands resolution, possibly using major theatre war. But it will be solved. The chances of Iraq posing a large scale conventional threat to its neighbours years from now are very small. To an extent, the same holds for North Korea. Pyongyang may be a threat to regional and global stability for a few more years, but the nature of that threat is changing. The likelihood of a massive conventional strike south is in decline. While that nation and its bizarre regime retain a massive military, China and Russia know that supporting North Korean aggression would be politically and economically disastrous. Plus, Russia has no ideological affinity with the regime in Pyongyang, and China only a titular one. With its economy in shambles, North Korea cannot even feed its own people. At the same time the South Korean military has become one of the most professional and effective on earth. Certainly North Korea still could strike south. So long as that nation is ruled by a regime that operates on ideology and delusional fantasy, the risk remains. But the chances of a successful North Korean invasion of the south are lower now than they have been since 1950 and continue to drop.

As the threat from Iraq and North Korea fades, no replacement "rogue states" with the incentive and the ability to invade their neighbours exist. States like China, India, and possibly Russia that have the economic and technological strength to field a military capable of conventional invasion of neighbouring states increasingly depend on integration into the global economy for capital and markets. Aggression would cut them off from the global economy and thus condemn them to potentially disastrous decline and isolation. Their leaders would thus recognize that any military victory would by pyrrhic. The emergence of new rogues cannot be ruled out, but nothing suggests that it is likely. Other factors also make conventional aggression increasingly risky and costly. One is the proliferation of nuclear weapons. As Martin Van Creveld wrote, the effect of nuclear weapons, unforeseen and perhaps unforeseeable, has been to push conventional war into the nooks and crannies of the international system. . . . The signs are that, faced by actual nuclear weapons or by the ability to build them quickly, states have grown wary not merely of territorial expansion but of conventional war itself.

The nuclear club is likely to increase in the future, further constraining large-scale, sustained conventional war. In such an environment, if a state does use force against a neighbour, it is likely to undertake a quick incursion, limited in duration and objectives. Decisive war between major states is rapidly moving toward history's dustbin. The cascading globalization of economies is also constricting states. This is changing behaviour at many different levels. At the "tactical" level, businesses now must have a global approach to markets, financing, trends, risk amelioration, partners, and suppliers. The "strategic" outcome is a linkage of economies around the world. "Economic downturns," notes the U.S. Commission on National Security, "that have usually been episodic and local may become, thanks to the integration of global financial markets, more systemic in their origins and hence more global in their effects." This is not a new phenomenon. Thomas Friedman points out that the period from the late 19th century to the middle of the 20th also saw substantial globalization driven by a decline in transportation costs arising from the invention of the railroad, steamship, and automobile. But the process of globalization underway today is immensely more powerful in terms of its impact on politics, economics, culture, and values.

Every state must choose between participation in the globalized economy or persistent poverty. Participation means that the state—not just businesses within a state, but the government itself—must follow certain rules of behaviour, including things like limiting corruption, opening markets, and implementing transparent budgeting and financial procedures.

Friedman calls this the "golden straitjacket." "Transparency," write Robert Keohane and Joseph Nye, "is becoming a key asset for countries seeking investments. The ability to hoard information, which once seemed so valuable to authoritarian states, undermines the credibility and transparency necessary to attract investment on globally competitive terms." This has immense implications. Decisions made by multinational financial institutions, overseas banks, or investors on the other side of the world now determine the economic health of a nation nearly as much as decisions made by its own leaders. As Jessica T. Mathews writes,

> National governments are not simply losing autonomy in a globalizing economy. They are sharing powers—including political, social, and security roles at the core of sovereignty—with businesses, with international organizations, and with a multitude of citizen groups, known as nongovernmental organizations.

In a sense, all states have taken on some of the weakness, vulnerability, and lack of control that traditionally characterizes small states. As the ability of the state to control its economy fades, it is likely to become weaker across the board, thus leading to a major, perhaps revolutionary, transformation of the global security system.

With the glare of the information age revealing the details of any military operation other than the very smallest to a global audience, interconnectedness increases the risks and costs associated with the use of force. The more sensitive a regime is to pressure from within and outside its country, the greater the constraints. Aggression is at least marginally viable for North Korea and Iraq because their regimes have built effective systems of repression and thus can tolerate the poverty and misery that comes from flaunting global norms. Most other states, even nondemocratic ones, recognize that overt aggression would cut them off from external capital flows and markets. The ensuing economic decline would undercut support for the regime and possible lead to its downfall. The demise of Slobodan Milosevic is a case in point. His aggressive policies cut Serbia off from investment, aid, and trade. Economic stagnation then undercut his political support. And so it continues: around the world globalization is tightening the "golden straitjacket" and increasing the costs of armed aggression.

American strategy since the end of the Cold War further decreased the utility of overt aggression. By retaining overwhelming military power, the ability to project and sustain it, and a willingness to assist states facing aggression, the United States has helped craft a global security system in which traditional cross-border invasion has little chance of success. This does not appear likely to change, at least in the short- or mid-term. Even though the U.S. military is significantly smaller than during the Gulf War, it remains capable of reversing traditional aggression unless constrained by political considerations. While strategic thinkers have warned that asymmetric methods such as anti-access strategies, terrorism, or weapons of mass destruction may prevent the United States from intervening to stop or reverse an invasion in the future, this remains speculative.

While large scale, conventional, state-on-state warfare will be rare, the tensions that generate violence will, if anything, increase. Three causes of armed conflict will be most prevalent in the coming decades. One is the continuing struggle for power and resources among ethnic groups, sects, and clans as the long process of decolonization continues. This may seem like a strange idea since it is common to think of decolonization as complete. But as Ralph Peters points out, the vast majority of national borders that exist today were drawn during the era of European and Ottoman colonialism. They more often reflect the administrative divisions of the colonial powers or diplomatic arrangements between them than they do social, economic, religious, and ethnic realities on the ground. The relationship between recent decolonization and large scale violence is clear. Of the 140 violent conflicts underway in the world today, only 10—all in North or South America—are not related to former colonial divisions and boundaries, or to the power structures that emerged from colonialism. As Peters argues, the rearranging of national borders to reflect current realities rather than colonial ones is likely to take several more decades.

Globalization will be the second major source of conflict in coming decades. Like any great shift, globalization has winners and losers in terms of regions, states, corporations, and individuals. As the losers see their standard of living, power base, influence, and prospects erode, they sometimes will lash out against those they hold responsible. This may be institutions like the World Bank or, more often, the United States. A loose network opposed to globalization is already taking shape and flexing its muscle. Eventually this could coalesce into a more formal movement and even spawn some sort of new, radical ideology. After all, communism emerged from the attempts to mobilize the losers from the process of industrialization. Globalization's losers are as frustrated and angry as 19th century Europe's industrial proletariat. If a new radical ideology does take shape, it could inspire violence ranging from terrorism and sabotage to full blown war.

In fact, a case can be made that this is already happening: the Islamic world has proven unable to adapt to modernization and globalization, and thus remains mired in stagnation, anomie, poverty, and repression. This leads to frustration, resentment, anger, and terrorism. But rather than changing the culture that causes the failure, radicals like those in al Qaida seek to bring down those who have succeeded in the globalizing world, particularly the United States. It is no coincidence that al Qaida targets the American economy, since its collapse would lessen the gap between the United States and the Islamic world and thus diminish the daily reminders that Islamic culture in its current form cannot provide a foundation for modern, powerful democratic states. Without an historical cultural shift in the Islamic world akin to the Protestant Reformation and Enlightenment in Europe, this will not change.

The third major source of conflict will be an intensified competition for resources, particularly in the poorer parts of the world. While the world's population is growing at a slower rate than a few decades ago, it will exceed 8 billion by 2030, with almost all of the increase in the poorer regions. Urbanization also continues unabated. By 2030 over three fifths of the world's people will live in cities. This growth is accompanied by degradation of the physical environment. The mounting stress on the world's water supplies, deforestation, desertification and the erosion of farmland are particularly troubling. These, in turn, fuel further urbanization and migrations. So far, attempts by governments to control and manage the adverse effects of these trends have proven ineffective. Should this continue— and everything suggests it will—the competition for resources, whether arable land, water, or capital, can provide a foundation for future conflicts. This might take the form of state aggression as regimes seek access to water, land, minerals, ports, or other resources. In most cases, though, states will realize that any gains attained this way will be negated by the high economic and political costs of aggression. Most resource-based conflicts, then, will be sectarian or ethnic, much like those in Western and Central Africa today.

Around the world, nation-states are hard pressed to meet the needs and demands of their population, whether for development or security. Again, the glare of the Information Age is a factor. Outside of North Korea, regimes have little success at preventing their populations from learning about conditions in others parts of the world, as well as the excesses and shortcomings of their rulers. The time is past when misery was considered normal and natural by its victims. The result is global disillusionment and frustration. A wide range of nonstate organizations are stepping into this void, providing everything from coherent ideologies that explain the source of the frustration and plan to alleviate it to more concrete goods like security. The information revolution and other factors like the expansion of the global market in arms serve to empower nonstate groups. In fact, one of the defining features of the information revolution is that the diffusion of knowledge and the multiple sources of information that it has brought tend to give small, versatile, and adaptive organizations a comparative advantage over large, ponderous, bureaucratic ones. This is most evident in the business world, but the same tendency holds for organizations that provide security and a sense of shared meaning and purpose—states are finding nonstate organizations to be more competitive and, in some cases, more threatening than ever before.

All this is increasing the role of nonstate entities in security and armed conflict. In combination with the constraints on the warmaking ability of states, this means that most future armed conflicts will involve nonstate entities either as major or secondary combatants. In fact, trends suggest that armed conflict pitting a state against nonstate entities, or even pitting one or more nonstate entities against each other will account for the overwhelming majority of wars in coming decades. As Ralph Peters phrases it, "20th century wars were fought between successful powers for hegemony; 21st century conflicts will be between successful states and unsuccessful entities over behaviours."

Nonstate entities necessarily fight differently than states. They are less bound by norms, rules, and laws. Terrorism and guerrilla operations are the norm. For protection, they attempt to be a poor target in the strategic sense, wrapping themselves in ethical, political, and legal ambiguity, using complex operating environments, and interspersing with noncombatants. Since finance is a major problem for them, they often blur the distinction between political and criminal organizations, forming "gray area phenomena." They attempt to build networks of support inside and outside their regions. And, they seek victory primarily by avoiding defeat. Simply surviving is an indicator of success; protracted conflict is to their advantage.

The dynamic changes in the global security environment point toward three macro-level shifts which will shape American strategy. The first is the demise of "stupid" enemies who commit aggression based on the assumption that the United States will not intervene. For a decade now, the United States has illustrated the capability and willingness to lead a coalition to stop or reverse overt aggression. Future aggressors, whether states or nonstate entities, will better understand the United States (due to information technology), expect American involvement and plan for it, attempt to stay below the threshold of U.S. intervention by disguising their aggression, seeking allies or protectors, constructing asymmetric defenses, or trying to deter the United States with terrorism or weapons of mass destruction. To sustain international and domestic support for intervention, the United States will increasingly seek to limit the unintended and second order effects of military operations. Victories in which the United States inadvertently alienates, destabilizes, or impoverishes neighbouring states or regions will, in the long term, prove counterproductive, even debilitating. To retain support and legitimacy, military operations must be as precise as possible.

Finally, most armed conflicts in coming decades are likely to be internal ones. The past decade has seen a tidal wave of economic and political reform around the world as state after state has undergone the transition to free enterprise economic systems and governments that are, to some degree, more open and democratic. While this is a tremendously beneficial trend, all indicators are that it has peaked. Many states are finding that sustaining an open government is more difficult than starting one. As fragile new democracies and the remaining authoritarian regimes struggle to meet the expectations of their publics—which are themselves growing due to the global information revolution—and to adjust to economic globalization, they are likely to face mounting frustration and outright opposition.

The outcome will be a plethora of internal conflicts (albeit with international dimensions, an inevitable byproduct of interconnectedness, globalization, and the profusion of information). As states themselves are constrained from overt military aggression, the armed forces of all nations will be involved in promoting internal stability and confronting internal enemies, whether separatists, militias, insurgents, terrorists, armed criminal cartels, or something similar. The first two decades of the 21st century will be dominated by protracted, complex, ambiguous armed conflicts rather than short, politically and ethically clear ones leading to decisive outcomes.

ARMED CONFLICT IN THE EMERGING SECURITY ENVIRONMENT

The emerging global security environment, then, will be characterized by a broad range of violent challenges to fragile states, but also by a United States which will use its own military power and that of allies to reverse or repel forms of aggression for which congressional, public, and international support can be mobilized and sustained. Recognizing this, aggressors, whether nonstate or state, will seek to prevent, deter, or complicate outside intervention by the United States and its partners. When this fails, aggressors will attempt to avoid rapid, decisive resolution of the conflict by using political, psychological, legal, and ethical ambiguity; complex operational environments including cities, mountains, jungles, the Internet, and the commercial cybersphere; interspersion among civilians; dispersion, not only within a country, but around the world as well; and asymmetric deterrents against the United States and other intervening powers, particularly the threat of attacks on the great power's homeland.

Within this environment, adversaries will open a new front, employing information warfare, through the Internet and flash journalism, to neutralize or diminish U.S. military power. They will attempt to portray the United States as a bully who kills arbitrarily and indiscriminately.

Using baited provocation attacks on U.S. forces, adversaries will use civilians as sacrificial lambs to energize the international community into restraining the United States. In this manner, adversaries can hobble U.S. power. Aggressors who do provoke a U.S. or U.S.-led response will seek to extend the conflict, recognizing that the United States cannot be matched at rapid, decisive outcomes but, because of the impatience that characterizes American strategic culture and the demands of global leadership, it is less adept at protracted conflicts, particularly those which take years or decades to resolve or peter out.

This future security environment will be dominated by four distinct but interrelated strategic battlespaces. The most familiar strategic battlespace will involve *direct interstate war* where state militaries are pitted against one another. It is regulated by 400 years' worth of laws, norms, and common practices. This is the strategic battlespace where things like the concept of "just war" and the international law of armed conflict come into play. This is also the strategic battlespace that American strategists have analyzed and wargamed in detail. Most of the force structure, equipment, technology, and operational concepts of the U.S. military were developed for major theatre war between states. It is also the realm in which rapid, decisive outcomes have occurred (although proliferation and interconnectedness are making it more difficult to attain decisive outcomes). The 1990-91 Gulf War is a classic instance of direct interstate war.

Nonstate war involves at least one combatant that does not have a fixed geographic base. A nonstate enemy would rely on information technology for core functions such as fund raising, intelligence collection, internal communication, command and control, and, potentially, attacks.

Nonstate opponents would select a physical location because of the inability or unwillingness of the host state to control the terrorist, insurgent, or criminal organization. This could be a result of the weakness of the state (e.g., the inability of the government of Colombia to destroy narcotrafficking organizations), of constraints that result from legal and civil rights (e.g., the ability of Al Qaida to operate cells in the United States or Germany), or of the state simply being unaware of the organization or turning a blind eye due to corruption, fear, or sympathy. The major point, though, is that a nonstate opponent does not depend on any *given* physical location. If a state acts against it, it could move to another location with a minimal erosion of capability. All this means that the state-to-state dimension of nonstate war is secondary.

Indirect interstate war entails proxy aggression by a state through the creation, encouragement, and support of insurgents, terrorists, armed criminal cartels, separatists, or militias which, in turn, undertake aggression against another state. It is a variant of state-on-state conflict, but one in which the aggressor camouflages its actions. The U.S. strategy of global engagement and the sustained effectiveness of the American military have made indirect interstate war an attractive option for aggressor states. Support for Al Qaida by the Taliban regime in Afghanistan is one example. North Vietnam's support for the

Viet Cong, Pakistan's support for Kashmiri insurgents, and Rwandan and Ugandan support for the rebels that overthrew Mobutu Sese Seke in the Democratic Republic of the Congo (formerly Zaire) are others.

Countering indirect interstate aggression requires a two-track strategy: one track is aimed at the terrorists, insurgents, or the like; the other at the sponsoring state. If the sponsoring state is skilful at disguising its role, has a powerful protector (as often happened during the Cold War), or has nuclear weapons, the second track may be purely political and economic. Always, though, the two tracks of the strategy demand distinct forces and operational concepts. Since the strategic effectiveness of the United States in a conflict decreases as the degree of ambiguity increases, it will invariably find that pressuring or coercing the state sponsor of indirect aggression is simpler than dealing with insurgents, terrorists, or other nonstate enemies themselves.

Intrastate war involves either a conflict between a state and a nonstate opponent such as an insurgency, militia, or separatist movement, or armed conflict between two or more nonstate entities. The international law and norms which regulate armed conflict apply only in part or not at all. This type of war, then, is delimited and controlled more by resource limitations or self-restraint on the part of the belligerents rather than any formal framework. As a result, it can take a variety of forms, from the mostly psychological and political maneuverings of the Chiapas uprising in Mexico through the pure terrorism of Basque or Irish separatists to the horrific massacres by drugged child soldiers in Sierra Leone. At the upper end of the spectrum, intrastate war can come to resemble state-on-state war when the insurgents are powerful enough to control and administer territory (for instance, Colombia and Angola).

Given the growing constraints on traditional interstate war and the pressures on states, a combination of indirect interstate war and intrastate war is likely to dominate the global security environment during the next three decades. At the same time, direct interstate war cannot be ruled out and may occur in some regions. Nonstate war will be a growing problem and will require the most extensive adaptation by militaries and other elements of state security forces.

AMERICAN STRATEGY IN THE EMERGING SECURITY ENVIRONMENT

Trends suggest that indirect and internal aggression will dominate the emerging security environment. The United States will seek to sustain its position of leadership, to include orchestration of security from both a regional and a global perspective. Despite the proliferation of weapons of mass destruction, the diffusion of technology, and the pursuit of asymmetric methods, the United States is likely to sustain military superiority over likely enemies *under conditions of ethical, legal, and political clarity*. With military transformation proceeding apace, when a discernible aggressor poses a threat to important or vital U.S. national interests and the military is unleashed, victory is likely. The problem will be sustaining the utility of military force in the absence of clarity, particularly when enemies discover that the use of protracted warfare in physically, ethically, legally, and politically complex environments offers protection against the terrible, swift sword of the American military.

Precision will be the key to both operational and strategic success in this environment. Taken alone, that is certainly not a new idea. Increasing precision has long been considered a central element of the ongoing revolution in military affairs. George and Meredith Friedman, for instance, rank the development of precision guided munitions along with the introduction of firearms, the phalanx, and the chariot as "a defining moment in human history." But many of the architects of the American revolution in military affairs view precision narrowly, defining it simply as the ability to hit the desired target with accuracy and limited collateral damage. Tactical precision grows from improved intelligence, guidance systems and, increasingly, from the ability to adjust or "tune" the effects that a particular weapon has. A proposed electro-magnetic gun, for instance, could be adjusted from a nonlethal setting to an extremely lethal one. This is indeed a useful capability.

But precision has at least two other equally important dimensions. One is *strategic*, specifically the ability to undertake military operations without damaging or disrupting neighbouring states, a region, or the global economy. Globalization and interconnectedness are increasing the importance and the difficulty of strategic precision. If the only option available to the United States is to crush an opponent by pummeling its infrastructure and economy as in World War II or the Kosovo operation, the result will be unintended damage to neighbouring states and the global economy, and thus a rapid erosion of support for the operation. Such operational methods may appear attractive, particularly if they are based solely on stand-off strikes and thus promise to limit U.S. casualties, but they will be counterproductive in the long term and contribute to a decline in American influence.

A third form of precision is *psychological*. This entails shaping a military operation and campaign to have the exact desired psychological effect. Like so much of the revolution in military affairs, this is a new variant of an old idea. Military thinkers have long understood that war is integrally, perhaps even essentially psychological. Sun Tzu, of course, crafted the quintessentially psychological approach to strategy, contending that "all warfare is based on deception." While some disciples of Clausewitz, particularly German military strategists, acted with disregard for the psychological dimension of strategy, the Prussian theorist himself clearly understood that war was a psychological struggle and the objective is to break the enemy's will. Psychological precision requires tactical precision but also other capabilities such as nonlethality, other new technologies, a certain pace and intensity of activity, or even refraining from the use of force if that is what is required to have the desired effect. Psychological precision often requires extended, direct human contact in order to gauge and adjust effects. It also demands extensive and intensive cross-cultural understanding of the psychological effect of an action which is, to some extent, culturally determined.

What causes fear in one cultural context, for example, might cause anger and intensified resistance in another.

Ironically, the United States has not been particularly adept at culturally-focused military operations. Instead we tend toward psychological "mirror imaging"—assuming that if we can take actions against an enemy that would collapse our will if they were done to us, they will have the same effect on the enemy. Much of the thinking on "effects-based operations" reflects this sort of psychological mirror imaging. By contrast, psychological precision demands long-standing, hands-on engagement with other cultures, and a willingness on the part of commanders and planners to incorporate the advice of cultural experts and social psychologists. Ultimately, though, U.S. strategy requires all three forms of precision.

To sustain global leadership, U.S. strategy must minimize the natural tendency of other countries to contain, balance, or oppose American influence. This is a mounting problem. Despite the fact that every time in history a single power has been dominant, other states have eventually become worried or fearful and attempted to contain, balance, or oppose it, Americans seem to feel this will not happen to us. It is as if we believe that the laws of history do not apply to us and that other states are as convinced that our power is as benign or beneficial as we are. This is simply not true. While the United States has some bedrock allies not intimidated by American power, many other states are not so sanguine.

Most of these became America's partners because Washington was the lesser evil during the Cold War or post-Cold War period when Soviet- equipped rogue states posed a significant risk. Many others thought that a strategic partnership with the United States would bring economic or diplomatic benefits. Such friends are often disappointed. By the summer of 2002, for instance, Pakistanis were growing disillusioned with the limited economic gains of their support for the United States in the war on terrorism. Later resentment grew when Pakistan's support for U.S. operations in Afghanistan did not prevent plans to require Pakistanis living in the United States to register with the government. Many less committed strategic partners will become distrustful, even fearful, if American power becomes oppressive. The pursuit of transformation by the U.S. military further fuels such fears. To many foreign observers, there is no reason for an already-dominant U.S. military to undertake such an effort unless it intends to impose its will on recalcitrant states.

Ultimately there is no way to prevent all attempts to contain, balance, or oppose American power. This is part of the price of dominance. But the way that the United States exercises its power will affect the extent and intensity of this process. The more that U.S. strategy is based on the imposition of force from afar rather than partnership and the pursuit of conflict resolution, the greater the effort to contain, balance or oppose American power. This should be a consideration in strategy and force development.

Robust and versatile American landpower will be essential in the emerging security environment. When the use of force becomes necessary, the United States will continue to prefer and seek rapid decisive operations with an extensive use of precise standoff strikes, but enemies will increasingly use protracted, complex, ambiguous, and asymmetric methods to counter these.

If the United States reaches a point where *all* that it can undertake are rapid decisive operations relying heavily on standoff strikes, it will be like a 16th century armored knight or mid-20th century battleship—extremely adept at a type of combat that has declining strategic relevance. Winning 21st century armed conflicts will require more than servicing targets. American military strategy should thus seek rapid decisive operations but also retain the ability to prevail in protracted, complex, ambiguous, and asymmetric warfare. To do this requires the versatility of landpower.

THE ROLE AND STRUCTURE OF THE OBJECTIVE FORCE

In the broadest sense, the Army will have three strategic functions in the future security environment.

First, it will remain an integral part of the Joint Team in traditional warfighting against an enemy state or other discernible enemy organization such as a paramilitary, militia, or guerrilla army. According to the *Objective Force White Paper*: In 2015, the Objective Force is an integral component of the Joint Force. It is organized, manned, equipped, and trained as a JIM [Joint, interagency, and multinational] force, possess[ing] common overarching doctrine, integrated training, commonality, and interdependency/ interoperability.

In particular, the Objective Force will bring a campaign quality to the Joint fight, "ensuring long term dominance over evolving, sophisticated threats . . ."

But as direct interstate war declines in frequency, the Army's special capabilities at protracted, complex, ambiguous, and asymmetric conflicts, particularly indirect interstate war and intrastate war, will become increasingly important.

The Army is likely to be called on to help stabilize challenged states and ungoverned regions—functions that require a ground presence rather than standoff strikes. The Army also provides the capabilities needed to consolidate battlefield success and turn it into strategic victory.

This is a vital point. Throughout history, military victory has not always led to strategic success. For example, Napoleon won a long series of stunning military victories but was unable or unwilling to undertake the alteration of Prussian, Austrian, or Russian societies that would have consolidated his triumphs. Similarly, in World War I the Western Allies won a clear military victory, but did not have the will to turn it into strategic victory by altering the elements of German society and culture that spawned armed aggression. In World War II, by contrast, military victory was transformed into strategic victory.

Strategic victory requires not only the defeat of the enemy military, but often occupation and a multiagency effort to change the society, culture, economy, and political system that undergirded aggression. This will be as true in the future as it has been in the past.

While it is conceivable (but unlikely) that the United States might attain military victory over some future enemy relying primarily on standoff applications of military power from the air, sea, or space, strategic victory always requires effective landpower. In some future wars, the United States may seek only military victory, particularly if the enemy has weapons of mass destruction or there is some rationale to leave the enemy regime intact (as was thought to be true following the Gulf War).

At other times, though, only strategic victory can assure the Nation's security. While the Army will be a vital component of the Joint Team in all future wars, providing the capability for strategic victory along with proficiency at protracted, complex, ambiguous, and asymmetric conflicts will be the Army's two *unique* strategic functions.

Trends in the global security environment suggest that there will be six strategically decisive characteristics for the Objective Force. One is *strategic speed.*

During the post-Cold War period, it became clear that the Army had unmatched capabilities once deployed but was, under some conditions, hindered by the length of time required for deployment. Given the fluidity of the emerging security environment and the advantages that accrue from having effective landpower availably quickly, the Army's leaders have made strategic speed a primary objective of the Transformation process.

"At the strategic level," according to the *Objective Force White Paper*, "the Objective Force deploys from either forward sanctuaries or the continental United States. The force has both expeditionary and campaign qualities; is configured for rapid deployment and ready at a moments [sic] notice for sustained operations."

A second strategically decisive characteristic for the Objective Force will be *full scale decisiveness*. This entails both military victory—providing "the essential capability to achieve decisive victory through the control of terrain, people, and resources without resorting to indiscriminate destruction"—and strategic victory, to include altering the basic social, political, and economic system that spawned aggression. The third strategically decisive characteristic for the Objective Force will be *broadband precision* including the tactical, strategic, and psychological dimensions.

The fourth strategically decisive characteristic for the Objective Force will be *proficiency at protracted, ambiguous, asymmetric, and complex conflicts*. This requires the continuing recruitment and education of soldiers and officers capable of decisionmaking in difficult environments and of understanding the psychological and cultural subtleties of this type of conflict.

It will also require the development of new operational and strategic concepts specific to protracted, ambiguous, asymmetric, and complex conflicts, and the building of networked Army units with appropriate technologies.

Robotics and nonlethality hold particular promise. Finally, success in such conflicts will demand seamless links between the Objective Force and other partners including the Joint Team, nonmilitary U.S. government agencies, and non-government entities, whether humanitarian relief organizations, international organizations, nonstate political movements, or corporations. *Compatibility with coalition partners* will be the fifth strategically decisive characteristic for the Objective Force.

Since the beginning of the Cold War, American strategy has stressed developing and nurturing partnerships as a mechanism for creating regional stability without the need for a U.S. military so large that it would be economically debilitating. This is unlikely to change.

The future U.S. military will be heavily involved in improving the capabilities of partners during peacetime, and supporting them and operating in conjunction with them during armed conflicts. To be successful, the Objective Force must be as compatible with coalition partners as possible—the goal is for multinational operations to be "business as usual for the Army." This entails overcoming technological problems, as well as developing common operational and strategic concepts.

Finally, *rapid conceptual and organizational adaptation* will be a strategically decisive characteristic for the Objective Force. The Information Age has made rapid, focused adaptation a determinant of success for any organization in a competitive environment. This was first seen in the business world with the movement away from rigid hierarchies toward networks, the building of "learning organizations," and the making of long-range strategic planning and change—even revolutionary change— continual rather than episodic.

During the Industrial Age large, hierarchical organizations held advantage over smaller, less formally organized ones. Firms like Standard Petroleum and General Motors could crush or absorb smaller competitors. Small states, unless protected by some quirk of politics or geography, could seldom compete militarily with large ones.

Today, the trend in the business world is toward macro-level integration and "strategic partnerships," but internal decentralization and the loosening of hierarchies. Technology is forcing a major shift in paradigms of scale with adaptability and speed as important as aggregate resources. By allowing multiple, cross-cutting connections between individuals and organizations, technology is dispersing power, creativity, and productive capability. Now successful commercial firms have a global perspective, a web of strategic partnerships, and internal flexibility based on project teams or work groups rather than hierarchies or bureaucracies.

This shift in advantage from large hierarchical institutions to adaptable, networked ones is migrating to the military realm. As indirect interstate war and intrastate war become dominant, many of the opponents faced by the Army will be nonstate ones. While these enemies will only be able to mobilize miniscule resources in comparison to the U.S. military, they will be relatively free of bureaucratic encumbrances, and thus very adaptable and flexible. To succeed against them, the Objective Force must become more adaptable and flexible than its predecessors.

This must entail the integration of modularity and "plug and play" capabilities from the squad to the strategic level. Specifically, the Objective Force must be much quicker than the Cold War or post-Cold War Army at developing new operational and strategic concepts, educating soldiers and officers to implement them, and developing organizations and technologies to make them work. Transformation must be continuous rather than episodic.

While the Objective Force must integrate all six strategically decisive characteristics, certain of these are linked to specific strategic battlespaces.

In direct interstate war, for instance, strategic speed will be vital, particularly the ability to deploy overwhelming force more rapidly than an enemy can. The "crucial measure of successful force projection is not the speed with which the first combat element engages, but rather the rate at which the United States and its allies are able to achieve overall operational superiority, depriving an enemy of freedom of action and making his ultimate defeat both inevitable and irreversible."

Broad band precision will be important to retain domestic and international support for American engagement in a conflict, and to prevent political pressure from forcing the United States to cease activity before its strategic objectives are met. And the ability to operate in coalition will be important because of the scope and size of direct interstate war.

Nonstate enemies will be the most adaptable and least encumbered by bureaucracy or international law and norms. This means that the ability of the Objective Force to itself adapt and to craft seamless links with other organizations, including private ones, will be the keys to victory.

In indirect interstate and intrastate war, broad band precision, the ability to operate in coalition, and the ability adapt rapidly will remain important, as will the development of concepts, organizations, and technologies applicable in protracted, asymmetric, ambiguous, and complex conflicts.

The ability of the Objective Force to sustain efforts over many months or years is particularly crucial in these strategic battlespaces since they are the ones where rapid, decisive operations will seldom, if ever, lead to strategic victory.

The trends shaping the emerging security environment and the roles which the Army will play in it suggest the need for two tracks to Transformation, one aimed at dominance in direct, interstate war, relying when possible on rapid decisive operations, the other aimed at dominance in indirect interstate and intrastate wars characterized by protractedness, ambiguity, asymmetry, and complexity. Clearly the two tracks of Transformation are intertwined. Many concepts, organizations, and technologies will have equal application in both.

But they also differ in some key ways. Indirect interstate and intrastate wars are not "lesser included instances." An Objective Force that can defeat a state military in rapid decisive operations, in other words, might not necessarily be able to undertake protracted stability operations. The Transformation process must assure that both tracks lead to success.

An Objective Force designed for both military and strategic victory in a security environment dominated by protracted, asymmetric, ambiguous, and complex conflicts would, in the broadest sense, have three components (see Figure 4). One would be the strike forces built around the Future Combat System.

This component would be characterized by rapid strategic mobility and be the master of rapid decisive operations. It would be the tool of decision in direct interstate war, but would also be used for the initial establishment of security in other strategic battlespaces when a discernible, armed enemy offers resistance. The second component would be Special Forces. These would be both numerically larger and more important to the Objective Force than to the Cold War and post-Cold War Army.

While the future of Special Forces requires detailed analysis and wargaming, the nature of the emerging security environment suggests a three way division here as well, with some Special Forces focused on protracted, ambiguous, complex, asymmetric (PACA) conflict, some on nonstate war, and some on direct action and support to strike forces, both in direct interstate war and in counterterrorism and counterproliferation activity.

As Special Forces play an increasingly important role in American strategy, they must undergo a fundamental redesign in order to match capabilities to emerging threats, and to erase the seams between them and other military and civilian organizations with which they must.

The third component of the Objective Force should be support forces. The idea here is simple: the more that partners can defend themselves and manage regional security, the better for the United States. Often partners need augmentation from the United States during crises or conflicts, particularly in specialized capabilities.

Currently if the United States sends engineers, intelligence specialists, information warriors, or military police to support a partner, these units must be stripped from a combat division, leaving it less effective or even undeployable.

To remedy this, the Objective Force should have units designed specifically to augment partners with the capabilities they are likely to be short of, particularly intelligence, engineers, medical units, military police, civil affairs, and psychological operations. This would improve the ability of the United States to support allies while retaining the readiness of the strike forces.

WHY AN ARMY?

It is ironic that nearly every analyst of the emerging security environment admits that it will be characterized by asymmetry and complexity, yet most assume that the solution is more technology and an even greater focus on a single type of military operation—rapid decisive operations. Ultimately only adaptability and versatility trump asymmetry and complexity. While all elements of the Joint Team play vital roles in the Nation's defense, the Army is the most versatile.

Only the Army can simultaneously contribute to rapid, decisive operations against another state's military, undertake stability operations during an intrastate conflict, and assure strategic victory by providing security while an aggressor's political, social, and economic systems are reformed. An American military without robust and effective land power capable of sustained operations would be like the 16th century armored knight or mid-20th century battlefield—very good but very limited.

If anything, the capability to attain *strategic* victory will become more important in the emerging security environment.

History is replete with instances where overwhelming military victory did not lead to strategic success, from Jena-Auerstadt through World War I to the Gulf War.

The terrorist attacks of September 11, 2001, demonstrate the need for strategic victory. Even today if the global war on terrorism only leads to military rather than strategic victory, the threat will simply reemerge. Strategic victory is nearly always more costly than simple military victory, so there may be times when national leaders do not seek it.

But when they do—and everything in the emerging security environment indicates the need to do so—robust and effective landpower will be vital. The Army, in other words, will be extremely effective at the type of armed conflict that will dominate the global security environment in the coming decade as Transformation continues.

As globalization and the information revolution rush ahead, the world is becoming even more interconnected. The repercussions of this are far reaching. For instance, the increased concern for the Palestinians in the Arab world—which is a factor in the anti-Americanism that was the foundation for the September 11 attacks—is due in part to the information revolution as satellite television networks bring daily reminders of the Arab-Israeli conflict into homes throughout the Middle East and the West.

Interconnectedness means that American military operations must be as precise as possible to sustain domestic and international support. When precision is understood as three dimensional, with tactical, strategic, and psychological components, the Army's contribution to an effective American strategy becomes clear.

Finally, American leaders must be sensitive to the natural and historical tendency on the part of other states to seek ways to balance, limit, or contain U.S. power. As Joseph Nye writes, "Throughout history, coalitions of countries have arisen to balance dominant powers . . ." The United States, however benign its power (and others do not see it as such), is not immune from the laws of history.

The way that America exercises its power will, in part, determine the intensity and the extent of attempts to counter it. As Stephen Walt notes, "if the strongest state acts in a benevolent fashion and its goals are broadly compatible with the interests of other major powers," the search for ways to keep it in check will be muted.

Given this, an American strategy that withdraws from the day-to-day (and often expensive and tedious) maintenance of regional security but instead simply applies force from afar as punishment will escalate efforts to balance, limit, or contain U.S. power. While such a strategy might appear attractive in the short term, it would ultimately prove less effective than one that commits the United States to deep engagement and shared responsibility with regional partners. The use of land power is the most effective expression of deep engagement and shared responsibility. For four reasons, then, the Army is vital to the type of strategy that would best promote American interests over the long term.

3

HISTORICAL PERSPECTIVES ON FUTURE WAR

Using historical perspectives on the future, this chapter addresses several fundamental questions. First, how did past futurists frame their arguments in historical terms and what common approaches did they adopt? Second, how have past approaches to speculation on future war influenced the way we think today? And, third, how have historical perspectives entered into the current debate about shifting paradigms in strategy and the revolution in military affairs (RMA)?

Before addressing these questions, a brief review of a few prominent European intellectual trends during the century and a half before World War I reveals emerging assumptions about change and progress that are basic to any analysis of why war has assumed its variety of forms. The modern fascination with cutting-edge technologies and their undeniable impact on war often obscures our view of war's other dimensions. Historians have widely noted the social, political and economic factors in shaping the evolution of conflict. Cultural and intellectual changes have played a powerful role as well.

Past patterns of thinking about the future have influenced the way we speculate about war-so much that we often use them subconsciously. First and foremost examples are our notions of change and progress. As noted by scholar J.B. Bury in The Idea of Progress, until the Middle Ages, Western cultures generally adhered to a static view of history. The ancient Greek philosophers did not perceive progressive development as natural to humanity. While they did grasp the cyclical rise and decline of city-states and empires, they perceived no general direction, and certainly no conspicuous or inexorable improvement, in unfolding human history. Even at the dawning of the Renaissance, when the intellectual preconditions for its appearance were taking form, the idea of progress in earthly affairs was yet to be born.

However, by the late 18th century, faith in progress was virtually a fixture in the outlook among all but the most pessimistic of Western thinkers. Period analysts founded this perception on an appreciation of comparatively recent but dramatic change brought about by scientific and technological advances. Progressive discovery in biology, botany, chemistry, physics and astronomy revealed dazzling patterns and regularities in the universe. Some inferred from the unlocking of nature's secrets that comparable tendencies might govern human affairs. A critical component of this revelation was the constancy of change and a fresh sense of the trajectory of historical development. Many looked boldly to a brighter future. For instance, Marquis de Condorcet wrote effusively in 1793 about the limitless perfectibility of humanity even as he was under death sentence and evading revolutionary authorities in France.

Contemporary thought about warfare reflected the spirit of the time and place. In his Essai general de tactique, written in 1770, Frenchman Jacques Antoine Hippolyte Comte de Guibert purported to make a science of tactics. Based on a historical review of the art of war, he professed to have established a series of enduring tactical principles that would transcend changes in weaponry. Along the way, he concluded that the states of the ancient world often exhibited a better grasp of the relationship between war and state institutions than kingdoms of contemporary Europe, although he held out hope for Frederick the Great's Prussia.

By the early 19th century, European interpretations of the historical development of human knowledge, warfare and social organization tended to share one distinctive characteristic: They saw human progress unfolding not in a perfectly linear fashion but in distinct stages. Each stage represented a fundamental transformation that built on the foundation left by its predecessor. Even the French Revolution's excesses, the Napoleonic Wars' horrors and conservative reaction across Europe did not stifle the optimistic profusion of new writings anticipating a bold new age. War, many believed, was crossing a historic threshold as well.

To forecast the path the future would take, those analysts who most influenced 20th-century perspectives attempted to use scientific methodology. Setting the pace were the "positivists" and Auguste Comte. Comte set aside the questions of causality and meaning. Believing that contemporary German idealists and romantics were wasting time in their preoccupation with such problems, he focused his attention on what could be known. Thus, Comte sought to ascertain the laws governing human and social development through empirical observation-the cornerstone of positivist methodology. Comte described history as inexorably unfolding in three intellectual stages: theological, metaphysical and positivist. The latter did not build on its predecessors but, instead, replaced them by virtue of its superior insight. Comte dubbed the application of positive doctrine to human affairs "social physics," the spirit of which incidentally pervades modern social science theory and warfare modeling. Accordingly, positivists anticipated that knowledge of the laws by which societies functioned would make it possible in the future to engineer a perfect society and even put an end to war. Not only was the future predetermined, humanity itself could self-consciously bring it to reality.

Even John Stuart Mill, the English paragon of classical Western liberalism and champion of free speech and free will, could not entirely escape the idea that certain laws actually governed the flow of history. Mill separated history into so-called organic and critical periods. The former represented periods of stability and the latter, disruption and change. The search for truth was the moving force in history. Overall, he contended that historical laws direct human action, and "the influence exercised over each generation by the generations which preceded it, becomes more and more preponderant over all other influences." Shaping the same logic toward a different end, German historicists and early philosopher-nationalists, such as Johann Fichte, argued that the present and future were governed by the past.

Fichte saw the unfolding of history in the evolution of the modern nation, viewing the state as the vehicle by which politically self-conscious peoples would secure their destinies. Similarly, German philosopher Georg Wilhelm Friedrich Hegel saw historical progression as a dialectical process involving creative destruction in which each stage produced the forces that would undermine it and synthesize a new stage. In this context, Hegel wrote, "Freedom is nothing but the recognition and adoption of such universal substantial objects as Right and Law, and the production of a reality that is accordant with them-the state." This logical foundation served as the point of departure for much of Carl von Clausewitz's interest in the state and its defense.

Against this common European cultural background, it is hardly surprising that popular philosophical concepts should have found their way into theoretical musings about warfare. Henri Jomini's works on warfare and his belief in the immutable principles that regulate it exhibit positivist influence. Although he was also influenced by empirical scientific precepts, Clausewitz expresses German philosophical concerns with "how we know what we know," the force of human will and a host of other problems. Clausewitz adapted the Hegelian dialectical method to his consideration of war. He recognized implicitly that Napoleon's crushing defeat of the Prussian army in 1806 demolished the military synthesis of Frederickian absolutism. Though cognizant of change, Clausewitz did not foresee the perfecting of humanity or a prescription for perfect soldiering. His grasp of friction-sand in the gears of the perfect Enlightenment rationalist machine-doubtless made him skeptical of positivist influence on the study of war. Still, he did believe that soldiers could improve their minds through experience and the study of history and theory.

Another perspective that affected interpretations of change and warfare surfaced in 1859 with the publication of Charles Darwin's Origin of Species. All the theoretical parts of Darwin's synthesis were well established before he wrote his book. However, no one had woven them together as distinctively as he did. When fully assembled, Darwin's theory of evolution offered a new paradigm for thinking about the world. This paradigm depended on the assumptions that change was constant and normal, the earth was far older than previously supposed and the mechanism of biological evolution was natural selection. The most explosive implication was that humans were the product of evolution.

Reactions to Darwin varied. To some, namely those who came to be called social Darwinists, "survival of the fittest" became the governing principle of peoples and states. This world view reflected a distinct notion of progress but certainly dispelled the optimism of preceding decades. The idea that struggle was integral to civilization's advance resonated widely and merged with another seminal 19th-century trend-nationalism.

A relatively recent phenomenon, nationalism was rooted in a late 18th-century cultural movement emphasizing the historical rise of distinct nations as expressed through ethnicity, language and heritage. Afforded political impetus by the Napoleonic Wars, nationalism became an incredibly potent social force in late 19th-century Europe, where the imagery of nations as living organisms fused with the concept of Darwinian struggle. A splendid example is Russia and Europe, published in 1869 by Russian Pan-Slavic theorist Nikolai Danilevski, which forecast a great war with Germany to decide whether Slavs or Germans would be masters of Central and Eastern Europe. With remarkable speed, the new nationalistic strain gained adherents among Europe's armies.

In the 1870s, Russian General Mikhail Skobelev remarked that only war, the highest manifestation of the life of the state, could stir a self-indulgent citizenry to the service of higher values. In 1911, in Germany and the Next War, retired German cavalry general and Pan-German publicist Friedrich von Bernhardi embraced the idea of struggle. War was not merely essential, it was the highest expression of civilization.

Not all, however, read Darwin the same way. To Herbert

Spencer, evolutionary theory implied that human nature itself was subject to change and therefore offered a renewed hope for the perfection of humanity. Civilization's development through natural selection was itself natural. In contrast to the social Darwinists, Spencer suggested that societies would evolve away from armed struggle toward harmony and cooperation. An industrial age of peace would supplant the age of militant struggle.

Marxism presented yet another competing interpretation. Though influenced by Comte and Hegel, Karl Marx predicated his views on materialist thought-all events and even intellectual processes have material or physical causes-and scientific social analysis. In 1848, Marx and Friedrich Engels wrote the Communist Manifesto, as well as several other works on the formation of social classes and proletarian revolution. They organized the past and future into stages of development from slave societies, through feudalism and capitalism, to communism. Marx looked ahead to the annihilation of capitalism, the withering of the state and the creation of a classless society. The engine of history was class struggle and periodic revolution against the prevailing order of economic relations in society. A historical determinist, Marx saw humanity's path toward this end as preordained.

After Marx's death, Engels applied the Marxian dialectic to the discussion of war. In 1887, Engels described a cataclysmic future European war that would lay waste to bourgeois societies and create the necessary climate for revolution and working class triumph. Vladimir Lenin borrowed Engels' vision to create a new typology of war. Drawing from Clausewitz and Marx, Lenin penned "The Principles of Socialism and the War, 1914-1915," an essay in which he contended that bourgeois-national wars, which had predominated until 1871, subsequently gave way to imperialist war, a distinctive and inevitable feature of mature capitalism. In 1917, Lenin forecast in War and Revolution that World War I would devolve into international civil war and revolution.

By the eve of The Great War, many believed change and progress had joined with biological metaphor to define the relationship among European states. This outlook steeled the will of peoples across the Continent to raise gigantic armies and justified virtually any sacrifice in the name of the nation.

SPECULATION ON WAR AND CHANGE

At the turn of the century, well before Lenin came to his revelation about war, Polish banker Jan S. Bloch published a radical non-Marxist critique of contemporary warfare. Employing only information that was available to professional soldiers of his day, Bloch contended that Europe's generals were wrong about what future war would hold. He wrote that ". . . war, instead of being a hand-to-hand contest in which the combatants measure their physical and moral superiority, will become a kind of stalemate, in which neither army being able to get at the other, both armies will be maintained in opposition to each other, threatening each other, but never being able to deliver a final and decisive attack. It will be simply the natural evolution of the armed peace, on an aggravated scale. . . . That is the future of war-not fighting, but famine, not the slaying of men, but the bankruptcy of nations and the breakup of the whole social organization."

Bloch, failing to appreciate nationalism's power, was not entirely correct, although he did discern some of war's dimensions with remarkable clarity. In the end, there was a decision, but only at a stupendous and irrational cost that toppled empires and pulverized a generation.

The point is to note Bloch's revolutionary view of war. Bloch appreciated that the arms evolution had reached a new threshold which would fundamentally alter the conditions of the next great European war. Aside from his skills as an economic analyst and his mastery of professional military literature, Bloch brought a different perspective to his examination. His paradigm was partially a function of his pacifist outlook, but it was equally attributable to his perception that the old way of thinking about warfare could not accommodate new realities.

Many military thinkers on the eve of World War I also recognized the importance of recent changes, but most construed them differently. As early as 1893, Russian Captain E.I. Martynov wrote a study titled "Thoughts about the Technique of Future Wars," in which he attempted to describe how future strategy would guide theatre-level war. Another forward-looking Russian was A.A. Neznamov, who served as an instructor at the Nicholas Academy of the General Staff from 1907 to 1912. Neznamov was among the leading proponents of unified military doctrine-a common approach to war for the Russian army.

Based on his Russo-Japanese War analysis, Neznamov identified four essential features that would characterize the next war and which competent future commanders would have to reckon with:

- The predominant role of fire-more lethal, accurate and voluminous.
- The lower quality of conscript soldiers.
- Mass armies.
- The unprecedented complexity of command and control.

Bloch shared most of Neznamov's projections. Both also pondered a question that had stirred great debate among generals and military theorists since the Franco-Prussian War: Was there a new relationship between technology and the human/moral factor in war? They both held to the radical view that "man was losing his grip on war." Future firepower would dominate combat and reduce soldiers to cogs in a vast, incomprehensible machine. Commanders would wrestle to control mass forces beyond the reach of communications.

Unlike many of his predecessors, Neznamov never referred to the power of genius in his writings. Whether or not he believed in genius, he did not expect to find it. What he sought were competent commanders-schooled leaders capable of properly executing any task in harmony with an overall battle scheme. Therefore, the Russian army's central problem was not a lack of genius but a parade-ground mind-set that stifled practical preparation and substituted templated courses of action for scientific analysis and artful judgment.

According to Neznamov, the education of a proficient general had to be based on self-study. He cited Russian Field Marshal

Aleksandr Suvorov's proposition that a good commander first mastered the regulations, then the principles of war and, finally, the history of recent and ancient wars. If the first two instilled a sense of what to do and why, the latter developed his critical faculties and an appreciation of the uniqueness of any situation. A commander had to create solutions, because every problem he would face in future war would necessarily be new, even if it was historically familiar in a general sense. In sum, Bloch rejected war because of its intrinsic futility, whereas Neznamov planned to prepare commanders to cope with future trials.

The problem confronting Bloch and Neznamov was no different than the one leaders face today. The social and political changes that reshaped military organizations were combined with rapid, incremental technological advances and seemingly normal evolutionary design improvements in existing weapons to produce jarring, disorienting changes on the battlefield. In Marxian terms, quantity became quality.

PARADIGM SHIFTS AND RMA

Current literature on policy and international security hails a paradigm shift in US foreign policy and strategy. The basis for this shift is the Soviet Union's collapse, the disintegration of the Eastern bloc and the dissolution of Yugoslavia. Since 1991, the United States has adjusted to a world without its principal political, ideological and military adversary. The implications are large and numerous.

What exactly do we mean by a paradigm shift, and how do we recognize one? Physicist and historian Thomas Kuhn brought the expression "paradigm shift" into common usage in 1962 with The Structure of Scientific Revolutions. He attacked traditional interpretations of scientific development that depicted a steady building process where each breakthrough added to an established knowledge foundation. Kuhn's thesis maintained that science advances alternately between the accumulation of discoveries within a given system of understanding and revolutionary changes which undermine the structure of existing knowledge and necessitate the building of a new conceptual framework. "Paradigms gain their status because they are more successful than their competitors in solving a few problems that the group of practitioners has come to recognize as acute."

During periods of so-called normal science, new discoveries flow logically from, and in turn support, the prevailing paradigm. However, Kuhn explains that ". . . the successive transition from one paradigm to another via revolution is the usual developmental pattern of mature science." Scientific revolutions occur because an existing paradigm cannot accommodate new discoveries or theories. "Normal science . . . often suppresses fundamental novelties because they are necessarily subversive of its basic commitments." In other words, people are more receptive to new evidence that conforms to previously held views than evidence which contradicts them. Ultimately, normal science approaches a crisis when the results of research can no longer be adapted to fit the established pattern. Ultimately, each paradigm generates the very research that will eventually undermine it.

Therefore, a scientific revolution must drive the old paradigm from centre stage to permit the advance of science. A revolution is not a mere reinterpretation of the existing paradigm. Rather, it leads to a fundamentally new comprehension of pre-existing knowledge. Thus, revelation and revolution demand a new paradigm.

Given the widespread adoption of Kuhn's terminology, it is appropriate to reconsider the extent of recent changes in the strategic environment in light of his definition. Has the American paradigm undergone a shift or merely a reinterpretation? The latter may be closer to the truth. Consider the continuities. NATO is still with us. The United States still seeks a world hospitable to free market economies and democracy, takes a proprietary interest in Western affairs and maintains highly capable military forces to protect its interests in the post-Cold War world. The lens of US-Soviet rivalry no longer distorts the American view of every regional conflict or Third World insurgency. Today, in terms of national security strategy, we are looking at the old post-World War II paradigm in an unfamiliar way.

The same is true of military strategy. Because US military forces can no longer focus on the former Soviet Union, a huge shift in emphasis is necessary. Still, the variety of missions proposed for US forces in the near term differs little from what we have done historically. US forces have engaged in low-intensity conflict and operations other than war since the founding of the republic and repeatedly in this century. Furthermore, if we look around the globe today, we see nothing unprecedented. Nationalist, religious and ethnic conflicts are hardly distinctive late 20th-century phenomena.

Yet, as the information age matures, some unfamiliar problems are likely to appear. For example, a determined adversary should be able to devise many insidious ways to sabotage, disrupt or contaminate the information highway upon which global and national commerce depend. Competition among multinational economic organizations could easily assume such a form. In addition, the advent of the alleged RMA will certainly influence how we practice war.

Historian Michael Howard recently posed a fundamental question: "Can technology change what has been, until now, the essence of warfare?" Many have attempted to answer this question. In the past several years, a host of books and articles have heralded the dawning of a new age in warfare. Characterized variously as the Third Wave, the Fourth Generation or simply the latest RMA, the new age in warfare has not escaped the notice of soldiers and scholars. The collective commentary has been impressive in its insight as well as its profusion. Perhaps no generation of military commentators has been so ready to embrace change and administer last rites to conventional wisdom about warfare.

One striking feature of the discussion is the periodization of history. Whereas most 19th-century observers periodized the past in terms of progressive stages of humanity's understanding of the world, social development or civilization, 20th-century writers typically focus on new technologies and the economic base that produces them. New technologies were central to the arguments of Liddell Hart and Julio Douhet. Even Soviet theorists, who relied on the Marxist description of historical stages, described the contemporary period-from World War II forward-predominantly in terms of technological change. Alvin and Heidi Toffler's War and Anti-War suggests that warfare is entering the Third Wave, in which power will be based on information technology. Eventually, they expect, technology and rationality will reduce the level of violence inherent in conflict to that of a hockey game. Could it be that the Tofflers and others are missing important continuities in the nature of war even as they offer provocative insights into the manner of its future conduct?

To be sure, the manner in which future war will be conducted is most relevant. In 1993, General Gordon R. Sullivan and Colonel James Dubik suggested five trends:

- Increased lethality and dispersion.
- Increased volume and precision of fires.
- Increased integration of technologies.
- Achievement of greater mass and effect.
- Refinements in invisibility and detectability.
- Russian forecasters recently identified a similar set of distinguishing features for future nonlinear war:
- Absence of well-defined spatial limits.
- Combination of offensive and defensive operations.
- Increasing reliance on information systems for coordination.
- Conduct of mass strikes by radio-electronic high-precision, laser and superfrequency weapons, large helicopter groups and radio-electronic suppression.

Upon close examination, each of these trends exhibits significant continuity with, or is rooted in, the evolution of warfare since the late 19th century. If we are in the midst of an RMA, historians can make a strong case that it has been unfolding for a long time. Viewing the same progression in another light, one could even argue that accelerating advance along the axes noted by Sullivan and Dubik constitutes one of the fundamental assumptions of the way we view warfare.

Perhaps it is just part of our 20th-century paradigm and not a new revolution at all. Warfare has been in a state of rapid change for the past two centuries, and many modern phenomena were born in that progression. The recent trends identified by Sullivan and Dubik and their Russian counterparts differ from those noted by Bloch and Neznamov more in degree than in kind.

Problems inherent in linking futuristic technological change and doctrinal concepts are much the same today as they were a century ago. Consider the US Army's 1950s' response to the nuclear age. Having retained a conventional focus after World War II, the Army suddenly revealed the Pentomic Division in 1956. Consisting of five battle groups, the new division stressed air mobility and dispersion to function better in a nuclear environment. The bold experiment failed because "the technology lagged behind the doctrine, and the strategic concepts raced ahead of tactical realities."

This time, the Army is valiantly attempting to prepare for change ahead of time. The future holds many eye-opening innovations, especially in technology. Recent dialogue has described future electronic combat as achieving spectrum supremacy which "will prove as critical as conventional battlefield preparation and air supremacy operations of past wars."

The near term also holds the prospects of cyberwar, robotic war and even neocortical warfare. Again, the underlying concepts are not altogether new. Most are consonant with J.F.C. Fuller's 1919 prescription for attacking the nervous system of the enemy. The imperative to gain spectrum supremacy might lead to escalatory scenarios reminiscent of the 1914 mobilization theory or Cold War nuclear logic.

Visions of new capabilities offer a glimpse of the future but leave even more unknown. In the Fall 1994 issue of Parameters, David Jablonsky asserted that the quantum leap in technology may actually increase the "fog of war," given compressed decision cycles and the increasing integration of the levels of war. Will we have more information than we can absorb? Will enemies find new ways to deceive us?

Because we cannot perfectly model future human behaviour and interaction, past wisdom may be more helpful than critics suspect. Recent attacks on Clausewitz stress his neglect of insurgencies and ethnic strife within his state-oriented, trinitarian framework; his inability to anticipate the flood of future technologies; and his failure to consider the role of culture in determining modes of conflict. Although these criticisms have some merit, they are based on a misconception of the Clausewitzian trinity, the constituent parts of which are violence, chance and reason. The army, the government and the people are merely the rough real-world correlates of the trinity. The actual trinity is not bound to any particular historical context. It is as relevant to Operations Uphold Democracy and Desert Storm as to Prussia. Perhaps the trinity is a nonlinear concept.

Were Clausewitz alive to comment, he might note that the idea of the state as Fichte knew it probably applies as well to the Palestinian Liberation Organization or Chechnya (which aspired to statehood) as to the United States. Furthermore, the passions and rationales that move states to roll the dice of war differ little from those which arouse tribes or insurgents. Finally, would a man who likened war to commerce really be unappreciative of the spectrum of conflict? Whatever features conflict assumes-urban operations, conventional air strikes, guerrilla fighting, psychological operations, random terror and even peacekeeping-all are discussable in Clausewitzian terms.

Like Sun Tzu, Clausewitz intuitively understood that the history of conflict revealed a dynamic tension among competing forces. Clausewitz, whose On War frequently bewilders American readers, drew heavily upon Hegelian dialectical reasoning, which sought synthetic truths through the resolution of opposing ideas or forces. It is this state of mutual opposition, regarded as perfectly natural by German philosophers, that characterizes the three parts of the trinity. Rather than ambiguity, Clausewitz saw in it flexibility and applicability to a many-sided reality.

Clausewitz did not describe in detail how future wars would be fought, but he was a futurist in his own right. In constructing a theory for thinking about war, he assumed that war's essential trinity would remain constant far beyond his lifetime.

As observed recently by Lieutenant Colonel Poncho Diaz-Pons, a historian formerly with the US Army Command and General Staff College, Fort Leavenworth, Kansas, "If you want to think outside the box, you want to know how the box was made." His point-and the point of this article-is that the writings of past thinkers have left us a legacy of intellectual constructs which we regularly apply to the study of change and future war. Thus, to paraphrase Liddell Hart, the "tug of war" between science and history remains a dynamic element in contemporary thinking on future war. The concepts of paradigm and revolution, rooted in past conceptualizations of history and progress, reflect this tension.

4

MILITARY THEORY AND THE FUTURE OF WAR

PLATO

As the world enters the twenty-first century, it appears to be in the midst of revolutionary shifts in the character of international security, with the forces of information technology and globalization seemingly transforming the theory and practice of war. In retrospect, it is now possible to see the decade between the collapse of Soviet communism in August 1991 and the attacks on the Pentagon and the World Trade Centre in September 2001 as an era of the unexpected. No one in the West expected, still less predicted, the fall of the Soviet Union; the Iraqi invasion of Kuwait and the Gulf War; the Asian financial crisis; the Indian and Pakistani nuclear detonations; or, of course, the events of 11 September.

Over the past decade, armed conflict has not remained within the traditional parameters of conventional warfare between rival states. From Somalia through Bosnia to Kosovo, East Timor, and Afghanistan, the face of war has assumed bewildering expressions. Under new global security conditions, the postmodern has collided with the premodern, the cosmopolitan has confronted the parochial, while the Westphalian state system has been challenged by new substate and transstate forces. Conventional high-tech Western armed forces have had to come to terms with a world of failed states populated by ethnic paramilitaries; of rogue regimes equipped with ballistic missiles and poison gas; and of radical extremists embracing a philosophy of mass-casualty terrorism.

For Western policy makers and military professionals these are deeply perplexing times; war seems more dynamic and chameleon-like than ever before. There are pressing questions: What is the future of war in conditions of great flux? Can traditional ideas of military power continue to dominate in an age of both globalization and fragmentation? What is the meaning of Western military supremacy in an era when democratic civilization—as demonstrated by the events of 11 September—is highly vulnerable to unexpected and unorthodox threats?

This article seeks to provide some answers to these questions. It adopts an approach reflecting a conviction that while events are always impossible to predict, it is possible to undertake intelligent analysis of trends in order to make some interim judgments about the kind of military conditions that might emerge in the near future. The article explores four areas. First, the fragmentation of the international system in the 1990s is analyzed in an attempt to demonstrate how new political conditions caused a diffusion of conflict modes that in turn have brought great uncertainty to the world of military analysts. Second, the main theories of war that emerged in the 1990s and the complexity these brought to traditional military thinking are examined. Third, a snapshot is provided of some of the most important challenges facing the West in terms of the theory and practice of the military art over the next decade and a half. Finally, some of the likely characteristics of warfare over the next decade are identified and subjected to tentative analysis.

WAR IN THE 1990S: THE DIFFUSION OF CONFLICT

In the 1990s there appears to have been a major transition in international relations away from a mainly state-centred system toward one marked by greater interdependence and interconnectedness. This trend toward interconnectedness was propelled by the dual impact of globalization and its handmaiden, the information revolution. Together, these two forces appeared to have altered the context within which modern states operate, bringing about an apparent redistribution of power among states, markets, and civil society.

From a military perspective, the globalization of the last decade is perhaps best described as a process in which space and time have been so compressed by technology as to permit distant actions to have local effects, and vice versa. The international system that emerged by the beginning of the twenty-first century was an interconnected world order in which regional and local military developments could be of global significance.

Defense analysts quickly discovered that conflict and disorder anywhere in the world could be quickly transmitted everywhere—and invested with crisis— by a pervasive global communications media, epitomized by the Cable News Network. It was also discovered that globalization is not a homogenous process but contains a striking paradox in that it brings about both convergence and divergence. The notion of interconnectedness and a heightened sense of global consciousness are paralleled by polarization and particularism. As President William Clinton put it in April 1999, the West finds itself engaged in "a great battle between the forces of integration and the forces of disintegration; [between] the forces of globalism and the forces of tribalism; [of the forces] of oppression against [those of] empowerment."

In effect, by 2001 the contemporary international security system had bifurcated—that is, it had split between a traditional twentieth-century, state-centred paradigm and new twenty-first-century substate and transstate strata. The great change in the early twenty-first-century international system from that of the last quarter of the twentieth century is the transition away from a dominant state-centric structure toward one marked by a greater number of substate and transstate actors. With bifurcation came a reduction in the relative significance of strategic geography, simply because the globalization of the information era appeared no longer to allow any state or society to retreat behind physical or moral borders.

It is very important to understand clearly what is meant by the "relative decline" of strategic geography. In no sense does such a phrase imply "the end of geography" in the same sense that Francis Fukuyama famously spoke of "the end of history." In terms of logistics, campaign planning, and topographical analysis, geography remains fundamental to the art of war, while geopolitics remains an important component of statecraft. Nonetheless, a shift away from territoriality toward connectedness has diminished the effect of strategic geography as a primary rationale for defining a nation's defense and national security postures. The process of this transformation-in which older forms of linear conflict have been supplemented by new forms of nonlinear conflict-has been recognized by both Western and non-Western strategists.

For example, the leading American strategic analyst Phillip Bobbitt has observed, "National security will cease to be defined in terms of borders alone because both the links among societies as well as the attacks on them exist in psychological and infrastructural dimensions, not on an invaded plain marked by the seizure and holding of territory. Similarly, two Chinese strategists have argued that we are entering an age of unrestricted warfare in which "there is no territory that cannot be surpassed; there is no means which cannot be used in ... war; and there is no territory or method which cannot be used in combination."

The result of globalization over the past ten years has been the development of an unpredictable and complex pattern of armed conflict. Under conditions of global strategic bifurcation the old distinctions-between civil and international conflict, between internal and external security, and between national and societal security—began to erode. It has become clear that in an era in which various transnational and substate forces were greatly empowered by technology, such issues as civil conflict, terrorism, and the proliferation of weapons of mass destruction could no longer be easily quarantined within states or regions. From the early 1990s onward, these phenomena emerged as global strategic threats precisely because they acted to blur the distinction between internal and external crises. Under new conditions, transnational and substate forces threaten not just states but entire societies and thus the fabric of international stability itself. Consequently, traditional ideas about warfare have come under challenge as the political, economic, and military dimensions of security have more closely merged and state-on-state war seems to have been supplemented by new forms of substate and transstate conflict.

The changing character of conflict and war mirrored the bifurcation of the international security system in the 1990s. The various views expressed about the future of military conflict reflected the post-Cold War fragmentation of international security and the diffusion of contemporary war into a variety of different modes. War became at once modern (reflecting conventional warfare between states), postmodern (reflecting the West's cosmopolitan political values of limited war, peace enforcement, and humanitarian military intervention), and premodern (reflecting a mix of substate and transstate warfare based on the age-old politics of identity, extremism, and particularism). It is important to note that none of these categories represents neatly divided compartments of activity; they overlap and interact with each other. The U.S. Marine Corps's recent doctrine of the "three-block war"—in which troops maybe engaged in a conventional firefight, peace operations, and humanitarian relief simultaneously in a single small area—captures the essence of this complex interaction.

However, if modern, postmodern, and premodern forms of war overlap with each other, each mode has distinctive features. Modern war remains symbolized by a classical doctrine of "encounter battles," collisions of rival states' armed forces moving on land, in air, and at sea. This is a mode of classical warfare that can be traced back to the first properly recorded battle in history, in which the Egyptians defeated the Hittites in a chariot and infantry battle at Kadesh in 1285 B.C. The most recent model (at this writing) of armed conflict by encounter battle is the 1991 Gulf War, when Western and Iraqi forces employing missiles, tanks, and mechanized infantry clashed in the deserts of Kuwait.

In the West's public consciousness, modern war is based on high technology and the conventional force-on-force warfare of the kind associated with the two world wars, Korea, and the Gulf. In contrast, postmodern war is mainly characterized by the extremes of Western risk aversion, since for the Western powers the stakes seldom involve issues of vital security or national survival. Postmodern war is based on high-tech aerospace power, casualty limitation, and cautious exit strategies, such as we saw during the Kosovo conflict of 1999. In many key respects, the war over Kosovo was the model of a postmodern conflict. It was, to borrow David Halberstam's ironic phrase, "war in a time of peace"—a conflict carefully calibrated, enabled by high-tech weaponry, with its course determined by Western opinion polls. However, postmodern conflict based around high-technology aerospace power has created its own antithesis—asymmetric warfare, including the threat of weapons of mass destruction, waged against Western society.

For its part, premodern war is symbolized by the images of "blood and iron" the West now allegedly abhors. Premodern war is essentially social rather than technological in character; it is an expression of the existential rather than the instrumental aspect of warfare. Those who wage such struggles may choose to sport middle-class suits and exploit the spread of advanced technology, but their mind-sets are mixtures of the antimodern, the millenarian, and the tribal. Such radicals embody what Pierre Hassner has called "the dialectic of the bourgeois and the barbarian."

Premodern conflict merges unconventional—to use the term du jour, asymmetric—warfare methods with the conventional or semiconventional military activities of failed states. The premodern model of conflict also tends to exploit the rise of nonstate actors, cultural identity politics, and ethnopolitical conflict. In many respects, premodern war represents a cultural revolt against the philosophy of Western liberal globalism; it is a conscious rejection of the universal values based on cosmopolitan democracy that followed Western victory in the Cold War. For many premodern radicals, the social order offered by globalization is anathema; it appears to them a facsimile of the secular, materialistic, and trivial world inhabited by Homer Simpson. For millenarian radicals of political Islam like Osama Bin Laden, the West's alleged cults of hedonistic individuality and intellectual relativism threaten societies that seek to define themselves by collective spirituality and timeless cultural traditions.

Premodern struggles embrace aspects of substate or intrastate civil conflict and ethnic cleansing ranging from Bosnia through Somalia to East Timor. Unlike the old national-liberation insurgents of the Cold War era, premodern radicals are more concerned with age-old cultural identity than the universal class ideology of Marxism; with a strategy of population displacement rather than winning popular support; and with sectarianism and secession rather than building inclusive model societies. One of the biggest changes in contemporary military affairs, then, has been the obsolescence of the Cold War political model of unconventional warfare and, as a result, of much of the West's counterinsurgency theory.

When distilled to basics, these three overlapping models of modern, postmodern, and premodern war provide us with two vividly contrasting images of future conflict—one that is mainly symmetric and one largely asymmetric. On one hand, we have the blend of modern and postmodern war seen in the 1991 Gulf War and waged in the air over Kosovo in 1999 to serve as a grim metaphor of Western supremacy in any conventional conflict. However, on another level, we are confronted with a strange mixture of premodern and postmodern conflict—a world of asymmetric and ethnopolitical warfare—in which machetes and Microsoft merge, and apocalyptic millenarians wearing Reeboks and Raybans dream of acquiring weapons of mass destruction. To use a Hollywood analogy, it is as if the West's Buck Rogers were now lined up against assorted road warriors from the devastated society portrayed in the "Mad Max" films.

MILITARY THEORY IN THE 1990s

The fragmentation of war has been mirrored in the world of strategic analysis. In the 1990s, military theory reflected the rapid diffusion of conflict following the end of the bipolar Cold War world. Multiple new theories of armed conflict appeared in the first half of the 1990s. At the beginning of the decade, the American analyst John Mueller gave us the "obsolescence of major war" theory, which argued that war in the advanced West was as outmoded as slavery and dueling. The Israeli scholar Martin van Creveld followed Mueller by declaring that the Gulf War was a historical freak, a throwback to World War II rather than a vision of twenty-first-century war. Van Creveld argued that the long era of interstate war first codified by the Prussian philosopher Carl von Clausewitz in the early nineteenth century had ended. What he described as Clausewitzian "trinitarian war"—based on the nexus between people, government, and armed forces—was dead, and Western military theory derived from classical warfare had become obsolescent.

The American futurists Alvin and Heidi Toffler then gave us the theory of "third wave" high-technology information warfare that helped initiate the "revolution in military affairs" debate. According to the Tofflers and the information-age warfare theorists who followed them, the Gulf War provided a glimpse of postmodern war as the realm of high technology. Precision strike, "dominant battlespace knowledge," and stealth platforms would shape future conflict. In the 1990s RMA-style ideas dominated American force planning for a future based on fighting two major theatre wars, as enshrined in the Pentagon's blueprint Joint Vision 2010.

In contrast, military writers like Robert Kaplan, Philip Cerny, and Ralph Peters proceeded to give us a vision of future war in which the form of social organization involved was far more important than the level of technology employed. For Kaplan, the war of the future was the "coming anarchy" of a Hobbesian world of failed states; for Cerny it was the "neomedievalism" of warlordism and violent disintegration; and for Peters it was a struggle by Western forces waged against a world of warrior cultures and paramilitaries from Mogadishu to Grozny. In 1996 Samuel P. Huntington published his seminal study of a coming "clash of civilizations" in which conflict between world cultures and "fault-line wars" would dominate the geopolitical future. Finally, in 1999, the British analyst Mary Kaldor put forward a theory of "new wars" in which identity politics and the privatization of violence would challenge the new global order. By the turn of the century, the West was awash in a world of competing ideas about the future of armed conflict. War and conflict had, in effect, split like an unraveling rope's end into a multiplicity of strands. War could be whatever one sought in the cookbook of theory: it could be desert combat in the Gulf, street fighting in Grozny, or something between the two. Armed conflict could be asymmetric or low-intensity style "fourth generation" conflict waged by guerrillas and terrorists against the West's conventional military supremacy. In addition, the ominous New Terrorism of nuclear, chemical, and biological warfare conducted by rogue nations and nonstate entities was also viewed by some analysts as representing a form of "nontraditional warfare.

THE CHALLENGE OF FUTURE WAR

Given the proliferation of military theory and uncertain political conditions, what are the possible contours of future warfare over the next decade? What cautious speculations can we make about emerging trends? In September 1999, the bipartisan U.S. (Hart-Rudman) Commission on National Security/21st Century stated:

> The future strategic environment will... be one of considerable turbulence.... The international system will be so fluid and complex that to think intelligently about military issues will mean taking an integrated view of political, social, technological, and economic developments. Only a broad definition of national security is appropriate to such a circumstance. In short we have entered an age in which many of the fundamental assumptions that steered us through the chilly waters of the Cold War require rethinking.... The very facts of military reality are changing, and that bears serious and concentrated reflection.

If the Hart-Rudman Commission's judgment about the facts of military reality changing is correct—and many, including the present author, believe it is—those concerned with preparing for armed conflict in the early twenty-first century must expect to confront a range of old, new, and hybrid forms of armed conflict. During the Cold War, the West confronted a unidimensional threat from the Marxist-Leninist Soviet Union-an adversary whose motives were certain and whose moves were predictable. In the new century, such conditions no longer apply. In the words of the present U.S. secretary of defense, Donald H. Rumsfeld, new military thinking is now required to arm Western societies "against the unknown, the uncertain, the unseen, and the unexpected."

It has become imperative that all concerned with security issues pay greater attention to the merging of previously discrete forms of war. The conceptual basis for the study of warfare in the West must now be broadened to include a rigorous study of the interaction between interstate, substate, and transstate conflict and of the diffusion of contemporary military capabilities. We have to recognize that in an interconnected age, linkage and interdependence seem to pervade all aspects of armed conflict. Military analysts and force-structure specialists need to concentrate on the multifunctional use of force in highly, complex operations. In addition, military professionals must learn to embrace the challenges of proportion, coercion, and dissuasion as well as the older tradition of battlefield destruction. In particular, what the U.S. Hart-Rudman Commission has described as "the spectrum of symmetrical and asymmetrical threats we anticipate over the next quarter century" must receive increased attention from both military theorists and policy makers. In short, the challenge is to prepare for full-spectrum conflict.

The task will be much harder than many defense analysts realize. The notion of a spectrum of conflict is not a new idea, but for most of the Cold War the Western understanding of war was based on generic intellectual categories of "conventional" (high-intensity) and "unconventional" (low-intensity) conflict. Most in the field of strategic studies thought in terms of separate worlds of conventional interstate (or high-intensity) and unconventional intrastate (or low-intensity) military activity. Unfortunately, the spectrum of conflict that is emerging in the early twenty-first century is distinguished by merged categories, multidimensionality, and unprecedented interaction.

In an era when all security issues are interconnected and when the national security of Western states has become critically dependent on international security, single-scenario strategies and rigid military force structures have become anachronistic. Traditional concepts of deterrence and defense need to be supplemented by new doctrines of security preemption, security prevention, and expeditionary warfare. Moreover, the clear separation of peace and war must be supplemented by an acknowledgment that modes of war have merged. In a new age marked by networks and instant communications, the need is for advanced military forces with skills useful across a range of tasks that may involve preventive deployment, preemptive strike, war fighting, peace enforcement, traditional peacekeeping and peace building, and counterterrorism.

However, the intellectual challenge facing military professionals is not, as Martin van Creveld would have us believe, to consign Carl von Clausewitz and two thousand years of Western military knowledge to the dustbin of history. Rather, the task is to learn how to fight efficiently across the spectrum of conflict. No responsible Western military theorist can accept at face value the thesis of the "obsolescence of conventional war" or the paradigm of asymmetric warfare as primary force planning or doctrinal determinants. In a dangerous and unpredictable world, military professionals and their political masters must prepare to fight in conditions of a "high-low mix"—to be ready to tame the big wildcats and not simply the vicious rodents, to be able to fight troops like Iraq's former Republican Guard as well as Taliban, al-Qa'ida militia, and terrorists. As every good operational commander knows, in the military art one can "trade down," but one can never "trade up." Moreover, all the evidence indicates that success in peace-support operations requires the kinds of conventional firepower, mobility, and force protection available only to military establishments that are optimized for conventional warfighting.

Readying ourselves for conventional war does not, however, absolve us from undertaking a major transformation in the way we think about the use of military force. The most pressing intellectual task at the crossroad of the old and new centuries is rapid adaptation to new and merging forms of conflict. In the West we have to reconcile how we would like to fight with how we might have to fight. We must try to synthesize relevant features from the massive literature on the classical Gulf War/ RMA model of warfare with the changing reality of conflict—both conventional and unconventional—as it presents itself. We have to undertake an intellectual exploration of the growing interaction between interstate, substate, and transstate conflict and conduct a rigorous investigation of the phenomenon of merging war forms—internal, international, postmodern, modern, and premodern.

The merging of modes of armed conflict suggests an era of warfare quite different from that of the recent past. Fighting in the future may involve conventional armies, guerrilla bands, independent and state-directed terrorist groups, specialized antiterrorist units, and private militias. Terrorist attacks might evolve into classic guerrilla warfare and then escalate to conventional conflict. Alternatively, fighting could be conducted on several levels at once. The possibility of continuous, sporadic, armed conflict, its engagements blurred together in time and space, waged on several levels by a large array of national and subnational forces, means that the reality of war in the first decade of the twenty-first century is likely to transcend a neat division into distinct categories, symmetry and asymmetry.

Indeed, it is arguable that the main reason for much of the intellectual confusion surrounding war at the turn of the century stems from the lack of a conceptual synthesis between the requirements of traditional conventional war and the emerging blend of interstate, transstate, and nonstate modes. It is no accident that the most productive areas of military theory have been those that have attempted to concentrate on the expanding phenomenon of war. The most interesting new approaches have come from those who have endeavored to examine the growing complexity of conflict, its holistic yet multidimensional character, its sociological as well as technological dynamics. Conceptual progress has come from analytical work into war's connection to society as well as to the state; from assessing the convergence of modes of conflict and the growing requirements to control armed violence in an age of instantaneous media imagery; and from developing multipurpose forces that can wage warfare across the spectrum of c onflict.

In short, it is the interactive character of war—Clausewitz's famous chameleon "that adapts its characteristics to the given case"—that has proven the most original avenue for analysis. The immediate future of war lies perhaps in two key areas. The first is the realm of multidimensional theories of war and conflict that call for multifunctional forces for intervention missions; the second is the evolving theory of counterwar, or "mastery of violence," which may assist military practitioners and policy makers to understand and deal with armed conflict as a multifaceted phenomenon.

A MULTIDIMENSIONAL APPROACH TO WAR AND CONFLICT

As twenty-first-century war becomes, in the words of the prominent Russian military theorist Makhmut Gareev, "a multivariant," advanced armed forces need to develop multidimensional approaches to conflict. The most interesting American and British military theory reflects a growing recognition that in a new age of multiple threats, discrete categories of conventional and unconventional conflict are eroding, along with corresponding legal and moral restraints.

Much of the West's preparation to meet an accelerating convergence of military challenges is shaped by three ideas. First, there is a general acceptance that armed forces must be able to adapt to differing modes of war, to become multifunctional. Second, as questions of both national and societal security merge and interpenetrate, reactive operational strategies alone become inadequate as means of deterrence.

Security in the new era of liberal globalism also requires a willingness to undertake interventions, as well as, correspondingly, proactive military forces. Third, if global political and technological conditions permit radical groups and rogue states to use ballistic or biological weapons to inflict mass casualties on democratic societies, this new challenge must be met by military preemption in ways not seen since the late nineteenth century. In other words, those who espouse the mass murder of innocent civilians in cities and suburbs must be destroyed wherever and whenever preemption is possible. As President George W. Bush put it recently, it is necessary for the West to act decisively against the new threat emanating from "the perilous crossroads of radicalism and technology." Specifically, the diffusion of advanced technology, from standoff missiles to commercial space systems to weapons of mass destruction, into the hands of smaller armies, paramilitaries, militias, and other armed groups puts a premium on Western expeditionary warfare.

Two leading American military theorists, Huba Wass de Czege and Richard Hart Sinnreich, have recently given an unequivocal view of the merging of conventional and unconventional conflict:

> Clear distinctions between conventional and unconventional conflicts are fading, and any future major conflict is almost certain to see a routine commingling of such operations. Similarly, once useful demarcations between front and rear or between theatre and strategic operations will continue to evaporate as the instrumentalities of war become more interdependent and, as is increasingly true of communications and space systems, less easily separable from their civilian and commercial counterparts.

As a result, the future requirement will be for joint forces designed for multidimensional, expeditionary-style operations—what the U.S. Army now refers to as "operational maneuver from strategic distance." Such operations are vital to control theaters where "high-low" threats and varied forms of conflict might be expected. Consequently, the main trends in contemporary Western military theory are toward operations with multinational and joint task forces with simplified headquarters structures—not simply corps and division, but increasingly force and formation. Smaller combat formations, such as the combined-arms brigades to serve modular building blocks for forces in the field, are needed. Force structures will become more modular and capable of rapid task force organization from "golf bags" of varied military capabilities.

In expeditionary warfare, the main need is to reconcile operational versatility with organizational stability. Western forces must be capable of undertaking joint, multidimensional missions ranging from shaping the environment to air-ground operational maneuver, to all-out conventional warfare. The demands of operational versatility are likely to place a premium on organizational change.

MULTIFACETED CONFLICT

Recent trends in European-American military theory toward multidimensional operations have also been applied to what some European military thinkers now call "counterwar theory," or the "mastery of violence" as an operational military strategy. In France, the development of counterwar theory reflects the perception that war in the twenty-first century has become "a mixture of phenomena." Some French military thinkers believe that in contemporary armed conflict it is largely impossible to treat war as merely a clash between rival forces; that the conventional cannot be separated from the unconventional; and that traditional lines of authority between military control and political responsibility are becoming blurred.

A military force may now be required to conduct intervention operations in conditions that correspond to neither classical warfare nor traditional peace-support operations. Extremely complex political conditions may arise in which law and order are lacking but the law of armed conflict must nonetheless, and at all costs, be upheld; in such a case a counterwar strategy, the disciplined control of violence, may have to be imposed. As French military analysts Brigadier General Loup Francart and Jean-Jacques Patry observe, "Military operations are now completely integrated with political, diplomatic, economic and cultural activities. Strategy is no longer simply a matter of defense. The problem is now, more than ever, to conceive military operations in a political framework."

General Wesley K. Clark, the American commander who prosecuted Nato's 1999 war against Serbia over Kosovo, has argued that politics in modern war now pervades all of the three levels of war—tactics, operations, and strategy. In the past, politics was mainly a factor at the strategic level, where statecraft guided the military instrument. However, in the early twenty-first century, politics also now impinges on the operational and tactical levels of war, Clark believes, to the extent that it may be necessary to speak of a "political level of war." If General Clark is right, the implications for future civil-military relations are profound.

In an age of increased military-political integration and twenty-four-hour electronic media, the goal of force may be not annihilation or attrition but calibrated "elimination of the enemy's resistance" by the careful and proportional use of counterviolence. The use of armed force in a surgical manner—the rapier rather than the broadsword—would require that military thinking and action be politically sophisticated, legally disciplined, and ethically correct. These needs were among the main lessons of the Kosovo conflict. As French military theorists have argued, the aim must be to ensure that the application of force in intervention operations—especially in an age of instant images—can be modulated and shaped by professional militaries to accommodate rapidly shifting politics and flexible operational and strategic objectives.

Given the growing complexity of the military art and of the use of force in statecraft, what are the characteristics of warfare most likely to be over the next decade? Four basic sets can be tentatively offered. First, war is likely to remain a chameleon, presenting itself variously in interstate, transstate, and nonstate modes—or as a combination of these. However, a word of caution is necessary: it would be a serious mistake to dismiss the possibility of interstate conventional war. If in some areas of the world, such as Western Europe, it is highly improbable, in much of Asia and the Middle East it remains a distinct possibility. Nonetheless, in general terms, the merging of modes of armed conflict does suggest an era of warfare in which national, transstate, and substate forces may coalesce or find themselves in mismatched confrontations. Moreover, the conventional and the unconventional, the symmetric and the asymmetric, may occur almost simultaneously, overlapping in time and space.

Second, advanced warfare will be largely joint-service in character. The revolution in information technology, especially as applied to command and control, long-range precision strike, and stealth, has so compressed time and space in military operations as to create an unprecedented nonlinear battle space characterized by breadth, depth, and height. During the 1990s, the concept of "battle space" replaced the linear battlefield that had defined armed conflict in the Western tradition from Alexander the Great to the Second World War. In essence, the concept of battle space has permitted a shift away from the organization of linear mass toward a simultaneous and "full-dimensional" concentration of effects. This is especially significant with regard to the cumulative impact of missile firepower from air, ground, and sea.

Third, most Western military experts believe that future operations will favour simultaneous attack by joint air-ground forces that are "situationally aware"—that have substantially complete and current views of the battlespace via computer and satellite. Advanced forces are also likely to be networked from "sensor to shooter"—that is, surveillance capabilities will be electronically connected to strike forces, and all of them to each other. There will probably be fewer troops deployed on the ground, but the individual soldier—the "strategic corporal"—will have a greater potential impact on events. Growing weapons lethality and increased ability of soldiers to direct long-range precision "fires"—as seen in Afghanistan, where ground forces acted as highly effective sensors for air strikes—are likely to become features of warfare over the next decade.

Fourth, the dominance of surveillance and strike means that joint operations by technologically advanced forces, capable of deep precision attack and quick maneuver, are likely to resemble large-scale ambushes. If an enemy can be remotely located, traditional movement to contact preceded by forward troops probing for the enemy will be replaced by well-prepared, deliberate, "deep" attacks using tactics that exploit rapid positioning for maximum effect. However, precision munitions are likely to be of limited use in close operations, in which infantry must be employed to finish off adversaries.

In the close battle, armored forces and artillery are likely to remain extremely useful in applying suppressive fire in support of troops in action. In the recent campaign in Afghanistan, American forces put their faith in air cover at the expense of both artillery and tanks. It was soon discovered that while precision munitions delivered from high altitude are effective against known point targets, they are much less useful in area attack, as is necessary against forces that are scattered, not precisely located. The majority of American casualties (twenty-eight out of thirty-six) in Operation ENDURING FREEDOM came from enemy mortar fire that could have been suppressed by armour or artillery. The lesson learned from fierce combat in the complex terrain of Afghanistan's Shah-i-Kot region is that for area suppression, field guns and tanks remain essential in twenty-first-century warfare.

The likely shape of war in the early twenty-first century essentially reflects the consequences of a bifurcated global system between an older state-centric world, on one hand, and new transstate and substate strata on the other. The West has entered a period in which classical interstate war has been supplemented by borderless threats from nonstate actors operating with the power of modern computers, ease of international travel, and, possibly, weapons of mass destruction, with which they can deal lethal blows to any society.

These trends, particularly the unholy alliance between new nonstate actors and advanced technology, collectively point to an urgent need for new strategic thinking. The shift toward connectedness and nonlinearity at the relative expense of territoriality and linearity has become perhaps the central reality of strategy in the opening years of the twenty-first century. Some international observers believe the strategic shift from territoriality to connectedness will be revolutionary in its consequences:

> We are at a moment in world affairs when the essential ideas that govern statecraft must change. For five centuries it has taken the resources of a state to destroy another state; only states could muster the huge revenues, conscript the vast armies, and equip the divisions required to threaten the survival of other states. . . . This is no longer true, owing to advances in international telecommunications, rapid computation, and weapons of mass destruction. The change in statecraft that will accompany these developments will be as profound as any that the State has thus far undergone.

The great danger to Western countries is no longer the threat of military invasion of the nation-state but an assault on the very foundations of our networked society. Western societies are now most vulnerable not from external invasion but from internal disruption of the government, financial, and economic institutions that make up critical infrastructures.

It was this great weakness that al-Qa'ida exploited with such devastating results on 11 September 2001. Increasingly, national security now depends on the protection of a specific set of social institutions and the information links between them. However, our reliance on critical infrastructures vastly exceeds our ability to protect them; it is therefore impossible to protect an entire society solely by "homeland defense."

To defend Western societies, the nation-state model of war based upon threat analysis and against defined enemies will have to be supplemented by new modes of strategic thought that concentrate on alleviating the vulnerabilities of modern states to new nonstate threats. As the French military analyst Phillippe Delmas has warned, "Today's world is without precedent. It is as different from the Cold War as it is from the Middle Ages so the past offers no basis for comparison. ... Tomorrow's wars will not result from the ambitions of States; rather from their weaknesses."

To meet the challenges of tomorrow's wars, Western countries will need highly mobile, well equipped, and versatile forces capable of multidimensional coalition missions and "mastery of violence" across a complex spectrum of conflict. They will need new national security apparatus for threat and vulnerability analysis and consequence management in the event of traumatic societal attack. They will need enhanced international intelligence and diplomatic cooperation to ensure that military force is employed with maximum efficiency. They will need new norms of international law that allow joint armed forces to be used, when the enemy can be located, in far-flung preemption operations.

The reality of Western societal vulnerability in conditions of liberal globalism represents a strategic transformation that obliges defense experts and politicians to think rigorously about the kinds of war that might lie ahead. We are confronted with a challenge of finding new ways of using force in merged modes of conflict in an international system that must confront simultaneously both integration and fragmentation.

The problems facing policy makers, strategists, and military professionals in the early twenty-first century, then, have changed dramatically and decisively from those of the twentieth. Military power and capability have expanded into a network of transnational interconnections. As a result, preparing for armed conflict is no longer only a matter of simply assembling battlefield strength to destroy defined adversaries.

Increasingly, military power is entwined in politics—as an instrument that shapes, polices, and bounds the strategic environment, that punishes, signals, and warns. The task for strategists is now one of disciplining available military power into a broad security strategy—one that embraces also diplomacy, intelligence analysis, and law enforcement—in a calibrated, judicious, and precise manner. In the prophetic words, written over thirty-five years ago, of the British strategist Alastair Buchan, "The real content of strategy is concerned not merely with war and battles but with the application and maintenance of force so that it contributes most effectively to the advancement of political objectives." At the dawn of a new century, of a new and uncertain era in armed conflict in a globalized yet deeply fragmented world, these words aptly describe the many dangerous challenges that lie ahead.

BISMARCK BATTLESHIP - GERMAN NAVY WW2

Battleship Bismarck, a 41,673-ton battleship, was built at Hamburg, Germany. First of a class of two heavy ships, with *Tirpitz* being the second, she was commissioned in August 1940 and spent the rest of that year running trials and continuing her outfitting. The first months of 1941 were largely devoted to training operations in the Baltic sea. *Bismarck* left the Baltic on 19 May 1941, en route to the Atlantic, accompanied by the heavy cruiser *Prinz Eugen*. On the morning of 24 May, while west of Iceland, the German vessels encountered the British battlecruiser *Hood* and battleship *Prince of Wales*. In the ensuing Battle of the Denmark Strait, *Hood* blew up and sank. The seriously damaged *Prince of Wales* was forced to break off contact. *Bismarck* also received shell hits that degraded her seakeeping and contaminated some of her fuel.

Later on 24 May, *Prinz Eugen* was detached, while *Bismarck* began a voyage toward France, where she could be repaired. She was intermittantly attacked by carrier planes and surface ships, ultimately sustaining a torpedo hit in the stern that rendered her unable to steer effectively. British battleships and heavy cruisers intercepted the crippled ship on the morning of 27 May. After less than two hours of battle, shells and torpedoes had reduced *Bismarck* to a wreck. She capsized and sank, with the loss of all but 110 of her crew of some 2300 men.

Nazi dictator Adolf Hitler's reaction to *Bismarck*'s loss produced a very cautious approach to future German surface ship operations against Britain's vital Atlantic sea lanes. In June 1989, just over forty-eight years after she sank, the German battleship's battered hulk was located and photographed where she lies upright on a mountainside, nearly 16,000 feet below the ocean surface.

CONSTRUCTION

Battleship Bismarck was Germany's first "real" post-World War I battleship, with guns and protection of similar scale to those of the best foreign combat ships. Built to a relatively conservative design, she featured a main battery of eight 38 centimeter (15-inch) guns in four twin turrets, two forward and two aft. Her secondary battery of twelve 15 cm (5.9-inch) guns, mounted six on each side in twin turrets, was optimized for use against enemy surface ships, especially destroyers. Her anti-aircraft battery, including sixteen 10.5 cm (4.1-inch) guns in eight twin mounts and several 37mm and 20mm machine guns, reflected the prevailing pre-World War II underestimation of the threat from the air, a failing common to all the World's navies.

The two ships of this class, *Bismarck* and her "sister" *Tirpitz*, were quite fast, at just over thirty knots maximum speed. Their steam turbine powerplants, producing some 150,000 horsepower, consumed a great deal of fuel oil, limiting their oceanic "reach" to a degree that was especially critical to a nation with Germany's geography. Future German battleship designs, which World War II aborted, featured diesel engines, intended to produce far greater endurance on the high seas.

Battleship Bismarck was very heavily protected against the gunfire of other battleships. With a standard displacement of well over 41,000 tons (about 50,000 tons fully loaded), she was also quite a bit larger than her European and American contemporaries. As shown by the photographs below, originally collected by the U.S. Navy's Office of Naval Intelligence, this ship's construction greatly interested foreign navies.

Built at the Blohm & Voss shipyard in Hamburg, *Bismarck*'s keel was laid at the beginning of July 1936. She was launched with considerable ceremony, including the attendance of Adolf Hitler, on 14 February 1939. Her outfitting, which included the addition of a new "clipper" bow (which the Germans called an "Atlantic" bow), lasted nearly two years. She was commissioned in August 1940, ran trials during the following months, and was not fully ready for service until late in 1940

GERMAN BATTLESHIP BISMARCK'S ATLANTIC SORTIE, MAY 1941

In the wake of the successful January-March 1941 cruise of the battleships *Scharnhorst* and *Gneisenau* against Allied shipping, and in keeping with Grand Admiral Erich Raeder's strategy of aggressively employing his heavy ships, another German Navy raiding expedition into the Atlantic was undertaken, employing the new battleship *Bismarck* and heavy cruiser *Prinz Eugen*. After many delays, these ships left the Baltic Sea on 19-20 May. Briefly stopping near Bergen, Norway, on 21 May, they then headed north, planning to enter the shipping zone by way of the Denmark Strait, between Iceland and Greenland.

British planes had photographed the German ships while they were in Norwegian waters, and the Royal Navy sent its own warships to sea in an effort to intercept the enemy and keep him from attacking the vital convoys. British cruisers began to shadow the Germans on 23 May, and *Bismarck* fired on HMS *Norfolk*. At about 6AM the next day, in the Battle of the Denmark Strait, the Germans fought and destroyed HMS *Hood* and drove off HMS *Prince of Wales*.

Battleship Bismarck was also damaged sufficiently to force her to abort her mission. British aircraft and ships continued to follow the two German vessels, which separated late on 24 May during an exchange of gunfire with their pursuers. *Prinz Eugen* continued into the Atlantic while *Bismarck* was to head toward France, where her damage could be repaired. That night, the British hit the German battleship with a carrier plane's torpedo, reducing her speed, but also lost track of her. Contact was regained on the 26th and the Royal Navy vectored its ships to attempt to sink *Bismarck* before she could reach the protection of Luftwaffe aircraft from France. Late that day, planes from the carrier *Ark Royal* scored at least two torpedo hits, one of which crippled *Bismarck*'s rudders.

Unable to maintain course toward France, and still out of range of friendly airpower, *Bismarck* now was at the mercy of her enemies. Torpedo attacks by destroyers on 26-27 May achieved no success, but on the morning of the 27th two Royal Navy battleships, *Rodney* and *King George V*, and two heavy cruisers arrived. Firing began before 9AM, with German gunfire accuracy quickly degrading to ineffectiveness. British fourteen and sixteen-inch shells gradually smashed *Battleship Bismarck*'s main guns, superstructure, hull and armour. Prompted by torpedoes and scuttling charges, the German battleship rolled over and sank somewhat after 10:30 AM on 27 May 1941, bringing to an end the most serious challenge that German surface warships would make to British Atlantic Ocean supremacy.

SHIP OF THE LINE

Following the War of 1812, the United States committed to building a strong navy. The U.S. Navy required ships which could hold the line of battle in conflict, hence the name ship-of-the-line or line-of-battle ship, later shortened to battleship.

The first of seven new ships approved by Congress, the three-masted square-rigger NORTH CAROLINA was considered the terror of the seas. Her keel was laid in 1818 in Philadelphia Navy Yard where she was built. She was launched in 1820 after being "fitted out" in Norfolk Navy Yard. Considered the most powerful vessel afloat in her day when commissioned in June 1824, NORTH CAROLINA was invited to many foreign ports.

From April 1825 until May 1827, NORTH CAROLINA served in the Mediterranean fleet as Commodore John Rogers flagship. Her powerful presence enhanced our nation's prestige and displayed our might, an important factor in the young country's national affairs.

She served as flagship once again in South America in May 1837. War raged between Chile and Peru and our relations with Mexico were strained. NORTH CAROLINA protected American commerce until March 1839.

Her great size limited the number of ports where she could be of service and so she returned to New York Navy Yard and served as a receiving ship for new sailors until 1866. She was sold for scrap at New York 1 October 1867 for $30,000.

Statistics

i. 196 feet 3 inches long

ii. 53 feet 6 inches wide at her beam

iii. weighed 2,633 tons

iv. 74 guns - 32 pounders and 42 pounders

v. complement of 820 men

THE LEGACY CONTINUES

The use of sea power to protect its shores and to project the power of a nation beyond those boundaries has been used since the early days of the Phoenicians, Greeks and Romans. Since ours is an island nation bounded by two oceans, naval heritage, within the maritime heritage context, has been an important element in our Country since its founding.

Over the centuries, maritime nations have developed major classes of seagoing combatants that have enabled them to effectively carry out the protection of its shores or the projection of power. Whether it was the ship-of-the-line or battleship, in their respective eras, these major combatants reflected the leading edge of technology of the period and the will of the nation.

The Battleship NORTH CAROLINA's heritage can be traced to a more recent event. In 1906 the British Admiralty commissioned a totally new design, DREADNOUGHT. With an increased number of larger guns in her main battery, a more capable secondary battery, larger designed displacement, better armour and increased speed, DREADNOUGHT became the prototype for subsequent battleships built by other nations, including the United States.

Historically, and until most recently, the most capable class of major combatants, or capital ships, in the U.S. Navy were named for States in the Union.

While the Battleship NORTH CAROLINA is a very visible, and powerful, example of a capital ship, her lineage is equally impressive. The first ship to bear the name NORTH CAROLINA was a ship-of-the-line in the 1820s. Following her was a Confederate ironclad in the 1860s, a World War I-era armored cruiser, a never-completed post-World War I battleship, the Battleship NORTH CAROLINA of World War II fame, and in 2007 a nuclear attack submarine.

While the focus is the Battleship NORTH CAROLINA, information on the others named for the State are included in this site.

- Ship-of-the-Line NORTH CAROLINA
- Confederate Ironclad NORTH CAROLINA
- Armored Cruiser NORTH CAROLINA (ACR 12)
- Battleship NORTH CAROLINA (BB 52)
- Battleship NORTH CAROLINA (BB 55)
- Nuclear Attack Submarine NORTH CAROLINA (SSN 777)

1863 - 1864

During the Civil War the Confederate States Navy commissioned an ironclad named NORTH CAROLINA. Berry and Brothers Shipyard, located here on Eagles Island (the Battleship Memorial is also on Eagles Island), constructed this ship. It was the first ironclad built in Wilmington and the largest ship built at Berry and Brothers, renamed the Confederate Navy Yard. She cost $76,000 to build and outfit.

The bulkheads above the waterline were slanted inward and covered or clad with railroad iron similar to the Confederate Ship Ironclad VIRGINIA (MERRIMAC). She had two gun ports on each of her four sides and carried six 8-inch guns that could be moved from one port to another. There was one pivot gun on her bow. However, her service was hampered because she was outfitted with old, defective engines confiscated from the United States' tug UNCLE BEN.

She participated in one engagement. At 8 o'clock on the evening of May 6, 1864, Commodore Lynch of the Confederate Fleet decided to send forth NORTH CAROLINA and two wooden gun boats, YADKIN and EQUATOR, to take reconnaissance of the blockading federal ships off New Inlet. The Commodore needed the federal ships to be dispersed or lured towards the guns of Fort Fisher. At this point in time, Wilmington stood as the only open Confederate port able to supply the rest of the Confederacy via blockade runners. Therefore, it was critical to bust this blockade of federal ships.

Thirty minutes after the three vessels disappeared from view of Fort Fisher, several shots from seaward were heard. The Confederates spent an anxious night wondering what had happened. Dawn finally came and they saw NORTH CAROLINA and the gun boats returning with the enemy following in the distance. The combatants exchanged gunfire. NORTH CAROLINA fired a shot through the smokestack of a charging federal ship. When the federal ships began to close in on the little confederate flotilla to finish them off, the three ships headed for the protective guns of Fort Fisher. The federal ships wisely kept their distance while the three confederate vessels steamed safely up the Cape Fear River.

NORTH CAROLINA was then stationed near Smithfield, present day Southport, as a guard vessel commanding the entrance to the Cape Fear River. While anchored there, she fell victim to the toredo, a sea worm that gradually destroyed her hull. She sank in 1864 after less than two years of service.

Statistics

- 165 feet long
- 33 feet wide at her beam
- 600 ton displacement
- six 8-inch guns, one pivot gun
- complement of 188 men

BATTLESHIPS

The term "battleship" that came into usage in the mid-1880s was derived from a term from an earlier 19th Century naval era, "ship-of-the-line." "Ship-of-the-line" described the primary warship classes that were characterized by large size, heavy armour, and carrying a main battery of large caliber guns as well as smaller caliber guns of varying sizes. "Line" referred to the battle line - the line of ships formed to attack another formation of ships. Since these battleships were considered to be the basic measure of a nation's naval power, they were also called "capital ships."

Over the next twenty years, the world's major naval powers built a series of classes of battleships, each subsequent class more powerful than the previous one. And while the early attempts were mere benchmarks for further improvements, it was not until the British Admiralty completed the all-big-gun HMS DREADNOUGHT in 1906 that there was a definitive example of what the battleship was to become. With her arrival, the term "dreadnought" became synonymous with the battleship type. All existing battleships and other similar major combatant types that came before were classified as pre-dreadnoughts, reflecting that their capabilities dropped them to a second class rating.

By the start of World War I the United States, Austria-Hungary, Britain, France, Germany, Italy, Japan, and Russia all had dreadnought battleships in commission, each country endeavouring to establish supremacy over the others. Two developments during the War significantly impacted future battleship design. Submarine development required naval architects to provide designs to protect against torpedo detonations and aircraft development caused them to consider antiaircraft gunnery and to provide heavier deck armour to minimize bomb damage. But a post-World War I treaty had an even more profound impact. World nations attempted to control the continuation of the naval arms races by enacting an arms reduction treaty in 1922. The Washington Naval Reduction Treaty, and the subsequent London Naval Treaty in 1936, established two basic limitations on capital ship design. Standard displacement was limited to a maximum 35,000 tons - standard displacement was the displacement of the completed ship, fully manned, equipped and ready for sea, including ammunition, provisions, fresh water for the crew, and miscellaneous stores, but not including fuel or reserve feed water for the boilers. The maximum size of the main battery guns was set at a 16-inch diameter bore. The 1922 treaty also declared a building holiday.

When the United States signed the treaty, they agreed to halt construction of thirteen new battleships and battlecruisers under construction, including battleship hull number 52 which was to be named NORTH CAROLINA. The United States also disposed of all pre-dreadnought battleships and several of the older post-dreadnought battleships.

The building holiday lasted until 1932 when, with the construction of the French battleship DUNKERQUE started, the race was on once again. Naval architects endeavored to meet the 35,000 ton displacement criteria, provide for powerful main and secondary battery armament, install armour and other means for protection against torpedoes and bombs, and still achieve a maximum speed of at least 27 knots, which was 5 knots faster than World War I-era battleships. The United States joined the race to construct the "fast" battleship.

The ten "fast" battleships built by the United States for service in World War II were split into three classes. First was the "fast" battleship prototype, NORTH CAROLINA (BB 55), and her sister, WASHINGTON (BB 56); then came SOUTH DAKOTA (BB 57) and her three sisters, INDIANA (BB 58), MASSACHUSETTS (BB 59) and ALABAMA (BB 60); and, finally, IOWA (BB 61) and her three sisters, NEW JERSEY (BB 62), MISSOURI (BB 63), and WISCONSIN (BB 64). While the armament and electronics were essentially the same among the three classes, the hull size and armour protection changed significantly. And although the type of propulsion plant was the same, the amount of horsepower increased dramatically. A thumbnail comparison of the three classes gives a clear picture of the evolution of the "fast" battleship.

Class	NORTH CAROLINA	SOUTH DAKOTA	IOWA
Length	728 ft	680 ft	888 ft
Full Load Displacement	46,000 tons	46,000 tons	57, 000 tons
Full Load Draft	34.6 ft	36.2 ft	36.0 ft
Shaft Horsepower	121,000 shp	130,000 shp	212,000 shp
Speed	27 kts	28 kts	33 kts

While the NORTH CAROLINA and SOUTH DAKOTA Classes were full of compromises to meet treaty requirements, particularly the maximum design displacement of 35,000 tons, the IOWA Class clearly was not weight dependent. In comparing the designs of the three classes, what becomes clear from an in-depth inspection of the space arrangements of the three classes, is that many of the design elements found in the NORTH CAROLINA Class were refined and further evolved for the follow on classes to make them more efficient and to enhance their effectiveness, whether it was the side protective system or the layout and access to the machinery and repair spaces.

Had they been built, the only class of battleship that would have been superior to the IOWAs would have been the post-World War II Montana Class. Although authorized, none of the Montana Class was constructed as the post-war emphasis was transferred to the new capital ship, the aircraft carrier.

During the era of battleships, the United States authorized construction of 71 capital ships of this type. While the historical impact varies greatly among battleships, a select few now serve their Country beyond their Naval service. ARIZONA, the most visible reminder of the Japanese attack on Pearl Harbor on 7 December 1941, and MISSOURI, the ship on which the Japanese surrendered in Tokyo Bay on 2 September 1945, are now memorialized in Pearl Harbor, Hawaii. Now acting as memorials in their namesake states are TEXAS in LaPorte, MASSACHUSETTS in Fall River, ALABAMA in Mobile, NEW JERSEY in Camden, and, of course, NORTH CAROLINA in Wilmington.

ARMORED CRUISER

1908 - 1920

The keel of the second federal ship named NORTH CAROLINA was laid in Newport News, Virginia, in March 1905. Constructed by Newport News Shipbuilding and Dry Dock Company, she was commissioned at Norfolk, Virginia, on 7 May 1908.

On her first assignment, she participated in an inspection tour of the Panama Canal in 1909 while it was still under construction. She then cruised the Mediterranean to protect Americans threatened by the Turkish Empire and provided a medical relief party to treat wounded and ill Armenians, victims of massacre.

In the years prior to World War I, she trained, maneuvered, and performed ceremonial and diplomatic duties in the Atlantic and Caribbean. It was NORTH CAROLINA that brought home the bodies of the dead crew of MAINE.

When World War I ignited, she protected Americans in the Near East, cruising constantly between Jaffa, Beirut, and Alexandria as a reminder of American might. She returned to Boston for overhaul in June 1915.

She next entered into the exciting period of her history when NORTH CAROLINA played a significant role in the development of naval aviation. She headed for Pensacola, Florida, for her assignment as a naval air station ship, arriving on 9 September 1915. On 5 November 1915, she launched a scout observation biplane by catapulting it from a ramp mounted on her deck. The steel catapult was constructed over the gun turret and fantail, or rear, of the cruiser. For the pilot, LCDR Henry Mustin, and the crew, it was a proud day. This marked the first time a ship launched a plane while under way. Her experimental work paved the way for use of aircraft on battleships and cruisers.

When America entered World War I, NORTH CAROLINA left Florida and headed north to escort troop transports plying the Atlantic between Norfolk and New York. After the war, she brought men of the American Expeditionary Force home in December 1918 and July 1919.

Renamed CHARLOTTE on 7 June 1920, so that her name might be used for a new battleship, she was decommissioned in February 1921. She was sold for scrap on 29 September 1930.

Statistics

i. 504 feet long

ii. 73 feet wide at her beam

iii. 14,500 tons displacement

iv. speed of 22 knots

v. armament of four 10-inch guns, sixteen 6-inch guns, twenty-two 3-inch guns, plus smaller guns and four torpedo tubes

vi. complement of 859

1919 - 1923

Battleship number 52 was to be called NORTH CAROLINA, but she was never completed.

Between 1919 and 1925, the United States Congress approved the construction of six battleships, one of which would be christened NORTH CAROLINA. She and her five sister ships, IOWA, INDIANA, SOUTH DAKOTA, MASSACHUSETTS, and MONTANA were monster ships. They would have been the most heavily armed capital ship in the world at that time.

While the construction of new ships was exciting, most people did not want a repeat of the arms race that contributed to the tensions leading to World War I. Therefore, President Warren G. Harding invited Great Britain, France, Italy, Japan and China to attend an international conference on the limitation of naval armaments. The group convened in Washington in November 1919 and the meeting became known as the famous Washington Conference producing the Five Power Treaty (included all attendees except China). The signing nations agreed to reduce the size of their navy and to cease building warships beyond an allotted number. In fact, there was a ten-year "holiday" declared on building battleships.

The keel for NORTH CAROLINA had been laid in Norfolk in 1919, but the signed treaty spelled her doom. She was sold for scrap in 1923 along with her five sister ships and WASHINGTON.

Statistics

i. 684 feet long
ii. 106 feet wide at her beam
iii. 33 ft. draft
iv. 43,200 tons displacement
v. speed of 23 knots
vi. armament of twelve 16-inch guns, plus 6-inch and 3-inch guns and two torpedo tubes

BB 55

When the keel of NORTH CAROLINA was laid in October of 1937, she was the first battleship to be constructed in sixteen years. She became the first of ten *fast battleships* to join the fleet in World War II. NORTH CAROLINA (BB 55) and her sister ship, WASHINGTON (BB 56), comprised the NORTH CAROLINA Class. Following them were the SOUTH DAKOTA Class – SOUTH DAKOTA (BB 57), INDIANA (BB 58), MASSACHUSETTS (BB 59), and ALABAMA (BB 60) – and the IOWA Class - IOWA (BB 61), NEW JERSEY (BB 62), MISSOURI (BB 63), and WISCONSIN (BB 64).

At the time of her commissioning on 9 April 1941, she was considered the world's greatest sea weapon. Armed with nine 16-inch/45 caliber guns in three turrets and twenty 5-inch/38 caliber guns in ten twin mounts, NORTH CAROLINA proved a formidable weapons platform. Her wartime complement consisted of 144 commissioned officers and 2,195 enlisted men, including about 100 Marines.

During World War II, NORTH CAROLINA participated in every major naval offensive in the Pacific area of operations and earned 15 battle stars. In the Battle of the Eastern Solomon's Islands in August of 1942, the Battleship's anti-aircraft barrage helped save the carrier ENTERPRISE, thereby establishing the primary role of the fast battleship as protector of aircraft carriers. One of her Kingfisher pilots performed heroically during the strike on Truk when he rescued ten downed Navy aviators on 30 April 1944.

In all, NORTH CAROLINA carried out nine shore bombardments, sank an enemy troopship, destroyed at least 24 enemy aircraft, and assisted in shooting down many more. Her anti-aircraft guns helped to halt or frustrate scores of attacks on aircraft carriers. She steamed over 300,000 miles. Although Japanese radio announcements claimed six times that NORTH CAROLINA had been sunk, she survived many close calls and near misses - such as the Japanese torpedo which slammed into the Battleship's hull on 15 September 1942. A quick response on the part of the crew allowed the mighty Ship to keep up with the fleet. By war's end, the Ship lost ten men in action and had 67 wounded.

Vital Statistics	
Hull Number:	BB 55
Keel Laid:	October 27, 1937
Launched:	June 13, 1940
Commissioned:	April 9, 1941
Decommissioned:	June 27, 1947
Length:	728 feet 5/8 inches long
Extreme Beam:	108 feet 3 7/8 inches wide
Mean Draught:	31 feet 7 inches normal, 35 feet 6 inches maximum
Displacement:	36,600 tons standard, 44,800 tons full load
Complement:	2,339 (144 officers and 2,195 enlisted)
Speed:	28 knots
Armament:	9 16-inch/45 caliber guns 20 5-inch/38 caliber guns 60 40mm/56 caliber guns 48 20mm/70 caliber guns

After serving as a training vessel for midshipmen, NORTH CAROLINA was decommissioned 27 June 1947 and placed in the Inactive Reserve Fleet in Bayonne, New Jersey, for the next 14 years until the 1958 announcement of her impending scrapping led to a statewide campaign by citizens of North Carolina to save the ship from the scrappers torches and bring her back to her home state. The Save Our Ship (SOS) campaign was successful and the Battleship arrived in her current berth on 2 October 1961 and was dedicated as the State's memorial to its World War II veterans on 29 April 1962.

PRE WAR

Authorized by an act of Congress on 3 June 1936, the keel of BB-55 was laid down at the Brooklyn Navy Yard on Navy Day, 27 October 1937. This was the first time the United States had started construction of a battleship in 16 years. A few new cruisers and destroyers had been built, but in general, the fleet was old if not obsolete at the time.

Ships are not built in a day. As they say, when you need ships it's too late to build them. Four years of design work, and three years and eight months went into her construction.

While building the NORTH CAROLINA, war broke out in Europe, and only four days before her launch Hitler's divisions occupied Paris. In the Far East, Japan had invaded China, and was threatening further aggressive moves in Southeast Asia.

On 13 June 1940, Governor Clyde R. Hoey of North Carolina's daughter, Isabel, to the strains of "Anchors Aweigh", smashed the traditional bottle of champagne against the bow and launched the ship. Then, on 9 April 1941, after completing her fitting-out, Secretary of the Navy Frank Knox commissioned the ship. After all work was done, the ship cost the taxpayers $76,885,750. Today, the sum would be vastly greater.

After commissioning, the North Carolina had an unusually extensive shakedown, lasting several months. During this long "shakedown" period, the North Carolina returned often to her building yard for adjustments and modifications. During this time, New Yorkers, and in particular radio commentator Walter

Winchell often witnessed the great new "battlewagon" entering and departing the harbor, and began to call her "The Showboat", after the colorful river steamer in a popular Broadway musical. The name has stuck ever since.

The Battleship returned to her building yard in New York for Thanksgiving and was inport on 7 December 1941. Completing her shakedown, NORTH CAROLINA remained in the Atlantic through early Spring when the decision was made to send her into the Pacific.

IOWA CLASS BATTLESHIP

The *Iowa*-class battleships were six battleships ordered by the United States Navy in 1939 and 1940 to escort the Fast Carrier Task Forces that would operate in the Pacific Theatre of World War II. Four were completed in the early to mid-1940s; two more were laid down, canceled prior to completion, and ultimately scrapped. They comprised the final class of U.S. battleships to be built.

Built with no regard for cost, the *Iowa* class was arguably the ultimate in the evolution of the capital ship. The ships topped the Discovery Channel's list of the ten "most fearsome vessels in the history of naval warfare." Yet even as these leviathans entered service, they were being eclipsed by aircraft carriers as the most important naval vessels.

The *Iowa*-class battleships served in every major U.S. war of the latter half of the 20th century. In World War II, they defended aircraft carriers and shelled Japanese positions before being placed in reserve at the end of the war. Recalled for action during the Korean War, the battleships provided artillery support for UN forces fighting against North Korea. In 1968, *New Jersey* was recalled for action in the Vietnam War and shelled Communist targets near the Vietnamese Demilitarized Zone. All four were reactivated and armed with missiles during the 1980s as part of the 600-ship Navy. In 1991, *Missouri* and *Wisconsin* fired missiles and 16-inch (406 mm) guns at Iraqi targets during the Gulf War. All four battleships were decommissioned in the early 1990s, and were removed from the Naval Vessel Register in 2006.

History

The *Iowa*-class battleships were shaped by the Battle of Jutland, by naval treaties signed by various countries during the 1920s and 1930s, and by the need to keep up with aircraft carriers and protect them from aerial attack.

The sinking of three lightly armored Royal Navy battlecruisers at Jutland in 1916 led the world's builders of capital ships to improve their naval armour.

The Washington Naval Treaty was proposed by U.S. Secretary of State Charles Evans Hughes and forged during a November 1922 conference attended by Great Britain, France, Italy, and Japan. The attending nations agreed to abandon ongoing construction of battleships and battlecruisers, to limit ships to 35,000 tons, to cap armament at 16-inch (406 mm) cannons, and to limit replacement tonnage. The London Naval Treaty further restricted battleship construction and banned new battleships through 1937. These treaties stopped U.S. construction of battleships and battlecruisers.

At the Second London Naval Conference in 1935, the Empire of Japan denounced the naval treaty and withdrew its delegates. The other conferees agreed that if Japan did not sign the treaty by April 1937, other nations would be free to build guns up to 16 inches (410 mm), the maximum size under the Washington Naval Treaty. Tonnage limits would also be relaxed.

That same year (1935), an empirical formula for predicting a ship's maximum speed was developed, based on scale-model studies in flumes of various hull forms and propellers. The formula used the length-to-speed ratio originally developed for 12-meter yachts: Speed = "1.408 * waterline length, and was later redefined as Capital Ship Speed = 1.19 * "Length at Waterline. It quickly became apparent that propeller cavitation caused a drop in efficiency at speeds over 30 knots (55.56 km/h). Propeller design therefore took on new importance.

In 1936, on the heels of the Empire of Japan's withdrawal from the Second London Naval Conference, President Franklin Roosevelt issued an executive order creating the Battleship Design Advisory Board (BDAB) and charged the new group with developing new battleship designs, in particular for a

45,000-ton battleship. The board, composed of renowned U.S. naval architects and headed by Captain Allan Chantry, played with various designs for the upcoming U.S. fleet of *North Carolina* and *South Dakota*-class battleships to help lessen the gap between the U.S. based battleships and those being commissioned in Germany and Japan at the time.

The United States began building the *North Carolina* and *South Dakota*-class battleships in the late 1930s. Designed mostly within treaty limitations, these new battleships could steam at 28 knots (52 km/h), fast for a battleship but not fast enough to keep pace with the aircraft carriers being planned.

Birth of the *Iowa* Class

The *Iowa* class, like the *South Dakota* class and *North Carolina* class, began in response to the need for fast escorts for the *Essex*-class aircraft carriers. Plans for fast battleships that displaced 45,000 tons had been under development since 1935, beginning with a study of the idea of creating an extended *South Dakota* class that would take full advantage of the escalator clause of the Second London Naval Treaty. When the Second Vinson Act was passed by the United States Congress in 1938, the U.S. Navy moved quickly to develop a 45,000-ton battleship that would pass through the 110 ft (34 m) wide Panama Canal. Drawing on the earlier speed equations and a newly developed empirical theorem that related waterline length to maximum beam, the Navy drafted plans for a battleship class with a maximum beam of 108 ft (32.9 m), which when multiplied by 7.96 produced a waterline length of 860 ft (262 m), permitting a maximum speed of 34.9 knots (64.6 km/h). The Navy also called for the class to have a lengthened forecastle and amid-ship, which would increase speed, and a bulbous bow.

Originally, the ships were to mount the Mark 2 16-inch (406 mm) / 50-caliber gun, which had been intended to arm the battleships and battlecruisers canceled in 1922. But due to a miscommunication between the Bureau of Ordnance and the Bureau of Construction and Repair that left the ship's barbettes too small, the Mark 2 guns were replaced in the design by the new, lighter Mark 7 16-inch 50-caliber gun. The Mark 7 was heavier and had a greater range than the 16"/45 Caliber Mark

6 guns used on the preceding *North Carolina* and *South Dakota* classes. The Mark 7 was originally intended to fire the same 2,240 lb (1,020 kg) shell as the 16-in/45-caliber gun, but as the design was being completed a new "super-heavy" 2,700 lb (1,200 kg) shell was developed for both guns. However, the *Iowa*'s armour was only designed to resist 2,240 lb (1,016 kg) shells, as adding armour would have pushed the ship's weight over the 45,000-ton limit.

At the time the *Iowa*-class had been cleared for construction the United States Congress had allocated only enough money to construct the first two ships (*Iowa* and *New Jersey*). Congress had not expected the *Iowa*-class to be so costly; with a price tag of $125 million per ship, the *Iowas* were 60% more expensive than the previously authorized battleship classes. Moreover, some policymakers were not sold on the U.S. need for more battleships, and proposed turning the ships into aircraft carriers by retaining the hull design but switching their decks to carry and handle aircraft. The proposal to build the *Iowas* as aircraft carriers was countered by Admiral Ernest King, the Chief of Naval Operations, and Congress' position on the funding for the *Iowa*-class changed after the Fall of France, when Roosevelt demand that Congress fund a two ocean navy to meet the threats posed in the Atlantic and Pacific Oceans. Concern over the German invasion prompted Congress to respond by allotting enough money to complete the last four *Iowa*-class battleships (*Missouri, Wisconsin, Illinois,* and *Kentucky*).

Under the direction of Secretary of the Navy Charles Edison, the design was finalized and a contract was signed with the shipyards in July 1939. Originally BB-61, BB-62, BB-63, and BB-64 were to be of the same design, while BB-65 and BB-66 were intended to be larger, slower ships mounting twelve 16-inch (410 mm) guns. But by late 1939, it was apparent that the navy needed as many fast battleships as possible and it was decided that BB-65 and BB-66 would follow the same design as their sisters.

Service history

When brought into service during the final years of World War II, the *Iowa*-class battleships were assigned to operate in the Pacific, primarily to provide anti-aircraft screening for U.S. aircraft carriers and perform shore bombardment. Among the *Iowas*, only USS *New Jersey* engaged a surface ship during World War II. At the end of the war, *Iowa, New Jersey* and *Wisconsin* were decommissioned and placed in the mothball fleet; construction on two uncompleted ships (*Illinois* and *Kentucky*) was halted.

The *Iowas* were recalled in 1950 with the outbreak of the Korean War, then returned to mothballs after hostilities ceased, in 1955.

In 1968, due in large part to congressional pressure, *New Jersey* was recommissioned and sent to assist U.S. troops during the Vietnam War. She did one tour on the firing line, then was decommissioned the following year.

In the 1980s, the battleships were recommissioned. President Ronald Reagan had vowed to rebuild the U.S. military and create a 600-ship Navy. With the *Des Moines*-class heavy cruisers worn out, the relatively low mileage *Iowas* were brought back to fill the offshore bombardment role. The ships also provided a counter to the new Soviet *Orlan*-class large missile cruisers, better known in the West as the *Kirov*-class battlecruisers. Each *Iowa* battleship was modernized to carry electronic warfare suites, CIWS self-defense systems, and missiles. They became the centerpieces of their own battleship battle groups (BBBGs). Their missions in the 1980s and early 1990s included the U.S. intervention in the Lebanese Civil War following the 1983 Beirut barracks bombing and the 1991 Gulf War, first as part of Operation *Desert Shield* and then as part of Operation *Desert Storm*. Decommissioned for the last time in the early 1990s, the *Iowas* were split into two groups: those retained in the United States Navy reserve fleets (better known as the "mothball fleet") and those donated for use as museum ships.

In 1996, the National Defense Authorization Act led *Iowa* and *Missouri* to be struck from the Naval Vessel Register. *Missouri* was donated to the Missouri Memorial Association of Pearl Harbor, Hawaii, for use as a museum ship. *Iowa* was set to be donated with *Missouri*, but was reinstated to the Naval

Vessel Register after the Strom Thurmond National Defense Authorization Act of 1999 allowed *New Jersey* to be donated as a museum ship. The last two *Iowa*-class battleships were removed from the mothball fleet in 2006, and are currently awaiting transfer for use as museum ships.

The Ships

The *Iowa*-class ships were built to steam at the same speed as the U.S. fleet of *Essex*-class aircraft carriers. Their main battery and secondary battery guns were designed to take on the ships of the Imperial Japanese Navy, and to shell beachheads in advance of U.S. Army and Marine Corps amphibious assaults. They carried a fearsome array of anti-aircraft guns to defend themselves and their carriers.

USS *Iowa* (BB-61)

Iowa was ordered 1 July 1939, laid down 27 June 1940, launched 27 August 1942, and commissioned 22 February 1943. *Iowa* conducted a shakedown cruise in the Chesapeake Bay before sailing to Naval Station Argentia, Newfoundland to counter the German battleship *Tirpitz.* Transferred to the Pacific Fleet in 1944, *Iowa* made her combat debut in the campaign for the Marshall Islands. The ship escorted U.S. aircraft carriers conducting air raids in the Marianas campaign, then was present at the Battle of Leyte Gulf.

During the Korean War, *Iowa* bombarded enemy targets at Songjin, Hungnam, and Kojo, North Korea. *Iowa* returned to the U.S. for operational and training exercises before being decommissioned. Reactivated in the early 1980s, *Iowa* made several operation cruises in European waters. On 19 April 1989, an explosion of undetermined origin ripped through her No. 2 turret, killing 47 sailors.

The turret remained inoperable when *Iowa* was decommissioned for the last time in 1990. In 1999, *Iowa* was placed in the mothball fleet as a replacement for sister ship *New Jersey*. Stricken from the Naval Vessel Register on 17 March 2006, *Iowa* is currently berthed at Suisun Bay in San Francisco, California, pending a decision on requests to turn the ship into a museum ship.

USS *New Jersey* (BB-62)

New Jersey was ordered 1 July 1939, laid down 16 September 1940, launched 7 December 1942, and commissioned 23 May 1943. *New Jersey* completed fitting out and trained her initial crew in the Western Atlantic and Caribbean before transferring to the Pacific Theatre in advance of the planned assault on the Marshall Islands, where she screened the U.S. fleet of aircraft carriers from enemy air raids. At the Battle of Leyte Gulf, the ship protected carriers with her anti-aircraft guns. *New Jersey* then bombarded Iwo Jima and Okinawa. During the Korean War, the ship pounded targets at Wonsan, Yangyang, and Kansong. Following the ceasefire, *New Jersey* conducted training and operation cruises until she was decommissioned. Recalled for action in 1968, *New Jersey* reported for duty near the Vietnam DMZ, and remained there until 1969, whereupon she was again decommissioned. Reactivated under the 600-ship Navy program, *New Jersey* was sent to Lebanon to protect U.S. interests and U.S. Marines, firing her main guns at Druze and Syrian positions in the Bekaa valley east of Beirut. Decommissioned for the last time 8 February 1991, *New Jersey* was briefly retained on the Naval Vessel Register before being donated to the Home Port Alliance of Camden, New Jersey, for use as a museum ship.

USS *Missouri* (BB-63)

Missouri was ordered 12 June 1940, laid down 6 January 1941, launched 29 January 1944, and commissioned 11 June 1944. *Missouri* conducted her trials off New York and shakedown and battle practice in the Chesapeake Bay before transferring to the Pacific Fleet, where she screened U.S. aircraft carriers involved in offensive operations against the Japanese before reporting to Okinawa to shell the island in advance of the planned landings. Following the bombardment of Okinawa *Missouri* turned her attention to Honshû and Hokkaidô, shelling the islands and screening U.S. carriers involved in combat operations against the Japanese positions.

She garnered international attention in September 1945 when representatives of the Empire of Japan boarded the battleship to sign the documents of unconditional surrender to the Allied powers. After World War II *Missouri* turned her attention to conducting training and operational cruises before being dispatched to Korea at the outbreak of the Korean War. *Missouri* served two tours of duty in Korea before being decommissioned in 1956. Reactivated 1984 as part of the 600-ship Navy plan, *Missouri* was sent on operational cruises until being assigned to Operation *Earnest Will* in 1988. In 1991, *Missouri* participated in the Gulf War by firing Tomahawk Missiles at Iraqi target and shelling known Iraqi positions along the coast. Decommissioned for the last time in 1992, *Missouri* was donated to the USS *Missouri* Memorial Association (MMA) of Pearl Harbor, Hawaii, for use as a museum ship in 1999.

USS *Wisconsin* (BB-64)

Wisconsin was ordered 12 June 1940, laid down 25 January 1942, launched 7 December 1943, and commissioned 16 April 1944. After trials and initial training in the Chesapeake Bay, *Wisconsin* transferred to the Pacific Fleet in 1944 and assigned to protect the U.S. fleet of aircraft carriers involved in operations in the Philippines until summoned to Iwo Jima to bombard the island in advance of the Marine landings. After the landings on Iwo Jima she turned her attention to Okinawa, bombarding the island in advance of the allied amphibious assault.

In mid-1945 *Wisconsin* turned her attention to pounding the Japanese home islands, a job she retained until the surrender of Japan. Reactivated in 1950 for the Korean War, *Wisconsin* served two tours of duty assisting South Korean and UN forces by providing call fire support and shelling targets of opportunity. Decommissioned in 1958, *Wisconsin* was placed in the reserve fleet at the Philadelphia Naval Yard until reactivated in 1986 as part of the 600-ship Navy plan. In 1991, *Wisconsin* participated in the Gulf War by firing Tomahawk Missiles at Iraqi targets and shelling Iraqi troop formations along the coast. Decommissioned for the last time 30 September 1991 *Wisconsin* was placed in the reserve fleet until struck from the Naval Vessel Register 17 March 2006. She is currently berthed in Norfolk, Virginia, pending a formal transfer of the battleship for use as a museum ship.

USS *Illinois* (BB-65)

Illinois was ordered 9 September 1940 and laid down 15 January 1945. Construction was canceled 11 August 1945 when *Illinois* was 22% complete. She was sold for scrap in September 1958. *Illinois'* design called for an all-welded hull, lighter and stronger than the riveted/welded hull of the four completed *Iowa*-class ships. A proposal to redesign the hull with a *Montana*-class type torpedo protection system was rejected.

USS *Kentucky* (BB-66)

Kentucky was ordered 9 September 1940 and laid down on 6 December 1944. Construction was suspended 17 February 1947 when *Kentucky* was 72% complete. She was informally launched 20 January 1950 to clear a dry-dock for repairs to *Missouri*, which had run aground. In 1956, *Kentucky*'s bow was removed and shipped in one piece across Hampton Roads, where it was grafted on the battleship *Wisconsin*, which had collided with the destroyer *Eaton*. Later, *Kentucky*'s engines were salvaged and installed on the fast combat support ships *Sacramento* and *Camden*. Nothing came of several proposals to complete *Kentucky* as a guided missile ship. Ultimately, *Kentucky* was sold to Boston Metals Co. for scrap on 31 October 1958. Like *Illinois*, *Kentucky*'s hull was of all-welded construction, lighter and stronger than the other *Iowas*, and a proposal to redesign the hull with a *Montana*-class torpedo protection system was rejected.

Armament

The *Iowa*-class battleships were among the most heavily armed ships the United States ever put to sea. The main battery of 16-inch (406 mm) guns could hit targets nearly 24 miles (39 km) away with a variety of artillery shells, from standard armour piercing rounds to tactical nuclear charges called "Katies" (from "kt" for kiloton). The secondary battery of 5-inch (127 mm) guns could hit targets nearly 9 miles (14 km) away with solid projectiles or proximity fused shells, and were equally adept in an anti-aircraft role and for damaging smaller ships. When commissioned these battleships carried a fearsome array of 20 mm and 40 mm anti-aircraft guns, which were gradually replaced with Tomahawk and Harpoon missiles, Phalanx anti-aircraft/anti-missile gatling gun systems, and electronic warfare suites. By the time the last *Iowa*-class battleship was decommissioned in 1992 the *Iowas* had set a new record for battleship weaponry: No other battleship class in history has had so many weapons at its disposal for use against an opponent.

Main Battery

The primary armament of an *Iowa*-class battleship is nine 16-inch (406 mm) / 50-caliber Mark 7 naval guns, which are housed in three 3-gun turrets: two forward and one aft in a configuration known as "2-A-1". The guns are 66 feet (20 m) long (50 times their 16-inch (410 mm) bore, or 50 calibers, from breechface to muzzle). About 43 feet (13 m) protrudes from the gun house. Each gun weighs about 239,000 pounds (108,000 kg) without the breech, or 267,900 pounds (121,500 kg) with the breech. They fire projectiles weighing from 1,900 to 2,700 pounds (850 to 1,200 kg) at a maximum speed of 2,690 ft/s (820 m/s) up to 24 nautical miles (39 km). At maximum range the projectile spends almost 1½ minutes in flight.

Each gun rests within an armored turret, but only the top of the turret protrudes above the main deck. The turret extends either four decks (Turrets 1 and 3) or five decks (Turret 2) down. The lower spaces contain rooms for handling the projectiles and storing the powder bags used to fire them. Each turret required a crew of 94 men to operate. The turrets are not actually attached to the ship, but sit on rollers, which means that if the ship were to capsize the turrets would fall out. Each turret costs US $1.4 million, but this number does not take into account the cost of the guns themselves·

The turrets are "three-gun", not "triple", because each barrel can be elevated independently; they can also be fired independently. The ship could fire any combination of its guns, including a broadside of all nine. Contrary to myth, the ships do not move noticeably sideways when a broadside is fired.

The guns can be elevated from "5° to +45°, moving at up to 12° per second. The turrets can be rotated about 300° at about four degrees per second and can even be fired back beyond the beam, which is sometimes called "over the shoulder." The guns are never fired directly forward because of the shape of the bow and risk that firing the guns forward would damage the ship; in addition to this concern, a satellite up-link antenna was mounted at the bow of each battleship when reactivated in the 1980s.

Secondary Battery

The secondary battery of the ship consists of 5-inch (127 mm) Mark 12 guns in 10 twin mounts, five each to port and starboard, and four Mark 37 Gun Fire Control Systems. These guns were introduced on destroyers in 1934, but by World War II had been installed on nearly every major U.S. warship. The secondary battery was intended to fight off aircraft.

Its effectiveness soon declined as Japanese airplanes became faster, then rose again toward the end of the war because of an upgrade to the Mark 37 Fire Control System and the proximity-fuzed 5-inch shells. During the 1980s modernization, four twin mounts were removed to make room for missiles, the two farthest aft and the two at mid-ship on each side. In the Gulf War, the secondary battery was largely relegated to shore bombardment and littoral defense.

Anti-aircraft Batteries

Since they were designed to escort the U.S. fleet of fast attack aircraft carriers the *Iowa*-class battleships were all outfitted with a fearsome array of anti-aircraft guns to protect U.S. aircraft carriers from Japanese fighters and dive bombers.

Oerlikon 20 mm Anti-aircraft Guns

The Oerlikon 20 mm anti-aircraft gun was one of the most heavily produced anti-aircraft guns of World War II; The US alone manufactured a total of 124,735 of these guns. When activated in 1941 these guns replaced the 0.50"/90 (12.7 mm) M2 Browning MG on a one-for-one basis.

The Oerlikon 20 mm AA gun remained the primary anti-aircraft weapon of the United States Navy until the introduction of the 40 mm Bofors AA gun in 1943.

Bofors 40 mm Anti-aircraft Guns

Arguably the best light anti-aircraft weapon of World War II, the 40 mm Bofors AA gun was used on almost every major warship in the US and UK fleet during World War II from about 1943 to 1945. Although a descendant of German and Swedish designs, the Bofors mounts used by the United States Navy during World War II had been heavily "Americanized" to bring the guns up to the standards placed on them by the US Navy.

This resulted in a guns system set to English standards (now known as the Standard System) with interchangeable ammunition, which simplified the logistics situation for World War II. When coupled with hydraulic couple drives to reduce salt contamination and the Mark 51 director for improved accuracy the Bofors 40 mm gun became a fearsome adversary, accounting for roughly half of all Japanese aircraft shot down between 1 October 1944 and 1 February 1945.

Phalanx CIWS

During their modernization in the 1980s each *Iowa*-class battleship was equipped with four of the United States Navy's Phalanx CIWS mounts, two which sat just behind the bridge and two which were fixed to a platform installed between the ship's funnels. *Iowa, New Jersey*, and *Missouri* were equipped with the Block 0 version of the Phalanx, while *Wisconsin* received the first operational Block 1 version in 1988. Phalanx CIWS mounts were used by *Missouri* and *Wisconsin* during the 1991 Gulf War; *Wisconsin* alone fired 5,200 20 mm Phalanx CIWS rounds.

Missiles

During the modernization in the 1980s, three weapons were added to the *Iowa*-class battleships. The first was the CIWS anti-aircraft/anti-missile system discussed above. The other two were missiles for use against both land and sea targets. At one point, the NATO Sea Sparrow was to be installed on the reactivated battleships; however, it was determined that the system could not withstand the overpressure effects when firing the main battery.

Tomahawk Land Attack Missile

The BGM-109 Tomahawk Land Attack Missile (TLAM) entered U.S. service in 1983. A long-range, all-weather, subsonic cruise missile, the Tomahawk could hit targets 1,350 nautical miles (2,500 km) away, more than 40 times farther than the 16-inch (410 mm) guns' 24-mile (39 km) range.

Harpoon Anti-ship Missile

For protection against enemy ships, the *Iowa* class carried Boeing RGM-84 Harpoon anti-ship missiles in four Mk 141 shock-hardened quad-cell canister launchers located alongside the aft stack, two launchers per side. At firing, the Harpoon weighs 1,530 pounds (690 kg), including a booster of about 362 pounds (164 kg). The cruising speed is Mach 0.87 and the range is 64 nautical miles (119.5 km) in Range and Bearing Launch mode and 85 nm (157.4 km) in Bearing Only Launch mode.

Armour

Aside from its firepower, a battleship's other defining feature is its armour. Battleships are usually armored to withstand an attack from guns the size of its own, but the exact design and placement of the armour—factors inextricably linked with the ship's stability and performance—is a complex science honed over decades. The *Iowas* benefitted from advances in steel technology that allowed mills to forge the steel at higher temperatures and heat treatment, which produced a much higher-quality, stronger and more elastic armour. The metal was a nickel-steel compound, classified as a stainless steel, that can bend easily and resists corrosion. Most of the armour was manufactured at Bethlehem Steel's main mill in Bethlehem, Pennsylvania, and Luken Steel's Coatsville mill just outside Philadelphia, Pennsylvania. The exception was the turret plating, which was forged at a plant built especially for the *Iowas*: the Charleston Ordnance Works in Charleston, West Virginia.

The *Iowa*-class battleships' armour can be divided into the part above the waterline, which is designed to protect the ship against gunfire and aerial bombing, and that below the waterline, intended to protect the vessel from mines, near-miss bombs, and torpedoes.

Overall, *Iowa*-class armour is essentially the same as on the earlier *South Dakota*-class battleships. Both have an internal main belt, a change from the previous two *North Carolina*-class battleships that was reluctantly adopted because it was difficult to install and repair. An external belt that could ward off 2,700 lb 16-inch (410 mm) shells would have required a belt incline of 19° and a beam too wide for the Panama Canal.

The underwater armour includes side protection and a triple bottom, both multi-layered systems designed to absorb the energy from an underwater explosion equivalent to 700 pounds (320 kg) of TNT—the Navy's best guess in the 1930s about Japanese weapons. However, unbeknownst to U.S. Naval Intelligence, the Japanese 610 mm (24 in) "Long Lance" torpedo carried a 490 kg (1,100 lb) warhead.

The *Iowa*-class torpedo defense is virtually the same as the *South Dakota*'s. Each side of the ship is protected by one tank mounted outside the hull and loaded with fuel oil or other liquid ballast, and an empty inboard tank, all running from the third deck to the bottom of the ship. The liquid tanks are to deform and absorb the shock from the explosion and contain most of the shards from the damaged structure. The inner void is expected to contain any leakage into the interior ship spaces. The armour belt is designed to stop fragments that penetrate the second torpedo bulkhead; however, tests in 1943 showed structural defects in the system.

Aircraft

The *Iowa* class used several types of aircraft for reconnaissance and for gunnery spotting. The early aircraft were floatplanes launched from catapults on the ship's fantail. They landed on the water, taxied to the stern of the ship, and were lifted by a crane back to the catapult.

Kingfisher

Initially, the *Iowas* carried the Vought OS2U Kingfisher, a lightly armed two-man aircraft designed in 1937. The ships typically carried three Kingfishers: two on the catapults and a spare on a trailer nearby. The Kingfisher's high operating ceiling made it well-suited for its primary mission: to observe the fall of shot from the battleship's guns and radio corrections back to the ship. The floatplanes also performed search and rescue for naval aviators who were shot down or forced to ditch in the ocean.

Seahawk

In June 1942, the U.S. Navy Bureau of Aeronautics requested industry proposals for a new seaplane to replace the Kingfisher and Curtiss SO3C Seamew. The new aircraft was required to be able to use landing gear as well as floats.

Curtiss submitted a design on August 1, and received a contract for two prototypes and five service-test aircraft on August 25. The first flight of a prototype XSC-1 took place 16 February 1944 at the Columbus, Ohio Curtiss plant. The first production aircraft were delivered in October 1944, and by the beginning of 1945 the single-seat Curtiss SC Seahawk floatplane began replacing the Kingfisher.

Helicopters

Around 1949, helicopters replaced floatplanes on the *Iowa* class. They operated from atop of Turret 2 until the catapults were removed, allowing helicopter operations to shift to the fantail. The aft guns are forbidden to fire when a helicopter is on the aft deck.

Helicopters added a logistics role to gunnery spotting and search-and-rescue; they ferried troops and supplies between ships and to and from land bases. Like the seaplanes before them, the helicopters had no hangar facilities, but the *Iowas* did have support facilities for five types of helicopters: the UH-1 Iroquois, SH-2 Seasprites, CH-46 Sea Knight, CH-53 Sea Stallion and the LAMPS III SH-60B Seahawk.

Mastiff

In 1975, Tadiran Electronic Industries introduced the Mastiff unmanned aerial vehicle (UAV) to the Israeli Defense Forces (IDF). The drone, designed for use in a reconnaissance role, proved its worth during the 1982 Lebanon War, when IDF personnel used Mastiff drones to aid in the location and destruction of Syrian SAM sites.

The Mastiff first came to the attention of the United States Navy after a botched American airstrike against Syrian air defenses in Lebanon in December 1983. During the operation, U.S. aircraft carriers operating off the coast of Lebanon sent out 28 aircraft to bomb targets in the Bekaa Valley in retaliation for anti-aircraft fire directed at F-14 reconnaissance flights operating from the carriers. The main target of the bombing run was a Syrian radar station, but before the aircraft could reach the site, two American planes were shot down by Syrian guns.

In an analysis of the incident, U.S. Navy Secretary John Lehman determined that the targeted SAM sites had been within the range of the battleship *New Jersey* and her 16-inch (410 mm) guns, but there had been no way for the battleship to accurately target the sites without an aerial observer to direct the ship's rounds to the target. In part because of the Israeli success with the drones, the U.S. Navy made a covert request for a Mastiff drone system. Israel responded by lending a drone to the U.S. in 1984. The success of the Mastiff system in tests ultimately led the Navy to develop its own UAV system, resulting in the creation of the RQ-2 Pioneer UAV.

Pioneer

In 1985, the United States Navy, impressed with Israeli successes with Mastiff unmanned aerial vehicle in the early 1980s, began looking for UAVs to provide imagery for gun spotters aboard the recently reactivated battleships. The result of this effort was the remote-controlled RQ-2 Pioneer, which made its first deployment in December 1986 aboard the *Iowa*.

Launched from the fantail using a rocket-assist booster that was discarded shortly after takeoff, a Pioneer used an aft-mounted, push-propeller engine to achieve speeds of up to 90 miles per hour (140 km/h) with a mission endurance of about four hours. The Pioneer carried a video camera in a pod under the belly of the aircraft, which transmitted live video back to the ship so that the operators can observe enemy actions or fall of shot during naval gunnery. Because it was difficult to land the Pioneer without damaging itself or the ship, a large net was strung up for recovery as for a volleyball game, and the aircraft is flown into it.

Each battleship could carry as many as eight Pioneers, sometimes referred to as remote piloted vehicles (RPVs).

Pioneer garnered international attention for its use during the 1991 Gulf War, when it saw extensive use from the *Missouri* and *Wisconsin*. The latter became the first ship to have enemy forces surrender to one of its remotely controlled observation drones.

Engineering Plant

The *Iowa*-class battleships are the fastest battleships ever launched, capable of sustained speeds of 33 knots (61 km/h) or better. The engineering plant consists of four General Electric double-expansion steam turbine engines, each driving a single shaft that turns one screw. The two outboard screws on the *Iowa* class have four blades and are just over 18 feet (5.5 m) in diameter. The two inboard screws have five blades and are about 17.5 feet (5.3 m) in diameter.

Eight Babcock and Wilcox M-Type boilers operate at 600 psi (4136.85 kPa) with a maximum superheater outlet temperature of 875 °F (468 °C)

The double-expansion engines consist of a high-pressure (HP) turbine and a low-pressure (LP) turbine. The steam is first passed through the HP turbine which turns at up to 2,100 rpm. The steam, largely depleted at this point, is then passed through a large conduit to the LP turbine. By the time it reaches the LP turbine, it has no more than 50 psi (300 kPa) of pressure left. The LP turbine increases efficiency and power by extracting the last little bit of energy from the steam.

After leaving the LP turbine, the exhaust steam passes into a condenser and is then returned as feed water to the boilers. Water lost in the process is replaced by three evaporators, which can make a total of 60,000 US gallons per day (3 liters per second) of fresh water. After the boilers have had their fill, the remaining fresh water is fed to the ship's potable water systems for drinking, showers, hand washing, cooking, etc. All of the urinals and all but one of the toilets on the *Iowa* class flush with saltwater in order to conserve fresh water.

The turbines, especially the HP turbine, can turn at 2,000 rpm; their shafts drive through reduction gearing that turns the propeller shafts at speeds up to 225 rpm, depending upon the desired speed of the ship.

Electricity

Electricity drives many systems aboard ship, including rotating the turrets and elevating the guns. Each of the four engine rooms has a pair of Ship's Service Turbine Generators (SSTGs) manufactured by Westinghouse. Each SSTG generates 1.25 MW for a total of 10 MW of electricity. The SSTGs are powered by steam from the same boilers that feed the engines. For backup, the ship also has a pair of 250-kW diesel generators.

To allow battle-damaged electrical circuits to be repaired or bypassed, the lower decks of the ship have a Casualty Power System whose large 3-wire cables and wall outlets called "biscuits" can be used to reroute power.

Radar & Electronic Warfare Systems

Since the first commercial radar system was installed aboard the battleship USS *Texas*, battleships have used radar for aerial reconnaissance, surface surveillance, and as part of the fire control system for the battleship's guns. Since their modernization in the 1980s, the four *Iowa* class battleships have also used electronic countermeasures systems for defense against enemy missiles and aircraft.

Radar

Each of the four *Iowa*-class battleships are equipped with the AN/SPS-49 Radar Set, an L-band, long-range, two-dimensional, air-search radar system that provides automatic detection and reporting of targets within its surveillance volume. The AN/SPS-49 performs accurate centroiding of target range, azimuth, amplitude, ECM level background, and radial velocity with an associated confidence factor to produce contact data for command and control systems. Additionally, the contact range and bearing information is provided for display on standard plan position indicator consoles.

The AN/SPS-49 uses a line-of-sight, horizon-stabilized antenna to provide acquisition of low-altitude targets in all sea states, and also utilizes an upspot feature to provide coverage for high diving threats in the high diver mode. External control of AN/SPS-49 modes and operation by the command and control system, and processing to identify and flag contacts as special alerts are provided for self-defense support.

The AN/SPS-49 has several operational features to allow optimum radar performance: an automatic target detection capability with pulse doppler processing and clutter maps, ensuring reliable detection in normal and severe types of clutter; an electronic counter-countermeasures capability for jamming environments; a moving target indicator capability to distinguish moving targets from stationary targets and to improve target detection during the presence of clutter and chaff; the Medium PRF Upgrade (MPU) to increase detection capabilities and reduce false contacts; and a Coherent Sidelobe Cancellation (CSLC) feature.

The *Iowa*-class battleships are also equipped with the Radar Set AN/SPS-67, a short-range, two-dimensional, surface-search/navigation radar system that provides highly accurate surface and limited low-flyer detection and tracking capabilities. The AN/SPS-67 is a solid-state replacement for the AN/SPS-10 radar, using a more reliable antenna and incorporating standard electronic module technology for simpler repair and maintenance. The AN/SPS-67 provides excellent performance in rain and sea clutter, and is useful in harbor navigation, since the AN/SPS-67 is capable of detecting buoys and small obstructions without difficulty.

The AN/SPS-67(V)1 radar is a two-dimensional (azimuth and range) pulsed radar set primarily designed for surface operations with a secondary capability of anti-ship-missile and low flier detection. The radar set operates in the 5450 to 5825 MHz range, using a coaxial magnetron as the transmitter output tube. The transmitter/receiver is capable of operation in a long (1.0 msec), medium (0.25 msec), or short (0.10 msec) pulse mode to enhance radar performance for specific operational or tactical situations. Pulse repetition frequencies (PRF) of 750,1200, and 2400 pulses/second are used for the long, medium, and short pulse modes, respectively.

Electronic Warfare

In 1967 Egypt sank the Israeli destroyer *Eilat* using a Soviet SS-N-2 STYX missile, prompting the Chief of Naval Operations (CNO) to consider creating a family of inexpensive Electronic Warfare suites to replace and/or complement existing and planned ship surveillance sensors in the early 1970s, a feeling increased when an analysis of the existing AN/WLR-1 and AN/ULQ-6 systems installed on most ships determined that neither system could counter an Anti-Ship Cruise Missile (ASCM) in time to prevent a hit. In addition, hard kill weapons were not effective because there was little early warning of an attack due to the characteristics of ASCMs. The resulting EW suite was the AN/SLQ-32(V), which debuted in 1979 and was capable of early warning of threat weapon system emitters and emitters associated with targeting platforms, threat information to own ship hard-kill weapons, automatic dispensing of chaff decoys, and Electronic Attack (EA) to alter specific and generic ASCM trajectories. This system, specifically the SLQ-32(V)3 variant, was fitted to the *Iowa* class battleships in 1980s for defense against enemy anti-ship missiles.

To counter the threat posed by enemy submarines the *Iowa* class were also outfitted with the AN/SLQ-25 Nixie, a towed torpedo decoy used on US and allied warships. It consists of a towed decoy device, and a shipboard signal generator. The decoy emits signals to draw a torpedo away from its intended target. The Nixie attempts to defeat a torpedo's passive sonar by emitting simulated ship noise, such as propeller and engine noise, which is more attractive than the ship to the torpedo's sensors. Active sonar is decoyed by amplifying and returning "pings" from the torpedo, presenting a larger false target to the torpedo.

During their modernization in the 1980s each of the *Iowa*-class battleships were outfitted with the Mark 36 Super Rapid Bloom Offboard Chaff (SRBOC) system, enabling the *Iowa*s to carry and fire chaff rockets which, when launched from their tubes, release missile decoys or lures. The decoys/lures are intended to act as an anti-missile shield by providing false targets for an enemy missile to attack. During the 1991 Gulf War, chaff was blamed for a friendly fire incident between the *Oliver Hazard Perry*-class frigate *Jarrett* and the battleship *Missouri*: during an Iraqi missile attack *Missouri* fired chaff into the air to confuse the incoming missile; however a Phalanx CIWS mount on *Jarrett* accidentally engaged the chaff fire by *Missouri*. Rounds from the Phalanx mount on *Jarret* struck *Missouri*, causing one minor injury to a crewman on the battleship; fortunately, no serious injuries or damage resulted from the attack.

Reactivation Potential

After World War II, the United States maintained the four *Iowa*-class battleships in the United States Navy reserve fleets, better known as the "mothball fleet", and on several occasions reactivated these battleships for naval gunfire support. The U.S. Navy has held onto its battleships long after the expense and the arrival of aircraft and precision guided munitions led other nations to scrap their big-gun fleets. The United States Congress is largely responsible for this. The lawmakers argue that the battleships' large-caliber guns have a militarily useful destructive power lacking in the smaller, cheaper, and faster guns mounted by U.S. cruisers and destroyers.

The Navy, which sees the battleships as too costly, is working to persuade Congress to allow it to remove *Iowa* and *Wisconsin* from the Naval Vessel Register by developing extended-range guided munitions and a new ship to fulfil Marine Corps requirements for naval surface fire support (NSFS).

The Navy plan calls for the extension of the range of the 5-inch (127 mm) guns on the Flight I *Arleigh Burke*-class guided missile destroyers (USS *Arleigh Burke* to USS *Ross*) with Extended Range Guided Munitions (ERGMs) that would enable the ships to fire precision guided projectiles about 40 nautical miles (70 km) inland. This program was initiated in 1996 with a preliminary cost of US $78.6 million; since then, the cost of the program has increased 400%. The results of the program have been similarly disappointing, with the original expected operational capability date pushed from 2001 to 2011. These weapons are not intended or expected to satisfy the full range of the Marine Corps NSFS requirements. The result of the latter effort to design and build a replacement ship for the two battleships is the *Zumwalt*-class destroyer program, also known either as the DD(X) or DDG-1000 (in reference to *Zumwalt*'s hull number). The DD(X) is to mount a pair of Advanced Gun System (AGS) turrets capable of firing specially designed Long Range Land Attack Projectiles (LRLAPs) some 60 miles (100 km) inland. The Navy currently expects sufficient numbers of DD(X) destroyers to be ready to help fill the NSFS gap by 2018 at the earliest.

> *"DDG 1000* Zumwalt *is [...] being developed by the Navy to serve as the backbone of tomorrow's surface Fleet. DDG 1000* Zumwalt *provides a broad range of capabilities that are vital both to supporting the Global War on Terror and to fighting and winning major combatant operations.* Zumwalt's *multi-mission warfighting capabilities are designed to counter not only the threats of today, but threats projected over the next decade as well." ---Statement of the DD(X) program on the United States Navy's Program Executive Office, Ships,*

On 17 March 2006 the Secretary of the Navy exercised his authority to strike *Iowa* and *Wisconsin* from the Naval Vessel Register, which has cleared the way for both ships to be donated for use as museums. The United States Navy and the United States Marine Corps have both certified that battleships will not be needed in any future war, and have thus turned their attention to development and construction of the next generation *Zumwalt*-class guided missile destroyers.

This move has drawn fire from a variety of sources familiar with the subject; among them are dissenting members of the United States Marine Corps, who feel that battleships are still a viable solution to naval gunfire support, members of the United States Congress who remain "deeply concerned" over the loss of naval surface gunfire support that the battleships provided, and number of independent groups such as the United States' Naval Fire Support Association (USNFSA) whose ranks frequently include former members of the armed service and fans of the battleships. Although the arguments presented from each group differ, they all agree that the United States Navy has not in good faith considered the potential of reactivated battleships for use in the field, a position that is supported by a 1999 Government Accountability Office report regarding the United States Navy's gunfire support program.

In response, the Navy has pointed to the cost of reactivating the two *Iowa* class battleships to their decommissioned capability. The Navy estimates costs in excess of $500 million, but this does not include an additional $110 million needed to replenish gunpowder for the 16-inch (406 mm) guns because a recent survey found the powder to be unsafe. In terms of schedule, the Navy's program management office estimates that reactivation would take 20 to 40 months, given the loss of corporate memory and the shipyard industrial base.

> *"In summary, the committee is concerned that the Navy has foregone the long range fire support capability of the battleship, has given little cause for optimism with regard to meeting near-term developmental objectives, and appears unrealistic in planning to support expeditionary warfare in the mid term. The committee views the Navy's strategy for providing naval surface fire support as 'high risk', and will continue to monitor progress accordingly."*
> *—Evaluation of the United States Navy's naval surface fire support program in the National Defense Authorization Act of 2007,*

Reactivating the battleships would require a wide range of battleship modernization improvements, according to the Navy's program management office. At a minimum, these modernization improvements include command and control, communications, computers, and intelligence equipment; environmental protection (including ozone-depleting substances); a plastic-waste processor; pulper/shredder and wastewater alterations; firefighting/fire safety and women-at-sea alterations; a modernized sensor suite (air and surface search radar); and new combat and self-defense systems. The Navy's program management office also identified other issues that would strongly discourage the Navy from reactivating and modernizing the battleships. For example, personnel needed to operate the battleships would be extensive, and the skills needed may not be available or easily reconstituted. Other issues include the age and unreliability of the battleships' propulsion systems and the fact that the Navy no longer maintains the capability to manufacture their 16-inch (410 mm) gun system components and ordnance.

Although the Navy firmly believes in the capabilities of the DD(X) destroyer program, members of the United States Congress remain skeptical about the efficiency of the new destroyers when compared to the battleships. Partially as a consequence the US House of Representatives have asked that the battleships be kept in a state of readiness should they ever be needed again. Congress has asked that the following measures be implemented to ensure that, if need be, *Iowa* and *Wisconsin* can be returned to active duty:

1. *Iowa* and *Wisconsin* must not be altered in any way that would impair their military utility;
2. The battleships must be preserved in their present condition through the continued use of cathodic protection, dehumidification systems, and any other preservation methods as needed;
3. Spare parts and unique equipment such as the 16-inch (410 mm) gun barrels and projectiles be preserved in adequate numbers to support *Iowa* and *Wisconsin*, if reactivated;
4. The Navy must prepare plans for the rapid reactivation of *Iowa* and *Wisconsin* should they be returned to the Navy in the event of a national emergency.

These four conditions closely mirror the original three conditions that the Nation Defense Authorization Act of 1996 laid out for the maintenance of *Iowa* and *Wisconsin* while they were in the Mothball Fleet. It is unlikely that these conditions will impede the current plan to turn *Iowa* and *Wisconsin* into museum ships.

Popular Culture

The *Iowa class*-battleships have been featured prominently in American culture. *Iowa* was the centerpiece for the book *A Glimpse of Hell: The Explosion on the U. S. S. Iowa & Its Cover-Up* which dealt with the events surrounding the 1989 explosion of her #2 turret. In 2001 the book was turned into a movie by the same name staring James Caan and directed by Mikael Salomon. *Missouri* was featured in the 1977 movie *MacArthur*, starring Gregory Peck, the 1983 television mini-series *The Winds of War*, starring Ralph Bellamy and Robert Mitchum, and Cher's music video "If I Could Turn Back Time". The 1992 movie *Under Siege*, staring Steven Seagal, was also set aboard *Missouri*, although the movie was actually filmed aboard the battleship USS *Alabama*. *Wisconsin* was featured prominently in the news during the 1991 Gulf War, when she became the first ship to receive the surrender of enemy troops on the ground when her Pioneer drone recorded Iraqi soldiers waving white flags after being shelled by *Missouri*.

5

FUTURE OF ARMS CONTROL

The Revolution in Military Affairs (RMA) presents two related problems for arms control. First, is the susceptibility of the RMA itself to credible and verifiable arms control measures, second the possible adverse impact of the RMA on existing efforts to control Weapons of Mass Destruction (WMD). If the RMA has fostered a measure of obscurity and uncertainty, rather than clarity, about the future of warfare, it has done no less when it comes to arms control.

The RMA has generated considerable, and inconclusive debate as to whether it is a "true" revolution in the nature of warfare or only part of a continuing "evolution" in weapons technologies, military organization and doctrine. It is closely associated with the post-Cold War national security policy of the United States which seeks to maintain America's dominant position and freedom of action at acceptable costs through the application of advanced technology to warfare.

The lessons of arms control during the Cold War suggest that arriving at a regime which could control elements of the RMA will be difficult given the inherent paradoxes of the arms control process itself and the particular nature of the RMA.

The fact that the weapons systems which comprise the RMA are considered "conventional" and the large role played by easily obtainable civilian technologies in these systems indicate that there is likely to be a "proliferation" of the RMA outside the West. Another factor promoting the spread of the RMA is the desire of countries to provide counters to the technological superiority of the United States and its allies.

While there is much that it is observable in the spread of the RMA, especially in terms of military organization and doctrine, existing arms control methodologies and technologies do not lend themselves to the establishment of a credible verifiable regime which could curtail the spread of the RMA. Given the nature of the weapons technologies, such a regime would require a level of intrusive, on-site verification measures which few countries would accept and which would be extremely difficult to sustain. Moreover, any international effort to control the spread of the RMA, which is led by the United States and its allies, will be seen as an unequal application of arms control norms in a manner similar to the perception of the Nuclear Non-Proliferation Treaty (NPT).

One of the major concerns with the RMA is the possibility of an "asymmetrical" response using WMDs by states or group against which RMA technologies are to be used. This in turn has contributed to efforts by the United States and its allies to deal with the WMD threat through multilateral arms control measures, such as the NPT and efforts to control chemical and biological weapons. The West has also adopted unilateral counter-proliferation efforts. Amongst the latter is the retention by the United States and NATO of the threat of nuclear response in the event that WMDs are used against them in response to their use of RMA technologies in future military action. Thus the West now has a new reason not to fully abandon nuclear deterrence, fear of asymmetrical responses to the RMA.

Examining scenarios in which the United States threatens or applies RMA against states withvarying degrees of conventional, RMA and WMD capabilities, suggests that the effectiveness of the RMA will vary according to the magnitude of such capabilities, the nature of any conflict and the political situation. States with large conventional forces and even an limited WMD capability can raise the cost of intervention to the United States or even deter it. But there is the threshold issue that complicates any predictions about how states will respond to RMA use and potential WMD counter-responses. Will small and weak states risk retaliation by nuclear weapons if they employ WMDs against American forces or the United

States itself? Will Washington cross the line if its troops are attacked by chemical weapons? Just as the various scenarios point to no conclusive answer on the action-reaction dynamic of RMA use, so too are the arms control possibilities varied. Some states may be amenable to arms control and abandon a WMD capability to respond to the RMA, while others, depending on their security situation and the character of their governments may wish to retain it and reject WMD arms control measures.

However, concern about WMD is very much on the international agenda and much has been done to establish new norms. In some areas of arms control, such as nuclear weapons, progress has been made. Given the other factors that affect the international security environment, and the very uncertainties associated with the RMA, there is reason to conclude that arms control will survive the RMA. Thus the future international security environment is likely to be one where *both* the RMA and arms control will present competing, but not always mutually exclusive, claims for the enhancement of international strategic and political stability.

INTRODUCTION

There has been much debate on whether or not the technologies, weapons and emerging doctrines associated with the Revolution in Military Affairs (RMA) constitute a true "revolution" in the nature of warfare. There has been less consideration of whether the RMA will engender a corresponding "revolution" in arms control. In part this is because there is the view that the weapons systems, doctrines and military organizational changes associated with the RMA are not trends whose control is possible, necessary, or even desirable. In other words, while there is general agreement that nuclear, biological, and chemical weapons are fit subjects for arms control, even by some of those states which possess them, the systems associated with the RMA has thus far garnered no such consensus.

The issue of controlling the RMA is linked with other aspects of arms control, for it has in a sense complicated or intruded upon older weapons developments and efforts to control them.

Thus no sooner did the end of the Cold War make possible the conclusion of the Strategic Arms Reduction Treaties (START I and II), than the RMA introduced a new class of weapons and warfare which in one sense has made strategic nuclear arms control less relevant than it had been. This is because nuclear weapons are no longer the dominant measure of military power for the United States and Russia. In another sense, however, the advent of the American RMA has heightened concern about the control of nuclear and other weapons of mass destruction (WMD). Efforts at arms control such as the Non-Proliferation Treaty (NPT), attempts to curb missile technology as well as chemical and biological weapons may well be more difficult as countries that lack the ability to respond to RMA systems in kind, will seek out alternative means of deterrence and defence. This in turn leads to a further complicating factor. Despite increased importance placed by the United States on the RMA, neither it nor its allies, seem prepared to entirely abandon nuclear deterrence in face of the spread of WMD capabilities.

The study below examines the RMA from an arms control standpoint. It discusses the question of whether the RMA itself can be subjected to arms control measures and what the impact of the RMA is on efforts to control WMDs. The paper does not take a position for or against the RMA or arms control. Rather, its objective is to provide an analysis of the various complicating factors that have arisen with regard to arms control as a result of the advent of the RMA. As with the previous Cold War era of arms control, wherein many of the paradoxes and uncertainties of nuclear weapons were never conclusively resolved, and where substantial disagreement existed over these issues, the arms control impact of the RMA points to a wide range of often self-contradictory scenarios and has likewise fostered differing views about the best policy choices.

Whatever its real-life impact, the RMA has generated considerable upheaval in the strategic studies scholarly community. But it is a debate which to many goes beyond academic interest since it is expected that how it is settled will have profound impact upon how nations develop and posture their forces for war. This is especially the case in the United States.

For the RMA, especially its strongest proponents, technology and its application to warfare is the dominant theme. Most share Martin van Creveld's opening premise in his book, *Technology and War*, '..war is completely permeated by technology and governed by it.' Warfare, particularly from the introduction of gunpowder in the 12th century, "has been captivated by technology." "Some historians could make a strong case that since the introduction of the wheeled chariot mankind has been obsessed with the search for that particular technology that would guarantee success on the battlefield."

War, however, is not, despite what so-called realists contend, entirely devoid of moral content. As Michael Walzer observed in his *Just and Unjust Wars*, "for as long as men and women have talked about war, they have talked about it in terms of right and wrong...aggression, self-defense, appeasement, cruelty, ruthlessness, atrocity, massacre-all these words are judgements, and judging is as common a human activity as...fighting." Over the centuries, norms about what should or should not be done in war have evolved, even as they have been violated, most spectacularly in the last century. One of the most important of these norms is the requirement to avoid unnecessary civilian casualities. Indeed, as noted below, one of the claims of the RMA is that in bringing ever advancing technology to bear on war, it can reduce "collateral damage." In this sense, the debate over the RMA is consistent with all past debates over the nature of warfare combining both moral and technological arguments. But, as in the past, the technological dimension is the overriding consideration.

Andrew Krepinevich's definition is often cited as that most closest to the mark. An RMA takes place when,

> *"...the application of new technologies into a significant number of military systems combine[d] with innovative operational concepts and organizational adaptation in a way that fundamentally alters the character and conduct of conflict. It does so by producing a dramatic increase- often an order of magnitude or greater-in the combat potential and military effectiveness of armed forces."*

A central tenet of the RMA, and the reason why it has fostered such intense debate, are the claims that only those states who will be able to master the changes will be confident of victory in future wars.

> *"The traditional, fundamental principles of war will still apply. Yet major departures are coming for two reasons. Many military forces are going to become more powerful and capable of high-technology warfare at the high end of the conflict spectrum. And a growing number of conflicts likely will be fought at the low end of the spectrum. Sophisticated technology may not be dominant in many of them. Both trends, and their interaction, will change warfare. ...This dynamic is hardly surprising. Warfare has continually evolved over the past two centuries. Military establishments that best anticipated change have generally been the most successful in war. By contrast, those that failed to foresee the future, and remained complacent and static, have often been surprised and defeated."*

Yet behind these general claims for the RMA is a more specific national claim, or rather expectation, that it will be the United States, the 'founding father' of the RMA which will reap the greatest benefits. While the RMA offers opportunities to other countries which will be able to afford the acquisition of "expensive modern weaponry and the skills to use it properly[...]only the United States, with its vast accumulation of military capital, better than four times the defense budget of the next leading power, and an unsurpassed ability to integrate large, complicated technological systems, can fully exploit this revolution."

The RMA offers America "the prospect of military power beyond that of any other country on the planet, now and well into the next century." This is why American theorists have embraced the RMA for it appears to afford the United States the opportunity to perpetuate its power. There is indeed about the RMA an American "boosterism," a profound sense of national uniqueness in the technology and doctrine of war. "The next century is confidently expected to be an American one where everyone follows our example: everyone must follow in our wake or fall apart. And that fact gives us a lasting information edge." By using the technologies, including information warfare, America will be able to confound and quickly defeat its enemies, striking at whole countries and destroying their will along with their forces and infrastructure, while they will be unable to strike back. These emblems of United States technological superiority, observes Blank, "taken together and multiplied in effectiveness" are alleged to "confer not just operational superiority, but a lasting American superiority and hegemony."

Writing in 1992, Van Creveld argued that a major break with the past was coming. He argued that as military technology, and the organizations needed to fully implement it advanced, the forces of the major powers came to resemble each other and "to see each other as their most dangerous opponents and, consequently, they acquired more and more powerful technology to smash each other." In the twentieth century, fewer and fewer countries were able to compete. "By 1914, only a few countries could still produce all their weapons, field first rate armed forces and incidently, divide the globe among themselves." With the advent of the Cold War, continued enhancement of conventional weapons and, above all, atomic power, this number was further reduced. With the end of the Cold War, and the cost of major weapons systems only one power capable of fielding the full array of modern forces was left, the United States.

But Van Creveld also contended that since the development of nuclear weapons, and despite improvements in conventional capabilities brought about by improvements in surveillance and accuracy, the era of large scale interstate conventional warfare was nearing its end. Both superpowers tried to develop nuclear and conventional arms in an effort to "decouple" them from full "scale strategic war," but gave up, whereupon one Superpower disintegrated and the other started bringing its forces home. With this example to follow, as of 1992, other countries seem to be following the same road, in the Middle East and South Asia, "proliferating nuclear technology was well on its way to putting an end to large scale, conventional conflict".

Van Creveld stressed that most of the conflicts since 1945 have been low intensity conflicts and most of them were waged "by or against political entities that were not states with the aid of armed forces not amounting to regular armies." He noted that none of the twenty conflicts then going on was being waged by "state-owned, regular, armies with the aid of heavy modern weapons or at least not on both sides". Because of this, military technology, "appears ready to shift gears. Technology in short will focus less on defending against an external threat by regular forces and more on providing security against an internal one. Its enemies will be guerillas and terrorist who in turn will often be indistinguishable from ordinary criminals; and indeed the shift is taking place right now."

Predictions of sweeping change, both in technology and especially in the nature of warfare, do not appear to have been entirely borne out as the century ended. The technology of war has evolved, but conventional forces, —air forces, navies and especially armies— have been used repeatedly, although not in major interstate warfare. More importantly, while the United States did bring its forces home from many foreign bases, they have not stayed home. Indeed, as stressed in this study, one of the key elements driving the RMA is that the United States seeks to continue to project its power abroad. In this regard, Van Creveld's other suggestion that the proliferation of nuclear technology will convince non-Western states of the disutility of large-scale conventional war, does not appear to be the main concern, rather it is that nuclear weapons and other WMDs will be used as counters to the RMA.

Although technological developments are key to predictions made by the RMA, a 1999 study by the RAND Corporation for the United States Defense Advanced Research Projects Agency (DARPA) suggests that the role of technological change needs to be placed in perspective. This is because, fundamentally, an RMA "involves a paradigm shift in the nature and conduct of military operations which either *renders obsolete or irrelevant* one or more core competencies of a dominant player or creates one or more new core competencies, in some new dimension of warfare, or both." For example, it could be argued that the introduction of the aircraft carrier constituted an RMA as far as naval power was concerned because it undermined the core competency of the dominant naval powers which had been large battleships. The advent of the Intercontinental Ballistic Missile (ICBM) shifted the paradigm by creating a dimension of warfare, intercontinental strategic warfare and creating a new competency, the long-range accurate delivery of nuclear weapons. The introduction of the machine gun shifted the paradigm by creating a "new tactical level model for land warfare," and "rendered obsolete" the competency in being able to "maneuver massed forces in the open." In some future conflict the employment of "cyberspace-based technologies" by one side against another sufficient to alter the course of the conflict, would be an RMA "since it would create a new core competency (information warfare) in a new dimension of warfare (cyberspace)." This is an important point, since if the RMA is to fundamentally change the nature of warfare, then it must in some sense provide one state or group of states advantages which negate previous advantages, even those held by the state introducing the new weapon.

At the same time, "transformation in one area of military affairs does not...mean the irrelevance of all others." The revolution brought about by the introduction of nuclear weapons did not "render conventional forces obsolete." While the rise of the aircraft carrier, made the battleship less central to naval power in the Second World War, the battleship was widely used in that war and in many conflicts since,including the Gulf War.

The RAND study also offers some cautions based on historical experience. RMAs can provide "immediate military advantage" to the first nation that exploits them in war but are not always brought about by dominant players. They are often adopted and more fully exploited by someone other than the nation inventing the new technology. This was the case with the tank, which originated with the British in World War I, but was first fully exploited by the Germans at the beginning of the Second World War. Not all RMAs involve weapons. Railways had profound impact creating a competency to move large numbers of troops further and faster. Not all RMAs are successful, at least not initially, some take time. All successful RMAs appear to have three components, technology, doctrine, and organization. Many of the new technologies associated with the RMA have yet to be fully proven in war. For example, it is argued by some that long-range, highly accurate weapons, cruise missiles or those launched from aircraft, will be able to deal with massed armored attacks, thus doing away with the need to counter such attacks with equally massed armour and traditional artillery. But there is as of yet no example to date of massed armour being halted by Precision Guided Munitions (PGMs).

The contemporary RMA is said to involve a number of "technology/ device/ system/ operational employment concept combinations" which have or could change ways of waging war. One of these is the capacity for "long-range precision fires." Here highly accurate long-range weapons employ ground, air, and space-based sensors and command and control system which can dominate warfare obviating the need to close in order to destroy the enemy. The RMA is also associated with "information warfare." The outcome of battles may depend on the ability to protect one's own information systems while at the same time disrupting those of the enemy. Then there is the concept of the RMA being a "system of systems." The idea here is that by combining a "vast assemblage of intelligence collection, surveillance and reconnaissance (ISR)" with "advanced command, control, communications, computers and intelligence processing (C4I)" and "precision-weapon systems," the result is a whole with capabilities "much greater than the sum of the parts." Beyond this would be the "network-centric warfare" concept which envisions the meshing of the information grid, the sensor grid and the engagement grid. Finally, the United States Navy (USN) has developed the concept of a "cooperative engagement capability." Here combat systems on geographically separated platforms would share "measurement date associated with rapid timing and precision to enable the battle group to operate as one..."

Because the impact of new technologies has not clearly resulted in paradigm shifts which have altogether rendered obsolete core competencies of major powers, it may be more useful, as Andrew Marshall of the U.S. Department of Defense's Office of Net Assessment does, to speak about a "potential" or "emerging" RMA "a hypothesis about major change taking place in the period ahead, the next couple of decades." At the same time many of the new technologies associated with the RMA are evolving at a "gradual rate," and "their sum total, when combined to form an integrated military force...could still prove revolutionary."

The present RMA does encompass certain new technologies that have evolved from previous ones. Indeed, it is "the culmination in modern military organizations of a variety of developments, some of them dating back decades." But "rapid, violent, and, above all, unpredictable change" has happened before and may yet happen with the RMA.

Stephen Biddle, in a lengthy analysis and critique of current claims that an RMA has already fundamentally altered the nature of war, also argues that the new technologies have yet to prove themselves. He points to the Gulf War noting that the new technologies employed would have been far less effective against a more skilled adversary which did not make so many errors as did the Iraqi forces. But Biddle also questions whether a fundamental revolution is going to take place. "A non-RMA projection, calling for a future of only incremental change is more consistent with the facts."

For Biddle, the key is not so much technology but the ability to skillfully use it. It was Germany's emphasis during the inter-war years upon training, education, and adaptation which made its use of tank warfare so effective in the early days of the Second World War.

He acknowledges that war has become more complex since 1900 and that those unable to "cope with this ever-increasing complexity have been exposed to the increasing lethality of modern weapons and have suffered increasingly severe consequences." Those that have, however, found ways to manage, have been much less exposed:

> *"The result has been a progressively widening gap in the real military power of organizations that can and those that cannot cope with complexity, but little change in the outcomes of wars fought between equally skilled opponents and no revolutionary discontinuities in the nature of warfare."*

Biddle agrees that technological advancement will "provide increasingly one-sided outcomes in major theatre wars." But he notes that, as the Gulf War demonstrates, "such wars are already very onesided" and "it is not clear that a continuation of this trend would provide any meaningful difference."

More importantly, Biddle contends that technological change in and of itself "is neither necessary nor even conducive to success." The relationship between technological complexity and battlefield success "has not been significantly altered by recent developments and is unlikely to be changed by technologies on the drawing board." As with Cohen, he points to the importance of skill in managing technological changes in warfare. In the 21st century, war will "be mainly a continuation of a century long increase in the importance of skill in managing complexity." The effectiveness of technologies will still depend on human behaviour "and especially on the counter-measures adopted by the technology's targets to reduce their exposure." Tanks have become more lethal and have greater ranges, but complex counter-measures can reduce the effects of their fire-power and compel them to move at less than capable speeds. And skilled combatants will learn to provide fewer lucrative targets for the deep attack technologies heralded by RMA enthusiasts.

Biddle's views on the importance of skill and human behaviour in managing technological to military advantage are confirmed in Timothy Thomas' recent analysis, "Kosovo and the Current Myth of Information Superiority." He points out that in spite of NATO's "near total information superiority, its battlespace awareness was manipulated by Serbian forces more often than expected. When human and software interpreters of intelligence information were fooled, it resulted in munitions wasted on fake or incorrect targets and in bad assessments of the actual situation on the ground." Mission tasks and damage assessments were also affected.

As revealed in Congressional testimony, the American and allied personnel were not prepared to conduct information operations. In some cases there was a lack of skills in targeting, intelligence analysis, and translation. "Information superiority" he concludes, "allowed NATO to know almost every thing about the battlefield, but NATO analysts didn't always understand everything they thought they knew."

Even if armed forces master the operational skills associated with the RMA, the outcome of warfare may not become more predictable. The spread of RMA related technologies will make it difficult to assess the balance of power to the extent that it is based on the expected outcome of armed confrontation. Opacity in the matter of military power may prove one of the most troubling feature of the RMA:

> *"As platforms become less important and the quality of munitions and, above all, the ability to handle information become more so, analysts will find it ever more difficult to assess the military balance of opposing sides...the revolution in military affairs may bring a kind of tactical clarity to the battlefield, but at the price of strategic obscurity."*

In other words, while the well-known physical attributes of the RMA technologies may make it easier to predict what weapons are capable of doing in specific military operations, the spread of those technologies will make it more difficult to assess what the outcome of conflict will be. In this sense, the spread of technology would introduce a new measure of uncertainty into power relationships, even on the part of those countries which nominally possess the most advanced of the RMA technologies.

This may impose caution on these states. At the same time, the general uncertainty engendered by this "strategic obscurity" may lead to a more unstable international strategic environment at odds with the interests of the United States and its allies.

As noted above, the enthusiasm about the RMA is only in part technological. Much of it is political and it is closely linked to the American desire to maintain its global dominance. This points to what some authors have called a fundamental asymmetry in the international strategic environment. The United States has overwhelming power in terms of the capability to intervene in foreign conflicts on a global scale. At the same time, "an asymmetry of interests" suggests "a policy of noninvolvement since so few contemporary conflicts seem to put in jeopardy key U.S. interests and therefore warrant the commitment of U.S. forces with the attending risk of casualties." But in fact the RMA can be viewed as being specifically tailored to a world in which America faces few direct threats to its vital interests, but may nevertheless wish to intervene in order to prevent a spread of conflict, to support allies, or for humanitarian reasons. It promises that technology can reduce the costs of unipolarism in both peace and war.

Integral with its technological implications for national security policy and the future of warfare, the American RMA has promoted much discussion about changes in doctrine and military organization. Doctrinally, the emphasis is on "decisive victory and friendly casualty limitations," in an effort by the military "to balance military and political power with military societal compatibility." The RMA doctrine also suggests that America will be able to apply force anywhere in the world even with reductions in overseas bases in peacetime and smaller forces, especially ground troops, in war. The lure of the RMA is that it "promises a way to overcome what many military men believed were the reasons for our loss in Vietnam." It not only results in minimal casualties but "even constrains the media's ability to portray the war other than the way the generals want it." [29] The RMA also fosters the notion that the United States can further reduce its overseas permanent bases. "How much nicer it would be," notes Michael O'Hanlon, "if U.S. troops could stay home until called upon in a crisis or conflict. Then according to RMA believers, they could lash out rapidly, intercontinentally, and lethally from bases" utilizing space power and long range air power.

The United States is rejecting preparation for a long war because of the dangers of a protracted conflict including public discontent. The National Military Strategy states explicitly that "Everything is staked on a short, decisive war," in which adversaries are rapidly defeated. "Failure to halt an enemy invasion would make the subsequent campaign to evict enemy forces from captured territory much more difficult, and costly. Such failure would also weaken coalition support, undermine U.S. credibility, and increase the risk of conflict elsewhere." The doctrine is said to be applicable in a variety of scenarios and that large scale, protracted war would become less likely, as the RMA "translated into more options in the application of military force in low intensity conflicts or operations other than war." (OOTW)

This doctrine may result in a new division of labour between the United States and its allies or coalition partners. Already somewhat apparent in the Balkan interventions, this trend would see the United States contribute high tech capabilities such as long-range precision strike, global logistics, space capabilities, and information dominance, while regional allies would provide the bulk of the troops, especially for peace-keeping duties after target country or groups were subdued by American RMA forces. This may well be what Washington, and especially the Congress and the people, are expecting from the RMA and what allies fear.

The doctrinal imperative of quick victory, combined with the impact of rapid communication, suggests that the lines between traditional levels of warfare, and their associated echelons of command, will become blurred or "permanently erased." There will be a melding of the strategic, theatre (operational), and tactical levels. Combined with the information warfare aspects of the RMA, this will create a requirement for commanders at all levels to know what is going on at all levels. This does not mean, though, that "micro-management" of these operations will disappear and more responsibility will fall to lower command levels. Indeed, as Cohen points out, the technologies associated with the RMA, which would literally allow the overall commander of an operation (and/or the politician) to see what the pilot in the cockpit sees, may actually increase the tendency of the highest echelons to involve themselves in tactics. Where conflicts are being fought for limited objectives, and where concern about collateral damage to civilians and high casualties could be important, the RMA may well make micro-management very tempting. This new doctrine is to be applied to all aspects of military operations, including various forms of peacekeeping and non-combat missions where decisiveness and political considerations will be particularly important.

In order to exploit the benefits of technology and achieve the doctrinally mandated decisive results, it has been argued that military organization will itself have to change. This is not to say that armies, navies, and, above all, air forces will disappear as distinct organizational entities. At the same time, the implementation of RMA technologies is likely to hasten an already apparent trend, at least in western armed forces, away from large conscript militaries to smaller forces wherein a premium will be placed not upon the combat experience of the personnel, especially the officer corps, but upon technical and management skills. And the RMA with its rapid transmission of information right down to the tactical level, may, as it has done in business, remove the need for layers of military middle management in the conduct of operations.

RMA advocates also argue that when forces need to be deployed, new technologies and organization will make them much more effective. For example, as Thierry Gongora notes, the United States Army has tried to integrate information technologies, by digitalizing the structure and equipment of its forces. In one 1997 exercise, the 4th Infantry Division showed that in comparison with regular formations, "the digitalized" division, "inflicted more than twice as many enemy casualties, in half the time, over three times the normal battle space using 25 percent fewer combat platforms." Western armed forces will seek this kind of capability "in the twenty-first century to make up for their decreasing size."

To implement RMA doctrine, much emphasis is placed in the United States upon "jointness" compelling the Army, Air

Force, and Navy to work together. Since the Goldwater-Nichols Act of 1986, and especially after the Gulf War, this has been almost dogma in U.S. defence planning for overseas operations. In October 1999, the United States Atlantic Command, based in Norfolk, Virginia was renamed, United States Joint Forces Command, (USJFCOM), The new command, is to serve as "the joint development owner" for the entire American military "responsible for developing the methodology to deploy all military forces for rapid and decisive military force power projection from the continental United States."

In 1994 Jeffrey Cooper argued that the United States must go beyond jointness to integration in order to obtain the full benefits of the RMA. The perspective must be changed "from improving the individual elements of combat power...to integrating and focusing the power of the 'whole'. Integration of the whole rather than enhancement of the parts is the central pillar of this RMA," and "the campaign plan and joint operations" are the "defining level for measuring effectiveness."

The short-war dominated RMA doctrines may be an "illusion" and a dangerous one. Trying to convert technology into "lasting" operational and strategic superiority may simply invite potential opponents to resort to strategic surprise or pre-emption as in the case of Japan's attack on Pearl Harbor. Strategic decisions have not been speeded or revolutionized by the RMA and Washington will be surprised again as it was in Somalia and Kosovo and with regard to ballistic missile proliferation. History shows, that "forces optimized for fast-paced, intensive, but brief war had to fight protracted and unwinnable wars of attrition that exacted enormous costs and domestic dissatisfaction. When the United States advertises its intention to avoid protracted wars, it makes that outcome more likely than not."

There are also doubts about a revolution in military organization. As the RMA has taken hold, it appears that predictions about fundamental changes in military organization have proven to be premature, especially in the United States. Stephen Blank notes that, "The continuing rivalry among the services is one aspect of U.S. military life that has not been revolutionized by the RMA." Each service now makes claims that it can deliver the sought-after decisive, cost-effective and bloodless blow. All three services have created new organizations for doctrine development. "In fact" observes Blank, "this atavistic squabbling contradicts the U.S. armed forces professed creed of jointness."

That there remains considerable academic debate about the RMA's technological, doctrinal and organizational aspects is not surprising. Similar debate has accompanied most major changes in the nature of warfare. Some of the predictions came true, others did not. In the absence of a major war involving states with RMA capabilities, much will remain in the realm of speculation, however well informed. The inconclusiveness of this debate notwithstanding, the RMA has already had an impact on the way states perceive the international security environment, including the future of arms control.

THE LESSONS OF THE COLD WAR

Absent from much of the debate over the RMA's meaning for the future of warfare is its impact on arms control. This has two dimensions. First can the elements associated with the RMA be subject to any kind of arms control regime? Second, how will the RMA affect efforts to control WMD? In considering these questions an overview of the lessons of the Cold War is instructive.

The advent of nuclear weapons at the end of the Second World War escalated the destructive potential of warfare to a new level and also gave impetus to the search for means to control this "absolute weapon." In theory, given the nature of nuclear weapons, it might have seemed that they would have been readily amenable to arms control for several reasons. First of all, relative to conventional weaponry, the number of nuclear weapons, and the platforms to deliver them was relatively small. Second, given the destructive power of a single device, the addition of more weapons to the arsenals did not seem to logically enhance national security. Third, while both the Soviets and Americans certainly planned to use these weapons in war, their utility was always circumscribed. Beyond deterrence, and if deterrence failed, the waging of central war, it was never clear how nuclear weapons could be employed effectively. As Henry Kissinger is said to have remarked when accused of giving the Soviets too many weapons during the Strategic Arms Limitation (SALT) negotiations, "What in the name of God is superiority? What is the significance of it, politically, militarily, operationally? What do you do with it?"

But if the nature of nuclear weapons seemed to make them so logically ripe for arms control, those same characteristics militated against control. Given the small numbers, it was difficult to agree on quantitative reductions for fear that, remaining forces would become vulnerable and that the surety of being able to inflict unacceptable damage on the side which struck first would be compromised. For many critics in the United States, Robert McNamara's decision to fix the number of ICBMs at 1054, left America vulnerable-a charge that would be repeated in the 1970s as President Carter sought to negotiate substantial reductions.

To be sure, inter-service rivalries in the United States, especially between the Air Force and the Navy, helped in part to drive force building, and increase the number of weapons. But concern about the stability of deterrence was also an important factor. In redundancy lay survivability and therefore the credibility of deterrence. This was the rationale behind McNamara's push for the development of nuclear-powered Ballistic Missile Submarines (SSBNs) with their Sea Launched Ballistic Missiles (SLBMs). In the 1970s, qualitative improvements to the relatively small arsenals, helped reduce the need for quantitative improvements. Thus both sides, sought to enhance the flexibility of their weapons and associated command and control systems in order that they would be able to hit a wider range of targets. But this in turn led to increased numbers as more weapons were needed to achieve flexibility. Developments in targeting combined with progress in satellite surveillance, allowed for greater accuracy, as with the advent of Multiple Independently-targeted Re-entry Vehicles (MIRVs), which at once reduced the need for more launchers while increasing the number of warheads, thus making arms control even more difficult. It was in fact Kissinger who worked to keep

MIRVs off the table during the SALT I negotiations. Throughout the Cold War, arms control was frustrated because both sides sought to enhance the survivability, flexibility and accuracy of their respective strategic nuclear arsenals.

There was another more intangible factor that militated against nuclear arms control, especially in the early part of the Cold War. Arms control had acquired a bad name during the period between the world wars. Not only had it failed to control arms, but it seemed to become part of the anti-appeasement lessons drawn by the western democracies from the history of those years. Faced with rising militarism and rapid rearmament in Germany and Japan, (the "rogue states" of the era) the West should have been building weapons if it wanted to avoid another world war, not trying to control them with what turned out to be useless treaties so disdainfully ignored by those bent on war. The watch word was, if you want peace, prepare for war, even nuclear war. This suspicion of arms control as a solution to meeting threats from states who cannot be trusted to keep agreements, colours current arms control efforts and lends support to the RMA.

In one important sense, though, concern about fostering instability through arms control, was a selffulfilling prophecy. While the nuclear arms race was surely primarily a product of the global rivalry between East and West, that rivalry was itself fuelled by competitive force building. Both sides viewed the growth and technologically improved sophistication of the other's arsenal as proof of intent, if not for war, then at least for the enhancement of political influence through the threat of war.

One of the key arguments of this paper is that the future is likely to witness *both* force building in support of the RMA and arms control efforts to mitigate some of its potentially dangerous and destabilizing effects. The history of the Cold War appears to support this view as it was a period which witnessed *both* nuclear force building, driven in part by technological innovation and continual efforts at control. Indeed, within a year after dropping the bombs on Japan, Washington was leading a campaign to bring about multilateral control of the spread of nuclear weapons. In 1946, the American government proposed the Baruch Plan, that advocated the supervised abolition of atomic weapons and the international monopoly of nuclear research and nuclear production for civilian purposes. The process was to be controlled by the International Atomic Development Authority (IADA). Though apparently generous, it would have subjected the Soviet Union to a nuclear world on American terms. Not surprisingly the offer was quickly rejected. Between 1955 and 1972, various attempts were made to bring out an end to the arms race. In general both superpowers perceived any offer for control as a political strategy to either eliminate a weapon category if one side felt behind, or freeze a weapon category if one side held a clear dominance.

The politics, indeed it might be said the theatre, of arms control politics, sometimes resulted in a temporary flurry of diplomatic activity with little substantive result. But, although reductions in superpower arsenals remained staled, arms control in selective areas was possible throughout the Cold War. Despite the demise of GCD (General and Complete Disarmament), a number of UN sponsored treaties were signed during the 1960s. In 1963, the Limited Test Ban Treaty denied states from conducting any further nuclear tests under water, in the atmosphere, or in outer space. This was followed in 1967 with the United Nations Outer Space Treaty .

Other important accords were also reached in the late 1960s. After five years of hard negotiations, the Latin American Nuclear Free Zone Treaty was finally signed in 1967, followed by the Non-Proliferation Treaty (NPT) in 1968. This treaty included extensive and intrusive on-site verification measures by the International Atomic Energy Agency (IAEA) for those countries which signed. France and China did not sign the NPT however, nor did several other near-nuclear states. In 1974, India exploded its first nuclear weapon, signifying the limits of the NPT in controlling the spread of nuclear weapons to countries and regions which posed a particular threat of further proliferation and possible use. Because the NPT also required the nuclear weapons states to seek reductions, something that was very slow in coming, the Treaty became for some states a symbol of the double-standard which the West, and especially, the United States applied when it came to arms control.

In the case of other weapons, such as chemical armaments, the United States "consistently" favoured "the strictest possible verification of arms control measures." It would present papers at disarmament conferences "which detailed the technological capabilities of the methods available and evaluated their strengths and weaknesses." As one academic noted,

"The degree of verification required by the United States was based upon its perception of the threat posed to national security by the arms in question and the likelihood of undetected violations. For example, the United States accepted the limited (and in U.S. opinion largely symbolic) verification provisions contained in the Biological Weapons Convention and the Environmental Weapons Convention, because it did not think it was likely that weapons of this nature would be developed for modern arsenals. Verification in these conventions consisted of procedures for cooperation and consultation between parties and recourse to the Security Council in case of unresolved complaints. The United States rejected similar proposals for verification of a chemical weapons accord, noting that the threat posed by these weapons, already in the arsenals of some states, demanded stricter, more assuring verification measures, including on-site inspection."

A renewed effort in arms control began in the early 1970s and was met with some success. The Convention on the Prohibition of Biological Warfare and of the Production of Biological Weapons was opened for signature in April 1972.

That same year, the United States and the Soviet Union finally reached agreement on the first Strategic Arms Limitation Treaty and the Anti-Ballistic Missile (ABM) Treaty. Reflecting the brief period of detente, SALT I, along with revisions concluded in 1974, essentially ratified the existing numerical balance, sanctioned nuclear parity yet left the door open for further modernization. Both sides were pressing ahead with MIRVs. Space-based and other surveillance technologies which had become part of the nuclear arsenals, were employed to assure National Technical Means (NTM) of verification. More important from an arms control perspective was the ABM Treaty which eventually limited both sides to one strategic missile defence system thereby assuring mutual vulnerability and, it was hoped, prevent an uncontrolled offensive weapons building race.

Having stabilized the strategic nuclear balance, the West now turned to the long-standing conventional imbalance in Europe, an imbalance which partly accounted for North Atlantic Treaty Organization's (NATO) continued reliance upon nuclear deterrence and its first use strategy. The talks on Mutual and Balanced Force Reductions (MBFR) in Europe began at the end of 1973. Difficult and protracted, the talks were bogged down in the definitions of balance and equal security. Further problems were encountered in the decision of which weapons to reduce, how reductions were to be phased, and the verification of these reductions. The negotiations met with little success.

After SALT I, the international political atmosphere became adverse to arms control. In the United States, critics charged that detente and the SALT process had been a ploy by the Soviet Union, which continued to modernize its strategic nuclear forces. Fears arose that the USSR was planning to fight and win a nuclear war and in a few years it would be able to use its SS-18 "heavy" Intercontinental Ballistic Missiles (ICBMs) to inflict a successful first strike on America. Moreover, Soviet activity in the Third World was seen as a violation of the supposedly implicit understanding that in exchange for ratifying parity through arms control, Moscow would behave and cooperate on other issues.

All of this made arms control particularly difficult for the Carter Administration which had come into office promising to achieve major reductions. Upon entering office President Ronald Reagan immediately adopted a hard line against the Soviet Union, commenting "both the current and the new Soviet leadership should realize aggressive policies will meet a firm Western response." Reagan replaced SALT with the Strategic Arms Reduction Talks (START) in the early 1980s, as his government perceived the former as an "offer to trade an apple for an orchard." Seeking to replace the long-standing policy of basing American security on the threat of retaliation, the Reagan administration launched the Strategic Defense Initiative (SDI) in 1983 and the Soviet Union spent much of the rest of the decade responding to SDI.

In general, arms control during the Cold War can be said to have had four broad objectives: to reduce the risk of atomic war, to reduce the damage should war occur, to reduce the burden of defence expenditure and to provide a greater measure of strategic and political stability between states. Efforts to reduce or control arms failed, or did not meet expectations, not because such attempts were always at odds with the objectives of force building, but on the contrary, because nuclear force building had the very same four objectives. It was supposed to reduce the risk of war by providing a credible deterrent to opposing nuclear forces and, in the case of NATO, to conventional attack. While predictions about damage limitation were always suspect, both the Americans and the Soviets devised systems whose purpose was to limit damage should nuclear war occur, either by striking first or by executing more accurate and limited strikes. The nuclear arsenals and associated command, control and intelligence infrastructures were expensive, but at least in the beginning they were viewed as less costly than conventional forces. Finally, the nuclear balance of terror, based upon mutual deterrence, was seen as providing for a measure of stability between the superpower antagonists and also within their spheres of influence.

Not only did arms control efforts and nuclear force building appear to have the same objectives, but the record of strategic nuclear arms control, at least until the rapid progress brought about by the end of the Cold War, tended to reinforce the centrality of nuclear force building in relations between the superpowers. Strategic nuclear arms control was possible in the early seventies because it meshed well with the security objectives of the superpowers. In this sense, the ABM Treaty and SALT I marked a significant step towards the establishment of parameters around which the superpowers maintained a balance of power. Neither side could seriously claim a first-strike capability. At the same time neither side was content to rest with the existing technologies that lay behind mutual deterrence. The search for new systems continued. The nuclear balance was never considered technologically static even if strategically a measure of stability appeared to have been achieved.

The SALT process, including the ABM Treaty, only served to entrench nuclear weapons, including advances in technology such as MIRVing, ever more firmly into the international system thus perpetuating the role of strategic nuclear weapons. The success of agreements rested upon the expectation that both sides would be left with what each believed was a necessary force level and composition, leaving the door open to further technological improvements. As Laurence Martin observed in 1979, "However frequently misunderstood, strategic arms limitation is not an alternative to giving nuclear weapons a major role in international politics, but merely one way of defining that role."

That nuclear weapons had a role in international politics was clear. What was not clear was how, where and when they would be used. The military balance was characterized by the 'usability' paradoxes of nuclear weapons, those, imponderable, self-contradictory concepts that were never resolved, and which clouded much of the thinking about security and strategy in the Cold War. Among them was the notion that while the Soviets and the Americans both sought to avoid waging nuclear war, the mutual deterrent postures created to achieve this end were based upon the capabilities and plans of each side which were designed to fight and win such a war. Whether the only outcome was MAD (Mutual Assured Destruction), each side adopted a NUTS (Nuclear Utilization Target Selection) approach. It was assumed that these postures lent credence to the threat of nuclear war because it was believed that nuclear weapons deterred only if there was a possibility that they would have been used. This, however, led to another paradox. Although deterrence was strengthened by mutual perceptions of use under certain circumstances, it was believed that it was dangerous to make nuclear weapons so usable that anyone was tempted to actually employ one. It was on this basis that arms controllers regarded the introduction of tactical nuclear weapons and so-called "flexible options," as inherently dangerous because they may have fostered the notion that nuclear weapons could be used and therefore would be.

But the paradoxes went further. Despite, and indeed perhaps because of, all their efforts to enhance the war fighting capabilities of their strategic nuclear arsenals, the nature of the weapons could not easily be ignored. There were few illusions on either side of the catastrophic risks that would attend the execution of nuclear war plans, which served to reinforce mutual deterrence. As Bernard Brodie observed: "It is the curious paradox of our time that one of the foremost factors making deterrence really work, and work well, is the lurking fear that in some massive crisis in might fail. Under these circumstances, one does not tempt fate."

To a certain extent the paradoxes of nuclear weapons made arms control possible, even while they restricted its scope. Quantitative limits were feasible, although qualitative improvements were continually sought, because numbers alone did not necessarily confirm advantages. The disutility of nuclear weapons in many conflict scenarios may have contributed to efforts to curb proliferation through the NPT process.

In the Cold War the role of strategic nuclear arms control between the superpowers, and to a certain extent general efforts to halt the spread of nuclear weapons through the NPT process, "was to confirm an international power structure. For this reason, agreements tended toward a general counting exercise." Moreover, what could be counted by national technical means or by agreements allowing for on-site inspection, were amenable to arms control where the political will existed to reach bilateral or multilateral agreements. Not surprisingly, attempts to limit conventional weaponry were impeded in part because of the difficulties associated with verification.

As the Cold War came to an end, arms control negotiation and verification entered a new phase. Real reductions in superpower weapons were now possible because of the changed international strategic environment. But it was how that environment changed that really accounted for both the pace and character of the new arms control measures. The 1987 Intermediate-Range Nuclear Forces (INF) Treaty eliminated a whole class of weapons on both sides of the European divide, but went a long way to achieving the NATO objective of removing the strategic and political threat posed by the Soviet SS-20s while leaving the Alliance with adequate theatre capabilities. Most importantly, the on-site verification measures of the Treaty not only gave it credibility, but clearly showed that the Soviets were abandoning their traditional aversion to intrusive measures. Moscow had to reduce defence spending and seek more stability as a result of domestic weaknesses that needed to be addressed.

In November 1990, after some unilateral Soviet withdrawals of conventional forces from Eastern Europe, the Conventional Forces Europe (CFE) Treaty (the post-Cold War successor to the MBFR talks) was signed. In mandated massive reductions in conventional forces in NATO nations and the by then unraveling Warsaw Pact. Its provisions included broad intrusive verification measures and transparency in future posture decisions. By September 1994, "over 18,000 items of treaty limited equipment (TLE) had been destroyed including 6,000 from the Russian Federation," with "no evidence of a concerted effort by any party to cheat or intentionally mislead inspection teams." Here again, the agreement seemed to favour NATO for whom the large Warsaw Pact land armies had been the prime strategic threat.

The end of the Cold War also allowed for real reductions in strategic nuclear weapons, once more on terms that benefitted the United States. Under START I, not only were overall levels brought down but the Soviets agreed to cut in half their heavy SS-18 ICBM arsenal, an objective Washington had been seeking since the 1970s. Under the unratified START II agreement, overall levels are be reduced to 3,500 warheads. Under the START III proposals, Presidents Clinton and former president Yeltsin agreed to negotiate reduced warhead levels to about 2,000 each. More importantly from the American view, START II eliminates all MIRVed ICBMs, including the remaining SS-18s. The treaty however, leaves both sides able to deploy MIRVed

Sea Launched Ballistic Missiles (SLBMs) and this provides the United States with an edge. Its fourteen Ohio-Class Ballistic Missile Submarines (SSBNs), which carry the Trident II D-5 SLBM constitute half of America's deployed strategic warheads. Moreover, the D-5 is a highly accurate weapon allowing "for targeting of hard and soft targets."

With the end of the Cold War American arms control concerns took on a new dimension in order to make sure that the weapons scheduled for destruction were in fact destroyed, especially given that many were now on the territories of newly independent states. The Nunn-Lugar Cooperative Threat Reduction Program provided, amongst other measures, for extensively intrusive U.S. on-site measures to supervise the denuclearization of Belarus, Kazakhstan and Ukraine. Other undertakings dealt with elimination of chemical and biological weapons in Russia, as well as "safe and secure"storage of fissile material.

The nature of the arms control measures were the result of the end of the Cold War and how it ended. The weakness and ultimate fall of the Soviet Union allowed the United States to obtain arms control agreements and associated verification measures, especially on site-verification, on the kind of favourable terms it had been seeking since 1945. This reinforced the idea that arms control and its methods of verification, are closely connected to, are a reflection of, the existing power relationships. The CFE Treaty and the START agreements, and the nature of the verification measures associated with them were seen, not without a certain justification, as the result of the West's "victory" in the Cold War.

This is not to argue that the CFE and START treaties were simply imposed upon a reluctant Soviet Union and now Russia in the way the Versailles Treaty of 1919 and the unconditional surrender of 1945 were forced upon a defeated Germany. These were mutually sought-after and beneficial agreements, as all successful arms control agreements must be. By the mid-1980s it was becoming clear that Moscow was interested in concluding arms control arrangements so that it could address important domestic matters. The Soviet willingness to consider more far-reaching agreements back-up by more intrusive verification measures, also undermined resistance to arms control within parts of the U.S. government and bolstered the views of American allies such as Canada that greater flexibility was possible without compromising Western collective defence. The fact that Russia has now ratified START II and continues to hold to the CFE, and appears willing to continue the arms control process, indicates that we have entered an era in which a new, broader consensus exists on what is possible and desirable.

For the West this consensus is important. Having obtained the kind of agreements that were made possible by the end of the Cold War, it also has stake in seeing them succeed for the sake of its own security interests. To be sure, the agreements represent both a desire to ease tensions with Russia and a latent, if not always openly stated, fear of a revival of animosity between East and West. It is because of the very difficulty and delicacy of the situation that arms control has become integral to allied security and its hopes for stability in Europe. The last thing NATO needs now, especially in light of its expansion eastward and Partnership for Peace (PfP) program is the uncertainty that would be brought out by a weakening of conventional and nuclear arms control measures arrived at during the last ten years. This mutuality of interests reinforces the reductions of the global threat that began in the early 1990s and holds out the promise that the Cold War will not soon return. In this sense arms control has both encouraged further stability even as it is a product of it.

In considering the history of arms control during the Cold War and its relevance to the RMA a number of considerations need to be kept in mind. First, these are "conventional weapons" and thus unlike the nuclear arsenals of the Cold War they do not fit into the usability paradoxes of nuclear weapons. They are being developed and deployed primarily on the expectation that they will be used and not as much on the basis of calculations about deterrence, mutual or otherwise. They are to be used in crisis rather than tempt fate by not acting. In this regard, they cannot be equated with the large conventional forces which

NATO and the Warsaw Pact maintained during the Cold War and which were reduced under the CFE Treaty. These forces were develop to complement the nuclear arsenals. The role of the conventional weapons in Europe in the presence of nuclear weapons suffered from its own contradictions and uncertainties. The most important "threshold" was not that between nuclear and conventional war, but between crisis and war itself. If deterrence had failed, it can be argued that it would have meant failure at all levels since NATO's nuclear forces were intended to deter conventional as well as nuclear attack. NATO's "flexible response" strategy always seemed to be more an agreement amongst allies not to disagree over strategy for the sake of allied unity than a prediction of how a war would actually be fought. While neither side wanted to rely entirely upon mutual nuclear deterrence, it was always highly suspect that there could be a protracted conventional war in Europe.

Second, there is the multiplicity of weapons systems and associated command and control technologies of the RMA as well as a variety of scenarios in which they might be used, something that was not the case with nuclear weapons. This suggests that any effort to control the RMA will encounter many of the difficulties associated with conventional arms control.

Third, while RMA forces cannot be considered the same as the strategic nuclear forces of the Cold War, it is interesting to note that similar claims are being made for them. That is they do have deterrent value, they limit damage if war takes place, they are cost-savings in terms of larger conventional forces and they have a positive impact upon global and regional stability. In other words, the RMA is attractive because it holds out the prospect of providing enhanced security for the leading RMA nation, the United States. This alone may make efforts to control it difficult, just as it did for nuclear weapons. Fourth, as with nuclear weapons, it is evident that, whatever its operational effectiveness, the mere existence of the RMA and its associated technologies, doctrines and military organizational changes are increasingly being entrenched into post-Cold War international politics. Finally, the record of arms control during the Cold War suggests that even if certain important agreements can be reached on a mutually beneficial basis, the technology of warfare continues to progress. This is something that needs to be kept in mind with regard to the RMA which has placed so much emphasis on the importance of pursuing continual technological innovation.

THE PROBLEM OF PROLIFERATION

Because of some of its characteristics, the RMA presents specific problems for arms control for which the lessons of the Cold War may be of limited value. To begin, the proliferation problems associated with the RMA cannot be separated from what Keller and Nolan call the "new proliferation"of arms world wide which they see as the direct result of the dominance of market forces, as opposed to political strategic considerations in the sale of arms. Whereas in the Cold War the transfer of arms and the technologies to build them were used to secure allies and influence, particularly by the United States. Today "almost everyone sells almost anything to just about anyone who can pay-and often to some who cannot." Without "enforceable multilateral restraints, the invisible hand has become the principal mechanism for allocating conventional weapons and associated technology on a global scale." Moreover, the globalization of weapons and technologies "is a form of proliferation that threatens the emerging framework of agreements on weapons of mass destruction..."

While many new sellers have entered the market, the United States with 43 per cent of world-wide arms trade remains dominant. Indeed, despite statements that Washington regards the spread of weapons as a threat and the establishment by Congress of a Presidential Advisory Board on Arms Proliferation, American policy since the mid-1990s has been to promote the sale of its weapons and advance technologies abroad in part to compensate domestic producers for reduced sales to the U.S. military. In announcing his policy in 1995, President Clinton "explicitly sanctioned" arms exports as a way "to enhance the ability of the U.S. defense industrial base to meet U.S. defense requirements...at lower costs." According to Keller and Nolan, "The absence of policy in the world's largest arms dealer has given way to a global frenzy of marketing." The market factors driving the current arms trade are particularly relevant to the RMA. In looking into the arms control and verification issues raised by the RMA, one important feature of the transformation, whether evolutionary or revolutionary, is the fact that many of the technologies that drive it are civilian in origin as indeed many technologies were in the past. As Cohen points out, the end of the Cold War and the "efflorescence of capitalism" in the U.S. and in many other countries, has in a sense "freed up the markets in military goods and services. Countries can gain access to a wide spectrum of military capabilities for ready cash, including the services of skilled personnel." Because of this "the potential will exist for new military powers to emerge extremely rapidly." Nations such as Japan and China will be able to "translate technology power into its military equivalent." During the Cold War, military industry was an "exotic and separate entity." With the RMA, "the pendulum has begun to swing back, and economic strength may again prove easily translatable into military power."

Another factor in spreading the RMA is that there is a certain "observable" characteristic about it. Progress on various systems, the results of research and development is widely reported in the specialized and popular press, especially the arms trade journals. Firms operating in the worldwide arms market, both legitimate and clandestine, have an incentive to spread the most recently available improvements. Military establishments which see themselves as inferior because they do not have the most recent technology, will attempt to "leap frog" the dominant players and may not necessarily do this covertly.

To a certain extent, the proliferation of RMA technologies, at least the most advanced versions, will be limited by resource and budget constraints. Some of America's European and Asian allies will be in the best position to follow the U.S. lead in acquiring the systems either through indigenous manufacture or, because they are allies, through transfer. This will especially be the case if Washington believes that such a transfer will enhance interoperability. Most countries, will be unable to afford or integrate the systems and may seek out cheaper systems, particularly where certain types of technologies can be adapted from those available in the civilian market. At the same time,

"while certain capabilities for intelligence, communication and targeting are becoming widely accessible, other remain highly specialized and at a degree of sophistication that isunavailable outside the higher military spheres, including the most advanced forms of systemintegration. In general there will be hybrid conventional capabilities, acquired selectively and in an uneven and uncoordinated fashion."

Because of concern that advantage may be lost, any attempt to limit the spread of RMA technologies will likely be the result of efforts on the part of those states, the United States and its principal allies, to try and curtail the spread of its most advanced technologies rather than with efforts "at international regulation of the relevant markets." Even here there may be difficulties and even once advanced systems become more readily obtainable.

As with Cohen, Lawrence Freedman also points to the cruise missile, "the paradigmatic weapon of the RMA." It can be launched from a variety of platforms. The Missile Technology Control Regime (MTRC) which seeks regulation through a common export policy and includes systems able to carry chemical, nuclear or conventional weapons, now has 29 states. But, other types of delivery systems, such as "aircraft and cruise missiles used with stand-off platforms" are outside the scope of the MTRC. The regime "cannot cope with aircraft-and many of the components of cruise missiles that are similar to those of aircraft."

In July 1996, 33 countries signed the Wassenaar Arrangement on Export Control for Conventional Arms and Dual Use Goods and Technologies. Efforts have been made to strengthen the agreement. But as Keller and Nolan noted, this agreement "has received scant attention from the policy community and ridicule from the arms lobby and it is presently languishing with no high-level involvement. Wassenaar does not have the 'teeth' to control arms exports."

As Freedman concludes "Most RMA-type technologies can neither be readily counted nor verified, and therefore do not fit into any of the traditional sorts of arms-control agreements." The problems of verification are compounded by the "civilianization of many important forms of collection and transmission." Only some of the "esoteric counter-measures and counter-counter measures may be kept from general release."

Presently, the United States is able to employ RMA technologies "to defeat most potential aggressors with disproportionately low casualties to itself, at least, in cases of interstate conflict of the type that directly affects its core national interests." Yet the technologies associated with the RMA could be adapted by powers "that fear U.S. military intervention" and want to find the means to deter or counter it. Because of the wide availability of at least some of the technologies, the RMA may well create "pockets of military capability" that will allow small states to frustrate the attacks of larger ones with overall more sophisticated militaries. Certain "microsystems" such as cruise missiles can inflict damage on aircraft carriers, while attacks on computer systems could hamper the transmission of information. As Krepinevich points out,

> *"...the growing threats posed by cruise and anti-ship missiles and ballistic missiles, advanced satellite technologies for communication that are available to any paying customer, sea mines and advance diesel submarines, physical and electronic vulnerabilities of information and communications systems on which the U.S. armed forces increasingly depend, and the proliferation of chemical and biological weapons..could make it much harder for the United States to reach foreign ports safely, keep those ports as well as airfields and other infrastructure safe from enemy attack, and protect its troops on the battle-field."*

As the technology spreads, it would come to benefit smaller and regional powers more than the United States. Indeed, continued development may "be more likely to erode U.S.

superiority than shore it up." John Arquilla of the Rand, argues that, "American military power lies so far beyond its nearest competitors today that it seems senseless to pursue the latest technological advances—especially as their introduction will no doubt lead to the erosion of existing advantages through process of diffusion to others." As Thomas asks, "What will happen when a real information warfare system confronts ours. Will our capabilities be degraded by a quarter, a third or more?" This might lead, over time, to "more multipolarity than U.S. leadership of world affairs," exactly what the RMA is supposed to forestall.

Not surprisingly then, the United States is working on developing counter-measures to the expected "counter-power projection strategies" of targets of American intervention. The *Joint Vision 2010* doctrine "as well as some recent technological solutions for early entry forces," indicates that the Americans "do not expect the next regional war to present conditions for power projection as auspicious" as those found in the Gulf War. And, according to Thomas, future conflicts may also be very different from the experience in Kosovo:

> *"Future enemies could possess some of all of the following: an adept air force; up-to-date air defense sites; precision-guided cruise missiles that can do to our bases and planes what we can to theirs (to include destroying AWACs); and the ability to reach the United States with weapons of mass destruction, precision missiles, or terrorists acts. When these threats confront US and NATO systems, what will information superiority do for us? Will it be even more unreliable when stressed by both nontechnical offsets and technological counters?"*

The diffusion of technologies has already promoted the search for the next generation of RMA to counter the existing and emerging technologies. From an arms control perspective, it is not the validity of all the claims about the RMA, or the persuasiveness of the many doubts that a revolution is taking place. Rather it is the fact that technologies are being developed which in turn may elicit responses, which will in turn heighten the search for ever more advanced versions of the RMA. In this sense, the proliferation of RMA technologies shares with the nuclear arms race the characteristic that it has acquired a technology driven momentum of its own which may not be entirely related to substantive military or political threats.

REGIMES, METHODS AND SYSTEMS

If the RMA has fostered a measure of obscurity and uncertainty, rather than clarity in the future of warfare, it has done no less when it comes to arms control. In part this is the result of the reality that, despite all the commentary and analysis, there is no consensus on what the RMA means. If it is in fact a revolution, then the force of technological change and what it offers, may be no more amenable to control that most previous innovations in weaponry. If what is taking place is just evolutionary, then it may be all the more difficult to subject to arms control since the RMA will involve continual incremental technological progress designed specifically to enhance force multiplier effects.

If the RMA is seen as a combination of weapons and associated technologies, military organization and doctrine, it is evident that arms control is primarily concerned with the first component. Yet, while arms control regimes may not deal directly with changes in military organization and doctrine the fact that these are generally observable can be said to support the control of the RMA to the extent that such changes may signal that countries are developing RMA-related capabilities. Here, arms control method of "collateral analysis" and two very simple "systems" of verification can be useful, literature survey and international information exchange through various methods, including public announcements. The organization of armed forces, particularly in the West is no secret. Governments including, and especially , the U.S. government, are quite open in terms of how their militaries are structured. Indeed, with regard to the RMA in particular, there is much public fanfare about the re-organization of services and commands to better utilize the technologies of the RMA. Moreover, there is a plethora of open secondary sources, such as *The Military Balance*, and various defence industry-related journals, which track in detail the world's militaries. As for doctrine, here too a great deal is in the public domain. The military services of a number of countries regularly publish doctrine in unclassified sources and the professional military journals are filled with various doctrinal debates on the RMA.

It is the technologies and the weapons based upon them that would need to be regulated if the RMA was to be subjected to any kind of verifiable arms control regime. Some of the problems with this have been discussed above. A good deal of the technology comes from the civilian sector, particularly the computer industry. Advances in micro-processing of information have been married to familiar weapons systems such as missiles, aircraft and naval platforms which are themselves acceptable weapons or already, as in the case of missiles difficult to control under existing regimes such as the MTCR. Then there is the large realm of command, control, communication and intelligence technologies that support the weapons and give them their improved accuracy and lethality.

The susceptibility of RMA weapons and technologies to traditional arms control methods, systems and regimes is presented in Table One which uses the approach taken by Cleminson's and Gilman's 1981 study, *A Conceptual Working Paper on Arms Control Verification.*

As indicated in the table there are many difficulties that would be encountered in trying to establish a regime that would be able to verify agreed upon controls on the RMA. As the platforms and the C4I technologies upon which they rely are clearly within the realm of conventional weaponry, negotiating a treaty would be problematic. What would be outlawed and why? Precision-guided weapons and cruise missiles and the ability to target and control them are at the heart of the RMA weaponry. Control of computer-related technologies would require more extensive and continual intrusive on-site verification than contained in the NPT and biological weapons agreements. There is space-based surveillance technology for NTM available to support any treaty, but what would it be looking for and could it find it? In the meantime, those countries which have an edge in this area, such as the United States, are interested in using it to monitor the spread of WMDS and rogue state advances in RMA.

Yet while it may not be able to subject the RMA to an verifiable arms control regime, this does mean that governments and international organizations are at a complete disadvantage when it comes to monitoring the proliferation of RMA-related weapons. As noted above, much is known and in the public realm. The problems would come when efforts were made to use this information to establish a credible arms control regime, one that would actually limit the spread of RMA weapons technology. The shortcomings of the traditional systems, including satellite surveillance and the need for unprecedented , and likely unacceptable, levels of intrusion to make the regime credible, strongly limit prospects for such an agreement.

Any effort to control the RMA would also encounter a major international political hurdle one directly related to the RMA itself with its American dominance and American concerns. As noted above, the United States has much to loose if the technologies which it now counts upon spread undermining its ability to apply force quickly and with minimal cost. To this extent Washington has an interest in curtailing the proliferation of RMA technologies. Moreover, any credible arms control regime for the RMA will require the surveillance systems and intelligence gathering techniques of the United States.

However, an American-led and dominated effort to create an international regime designed to curtail the spread of the RMA would have many of the problems now associated with the NPT. It would in essence seek to deny to other countries the weapons systems which the United States and its allies believe they should maintain for the sake of their own interest.

In addition, Washington is likely to be selective on the issue of proliferation. It will want its allies to have some of the RMA capabilities it now has in order to solidify security ties and enhance interoperability. In other words, an arms control regime which truly limits the spread of the RMA will work to the advantage of the United States.

RESPONSE TO THE RMA, NUCLEAR WEAPONS, WMD AND COUNTERPROLIFERATION

The difficulties of controlling the RMA might be acceptable if other dimensions of arms contol were not adversely impacted. This brings up the second major consideration associated with the RMA, the problem that it will undermine efforts to control nuclear weapons and other WMDs.

The end of the Cold War made progress in nuclear arms control possible, but it also raised questions about the continued utility of nuclear weapons. Some of those raising these doubts, offer the RMA as the solution. Krepinevich argues that the new military technologies and the nature of post-Cold War threats, "principally regional Bosnia-type ethno-nationalist conflicts or Iraq-type regional conflicts...mean that the utility of the U.S. nuclear arsenal will likely be eclipsed by the capabilities of a host of emerging conventional and electronic weapons." Former State Department Advisor and the author of *Toward a Post-Nuclear Ethic*, Robert Manning, suggests that America's "emerging high-tech" conventional capabilities "point to a sharp de-emphasis of nuclear weapons in U.S. defence planning."

Much has been done to de-emphasize nuclear weapons. Manning cites the INF treaty of 1987, the near ninety per cent reductions in American and Russian arsenals under the START treaties, the Nunn-Lugar program, the indefinite extension of the NPT and the Comprehensive Test Ban Treaty, (CTBT) as reasons for optimism.

The nuclear complications of the RMA are part of the larger WMD problem. Along with the hopes and confidence inspired in America by the RMA, its doctrine and efforts at new military organization, has come what Gongora calls "the nightmarish prospect of asymmetric conflicts." Manning, refers to a new "wave of proliferation" brought about by the very success of the Gulf War, arguing that countries "who lack major power allies and are faced with overwhelming conventional force may seek utility in the logic of deterrence that guided the superpowers in the Cold War." Bates and McHorney state explicitly that the "dominance of the American military may...actually *encourage* the acquisition and use" of WMD. Moreover in considering the arms control implications of the RMA, it is important to examine the "complex links between the proliferation of weapons of mass destruction and the trade in conventional weapons."

As German scholar, Oliver Thranert notes, the proliferation of biological weapons to countries in the southern hemisphere "might give the later the idea that they can use such weapons as an effective tool against the superior armed forces of the U.S. and other industrialized countries." The United States as "the only remaining globally active superpower is especially affected by the threat of the proliferation of biological weapons, because a major dimension of American strategy is the "prospect of being able to exert influence in areas of conflict in which U.S. national interests are considered at stake." But it is the fear that certain "rogue" states may "adopt an asymmetric strategy" as a means to counter "American conventional military prowess" and thus "make it hard or even impossible for American forces to gain access to theatres of conflict by resorting to biological warfare."

The use of biological weapons would make it difficult for Washington to contain a regional conflict. Had Iraq used such weapons against Israel, it may have called forth a Israeli nuclear reprisal. In addition, Washington might find it difficult to rally coalition partners in any effort in which biological weapons might be employed by a country as they could be subjected to retaliation. "In sum," notes Thranert, "the time is past when industrialized countries could intervene in conflicts far from their own shores at relatively low cost." He adds that because of the so-called "'CNN effect' the American public will reject interventions, whether at the outset or after considerable losses have been sustained in biological weapons campaigns." In other words, the proliferation of biological weapons directly calls into question the claims made by proponents of the RMA".

> *"Moreover the control of biological weapons in the presence of the RMA is particularly problematic. They are more of a threat than chemical weapons given that they are relatively inexpensive and uncomplicated to produce, use techniques available in the open market for civilian biotechnology products, do not*

need to be stored in large quantities and are "incomparably easier to conceal than are nuclear or chemical weapons programs." "Without doubt" he concludes, arms control cannot be the only instrument for countering the threat posed by the proliferation of biological weapons."

In a recent study published by the Brookings Institution, *Technological Change and the Future of Warfare*, Michael O'Hanlon also raises doubts about the prospects of new methods of controlling WMD. He argues that existing technologies and those likely to emerge in the next twenty years will be insufficient to detect concerted efforts to develop WMDs on the part of those states who wish to develop them. Sensors have limited ranges when it comes to the detection of nuclear materials.

With regard to biological threats, lasers and other electromagnetic beams that might be used against deadly aerosols once released, cannot penetrate the buildings, vehicles and containers where they would most likely be stored, while finding them in a timely fashion presents difficulties as the United Nations Special Commission (UNSCOM) " on-site experience in Iraq has demonstrated." And UNSCOM, one of the most comprehensive and intrusive arms control efforts, unlike most international inspections, was initially backed up by the threat of retaliatory air strikes when Iraq balked. Even then, it was eventually forced to withdraw.

One approach to the perceived problems of arms control in dealing with WMD which has been adopted, particularly by the United States, is what is referred to as "counter-proliferation". The distinction drawn by Washington between nonproliferation policies and counter-proliferation policies is subtle but not insignificant in terms of multilateral arms control efforts. A 1994, memo from the National Security Council (NSC) Special Assistant to the President and Senior Director for Non-proliferation and Export Controls to the Assistant Secretary of State for Political-Military Affairs and to Ashton Carter, then Assistant Secretary of Defence for Nuclear Security and Counter Proliferation stated that:

> *"Proliferation is the spread of nuclear, biological and chemical capabilities and the missiles to deliver them. ...Non-proliferation is the use of the full range of political, economic and military tools to prevent proliferation, reverse it diplomatically or protect our interests against an opponent armed with weapons of mass destruction or missiles should that prove necessary. Non-proliferation tools include intelligence, global non-proliferation norms and agreements, diplomacy, export controls, security assurances, defences and the application of military forces. ...Counter-proliferation refers to the activities of the Department of Defence (DOD) across the full range of U.S. efforts to combat proliferation, including diplomacy, arms control, export controls and intelligence collection and analysis, with particular responsibility for assuring U.S. forces and interests can be protected should they confront an adversary armed with weapons of mass destruction or missiles."*

The Clinton administration's latest national security strategy statement declares the "spread of dangerous technologies" as a threat to American interests and pledges to support arms control measures to address this threat. In 1994, the President declared it to be "an unusual and extraordinary threat to the national security, foreign policy and economy of the United States." A September 1999 report by the National Intelligence Council warned that the spread of medium-range missiles represents an "immediate, serious and growing threat" to American and allied forces.

While non-proliferation policies have been adopted to deal with these threats, the American view is that the spread of WMD and missiles to rogue states and possibly terrorist groups, constitutes the "failure" of non-proliferation policies in these cases and thus the need to resort to counter-proliferation. In a 1993, speech to the Committee on International Security and Arms Control of the National Academy of Science, the U.S. Deputy Assistant Secretary of State for Counter-proliferation announced the launching of the Counter proliferation Initiative (CPI). This was reflective of then Secretary of Defence Les Aspin's Bottom-Up Review (BUR) of defence policy which took note of the changed international circumstances brought about by the ending of the Cold War and the "ability of the United States to limit the proliferation of weapons of mass destruction." Aspin concluded "that preventing proliferation with the policies of persuasion and denial would be less effective in the 21st century for the United States." Thus the BUR identified the need for counter-proliferation of WMD.

The CPI seeks to prevent the spread of WMDs, to "roll-back" their acquisition, to deter their use, to adopt defensive measures, such as greater protection for U.S. forces, when they were used and if necessary to take "offensive measures" to deal with proliferation. It called the changes to the strategies and composition of American forces to allow them to "successfully" respond "to major regional contingencies that involve" states who might be armed with WMDs. In the 1995 Unified Command Plan, the Joint Chiefs of Staff issued a memo which "delegated the mission of countering proliferation" of WMDs "to the military commanders responsible for regions considered to be at high risk."

The Clinton administration is planning to spend as much as $12 billion on protecting its armed forces and civilian population from WMD attacks. This includes a program to "prepare large and medium size cities for handling chemical and biological attacks." In May 2000, the Justice Department and the Federal Emergency Management Agency "simulated a series of mcok biological and chemical terrorist attacks in program involving thousands of people and closely watched by top U.S. officials-to test the readiness of local, state and federal governments to handle potential crises involving WMD attacks." There is the growing view, expressed by Central Intelligence Director George Tenet that the counterproliferation efforts against the spread of WMD weapons, "has been gradually losing ground." The "challenge is to find policies to deter the use of these weapons, develop countermeasures," such as NDM, "and plan on handling crises that might arise should WMD be released." The new United States Joint Forces Command has been given responsibility for "homeland defense" including "providing military assistance to civil authorities for consequence management of weapons of mass destruction incidents within the continental United States, its territories and possessions." It will also "support the WMD consequence management efforts of the other combatant commands" through the world. In setting up USJFCOM, Secretary of Defense William Cohen, appointed an Army National Guard Brigadier-General as the first commanding general of Joint Task Force-Civil Support (JTF-CS). "The JTF-CS will ensure Department of Defense assets are prepared to respond to requests for support from a Lead Federal Agency such as the Federal Emergency Management Agency."

The CPI includes working with other countries and international organizations, and Presidents Clinton and Yelstin issued a declaration on the need to deal with proliferation. These U.S. policies were adopted by NATO, which established three proliferations groups, the Joint Committee on Proliferation, the Senior Political Military Group on Proliferation and the Senior Defence Group on Proliferation. But while the CPI found support amongst American allies and developed countries, the developing world saw it as "exacerbating national security concerns by widening the gap between the military capabilities of the developed and developing countries." John Simpson points to "the development by the U.S. of military options for counter-proliferation purposes" and the development of tactical and strategic defence systems, as a source of friction between the nuclear weapons and non-nuclear weapons states, with regard to the future of the NPT.

Of interest from a non-proliferation standpoint, is the relationship between the RMA and the CPI. It is evident that the United States will employ its RMA technologies in defensive and offensive measures designed to deal with states or groups who might acquire and use WMDs. In this sense, the salience of nuclear weapons would diminish and further cuts would be possible. This in turn could assist the NPT by allowing for further cuts in the American nuclear arsenal. But as discussed below, it also appears that the counter-proliferation objective could serve to reinforce the continuing utility of nuclear weapons, thus in turn undermine non-proliferation efforts.

The failure of the Senate to ratify the CTBT indicates a reluctance in some quarters in the United States to go further on arms control. Moreover, as Manning himself notes, average annual spending on nuclear weapons research and development in the United States by the Department of Energy (DOE) and the Atomic Energy Commission, which was $3.7 billion during the Cold War, is expected to average $4.6 billion over the period 1998-2008.

And this does not include Department of Defence costs "or those associated with the production of nuclear weapons materials." In 1996, "DOE's research development, testing and materials production programs were reclassified as 'stockpile stewardship' and weapons production was reclassified as 'stockpile management'."

Perhaps more importantly, several studies done in the United States have suggested the need to retain a nuclear weapons capability, including a first-use option, against adversaries with the potential for WMD or even conventional forces that could inflict damage on American forces and interests. In 1992 The Strategic Deterrence Study Group, argued that the United States could not "count on [conventional deterrence] to deal with many lethal Third World threats...and also supported the 'first-use' of nuclear weapons if American military forces are confronted with superior conventional forces 'at remote places around the world'."

In November 1997, President Clinton issued a new U.S. Nuclear Weapons Employment Guidance as contained in Presidential Decision Directive 60 (PDD-60). It declares that the United States would no longer be required to fight and win a protracted nuclear war. Bates and McHorney point out that PDD-60 is "relevant to counter proliferation because it supports the possible employment of nuclear weapons against a country that uses chemical or biological weapons against American military personnel or civilians." The exact contents of the document remain secret but,

> *"If available information about PDD-60 is accurate, the new policy would definitely lower the threshold for the use of nuclear weapons. Some analysts fear that PDD-60 may encourage other nations to acquire nuclear weapons as a means of deterring chemical and biological attacks. The use of nuclear weapons against a non-nuclear weapon state would invalidate security assurances given by the United States to signatories of the Nuclear Nonproliferation Treaty."*

The Clinton administration has tried to allay fears about PDD-60 and its impact on nonproliferation policy. In 1998 it openly assured allies and Russia that it has "no plans or intention of using nuclear weapons against Iraq." However, it also stated that it "did not rule out in advance any capabability available to use." "Thus,"conclude Bates and McHorney, "the Clinton Administration failed to rule out the use of nuclear weapons against a non-nuclear-weapon state." And this option remains part of the counterproliferation approach.

Even authors who stress the disutility of nuclear weapons in view of the Bosnia-type conflicts and the threat of non-state actors that are likely to be the norm, suggest a use for nuclear weapons. Manning, for example, points out that nuclear weapons might still be needed in a "counter-proliferation mission" such as "a preemptive attack upon a buried weapons of mass destruction research facility that would be invulnerable to conventional weapons."

Thranert agrees that giving nuclear weapons a role in deterring biological weapons for example "runs counter to other nonproliferation and arms control aims." Not only would such a policy set a problematic example for curtailing the spread of nuclear weapons, it would indeed go against long-standing American pledges (in support of the NPT) not to use nuclear weapons against a non-nuclear weapons state. Nevertheless,

> *"Strategically, it is understandable that the US would not wish to rule out nuclear deterrence against the use of biological weapons. Were it officially to renounce the resort to nuclear weapons as a counter to the use*

> *of biological weapons by hostile forces, this could be taken by some countries as a virtual invitation to concentrate on the development of biological weapons. There remains, therefore, an irresolubly conflicting relationship between the objectives of arms control and the requirements of strategy. Seen in this light a...nuclear order in which such weapons have been abolished, seems many years in the distance if for no other reason than that the US believes it needs nuclear weapons for reasons stemming from its quest to deter the use of biological weapons."*

O'Hanlon also doubts that American military superiority "is great enough to permit strictly conventional military responses to any battlefield use of weapons of mass destruction against American forces." There are uncertainties about whether the U.S. military can maintain its present superiority or whether it could cope with chemical, biological or nuclear attacks on its forces and bases. He agrees that the U.S. "military advantage over most potential foes is great enough that American forces could probably prevail without resorting to the use of nuclear weapons."

> *"However, they would most likely do so at a price of high U.S. casualties. Rather than accept high casualties, the United States would have powerful reasons to use nuclear weapons against an enemy's forces and military infrastructure in response, both to save its own troops' lives and to deter further enemy attacks of that kind in the future. Making the possibility of such a response known in advance, as it did before Operation Desert Storm, could also have deterrent benefits. It could discourage a foe from the belief that it could keep the casualty-adverse United States from responding to its aggression."*

Paul Schulte of the United Kingdom's Ministry of Defence, argues that despite problems with onsite verification, exacerbated by the failure of the United Nations to continue inspections in Iraq, multilateral efforts should continue to support the Chemical Weapons Convention. But he also stresses the need for counter-proliferation. He points to the efforts by NATO's Senior Defence Group on Proliferation to improve the Alliance's training and equipment to operate in a chemical and biological weapons (CBW) environment.

"This," he argues, "is a practical and valuable modification of the strategic landscape that does not need complicated multinational negotiations. These improved defenses bolster arms-control agreements" by making the use of chemical and biological weapons "less attractive to proliferators." [103] He also calls for NATO to issue a "specific declaration" at the start of "any crisis that it would reserve the right to take proportionately severe action against, or even to remove, any regime that used CBWs against it or its forces and to try the leaders as war criminals."

What Schulte is saying is that the West reserves the right to employ the most technologically advanced weaponry which the RMA can provide, but that it also reserves the right to deny potential adversaries WMDs and, if they are used, to retaliate with its own WMDs. Even he acknowledges the implications of this position:

> *"In the future we must expect that states or groups who see the United States-backed Western dominated world order as fundamentally unjust will feel entitled to search for equalizers against the military superiority that is the backbone of that world order. In this regard, we should not underestimate the importance of frustration and rage as drivers of chemical and biological developments...CBWs, because of their intrinsic nastiness, can act as conflict intensifiers and avenging symbols. The drive to ban CBWs, which is heavily supported by the Western allies, may appear to be a means of canceling out all remaining asymmetries that might threaten the West and thus make the world safe for dominance by high-technology conventional weapons, backed by American (or Israeli) nuclear power. Those who feel this way are*

not very interested in being dissuaded, and their arguments may even gain some support from the anti-nuclear lobby."

There is yet another complicating factor in regards to the arms control implications of the RMA. Non-Proliferation efforts focus on "so-called" weapons of mass destruction, nuclear chemical and biological and in recent years on their delivery systems long-range ballistic and cruise missiles. From time-to-time there are also efforts to control "weapons of ill repute," such as antipersonnel mines and fragmentation devices. But, "in a gaping logical disjunction, shorter-range missiles, combat aircraft, surface ships and submarines-all of which can deliver" WMD, "continue to be traded widely." Moreover, "a coordinated conventional attack can achieve levels of devastation associated with weapons of mass destruction, even on the battlefield." This was demonstrated in the Gulf War and the attacks on Yugoslavia. The RMA promises to increase the accuracy and lethality of conventional weapons "as future generations of platforms incorporate more sophisticated electronics, mostly from commercial sectors of the global information economy."

In this sense, the distinction between advanced conventional weapons and WMDs, becomes harder to maintain. As Keller and Nolan argue, "It is not a simple dichotomy, conventional on one side and unconventional on the other. Amongst nuclear, chemical and biological weapons there are differences in technology, levels of lethality and delivery requirements, with nuclear being harder to acquire but not to deliver":

"In short, the category "weapons of mass destruction" is based more on historical usage than on logical grounds or on an analysis of the characteristics of various weapons. But the false dichotomy between weapons of mass destruction and conventional weapons has helped to legitimize arbitrary limits on non-proliferation, both intellectually and in terms of specific treaties and regimes. If it is not a weapon of mass destruction or a missile to carry one or occasionally a weapon of ill repute, then it is presumed to have

a legitimate place in commerce and warfare. Consequently, there are few if any controls over the sale of such weapons or the transfer of their underlying technologies."

This brings up the moral dimension of the RMA. Why should its technologies be regarded as more just in terms of the conduct of war, than WMDs? While it promises to reduce civilian casualties because of the accuracy of the weapons systems, it can inflict great suffering on civilians as the weapons seek to cripple military and governmental infrastructures. So-called "minimal collateral damage" is a relative term, usually employed by the attacking forces. The NATO campaign against Yugoslavia have led some to call for allied leaders to be tried on war crimes.

Even discounting the morality of the weapons, the distinction which the United States and its allies hold to seems to make even less sense when it is considered that the exports of conventional weapons technology, which they promote, could lead to improvements in capabilities which will approximate the kind of WMDs whose proliferation they wish to stop. Combined with the moral considerations, this would seem to suggest the need to put in place the same kinds of transparency and controls on end-use for sensitive dual-use civil-military technologies which are applied to nuclear, chemical and biological weapons and some missiles. But these have proven difficult in the past and, as noted above, may be even more so given the globalization of high technology trade and its relationship to the RMA.

All of this highlights another of the central arguments of this paper, which is that the RMA in promising to provide the West with security in a way that diminishes the salience of nuclear weapons and thus enhance the prospects of arms control, has in fact raised its own host of complications and uncertainties about the future of warfare and particularly for the control of WMD proliferation. In the post- Cold War era, given the nature of possible threats and military operations, nuclear weapons seemed to lose their utility and the RMA was encouraged. The United States had developed the RMA to allow it to apply forces quickly, accurately and with minimal cost in instances where its interests require it to intervene against distant adversaries. America also, though, has raised the issue of the proliferation of weapons of mass destruction especially with regard to rogue states. Yet it is operations against these very states which is used to justify the RMA. To complete the circle, it turns out that nuclear weapons do have a utility, to deter the use of biological weapons against the United States and its forces in the event that it has to apply RMA technologies against these states.

Thus, like the nuclear arsenals of the Cold War, the RMA has its own intractable paradoxes and uncertainties, despite the fact that it involves conventional weaponry, especially with regard to questions of threshold—the point at which an RMA conventional attack would elicit a WMD response. How much damage from a conventional attack would be considered "unacceptable"? What level of likely WMD response would compel the United States not to intervene militarily?

While fear of WMD response to an RMA attack is driving much thinking in the West, it is hard to imagine any government or group tempting fate by employing WMDs against the United States or its allies. It may well be possible for small, weak states to employ chemical and biological weapons, but once this threshold is crossed, yes, all the advantages go to the larger attacking country in terms of response and in terms of the reaction of neighbouring states and the international community. "Ugliness is no proof of military utility."

Yet this only brings up the question of whether in fact the United States would cross the nuclear threshold in response to a chemical or biological attack, especially one confined to American forces in the field. If deterrence fails, how usable are limited nuclear strikes? What level of attack on American forces would be sufficient? In one sense, they are more usable simply because their use against a rogue state would not carry with it the prospect of escalation to a global strategic nuclear war. Moreover, while the use of any nuclear weapons would risk global condemnation, so would an attack upon American and allied forces that employed chemical and biological weapons. Indeed, an American nuclear response might well be viewed as a justifiable means of ending, or forestalling, further attacks and reinforcing deterrence to others who might contemplate them.

On the other hand, Blank points the particular problems of associated with a nuclear response to an RMA attack.

> *"All nuclear threats challenge the United States' thinking about war. U.S. doctrine and strategy aims to control war and force it into congenial forms, however nuclear war's danger lies not just in its frightful devastation, but in its inherent unpredictability and freedom from true strategic control by the governments involved. While nobody knows what objectives justify nuclear use other than retaliation against nuclear weapons or against strikes upon them, a government that did not so reply to a nuclear attack would fall. That war would then become an uncontrollable total war fought for objectives far transcending the supposedly limited means and objectives that the United States professes to employ."*

It is evident that responses to the RMA, by the West and by potential WMD proliferators, will complicate existing arms control measures. However, this situation should not be considered the death knell of arms control. Indeed, there may well be reasons to expect renewed emphasis on controlling WMD in the new strategic environment of the RMA. That RMA-related technologies will not likely be subjected to arms control efforts, will upset some countries, but this will not bring a halt to efforts to control WMDs. Moreover, as noted above, the United States, for its own self-interest, is pressing for tighter controls on WMD and adopting counter-proliferation policies in the expectation that some states will use the RMA as a reason to ignore or challenge existing multilateral arms control regimes.

To argue that the advent of the RMA has the potential to encourage the proliferation of WMDs and thus create difficulties for future arms control and associated verification efforts, does not mean that this will necessarily take place. A key factor will be the relationship between individual states and neighbouring countries as well non-regional states which for varying reasons may become adversaries and threaten intervention. A region of relative intra-state stability which provides no reason for intervention by major outside powers may be unaffected by any adverse effects of the RMA. Latin America may be considered in this category.

As discussed above, the real focus for concern about the impact of the RMA is with the relatively small number of so-called rogue states which are viewed by the United States, and depending on the region or country, by U.S. allies and others, as presenting a threat to their neighbours and to broader international stability. The view is that existing judicial and political arms control methods may be insufficient. It is the expectation that force may be needed to check these states that has driven much of the RMA in the United States. But it is these states which are crucial for the integrity of future arms control efforts. If the RMA should make those efforts more difficult, then the fact that proliferation is not taking place more widely may be of little significance.

THREE ALTERNATIVE STRATEGIC AND ARMS CONTROL SCENARIOS

One way of looking at the implications of the RMA on arms control is to examine three broad categories of states that the United States may face: 1) a state with significant conventional capabilities, limited RMA capacity, but an advanced WMD capability; 2) a state with less conventional capability but significant WMD capacity; and 3) a state with *both* a limited conventional capability and limited WMD capacity. Each case can be examined from the standpoint of the effectiveness of the RMA, the possible responses by the target state and the implications for arms control. The connecting thread in all three scenarios from an arms control standpoint is that the RMA appears to provide increased, although not absolute, advantages to the United States in terms of power generated through either the latent or applied use of force compelling potential target states to either acquire RMA capabilities themselves or develop and retain WMDs.

A state with significant conventional capabilities and some RMA capacity, as well as advanced WMD such as Russia, China (and in the future perhaps India and Iran) will pose the greatest challenge to the use of the RMA and perhaps to arms control. In the Russian view, the RMA "degrades strategic stability." Recent changes in Russian doctrine which, as a result of Kosovo, suggests the use of tactical nuclear weapons "in a first strike response to conventional attack." Here the enlargement of NATO only contributes to this trend since it is viewed as "preparation for a future military threat that can only be countered by the threat or use of tactical, if not strategic, nuclear weapons." They fear the very type of attack which the Americans hope the RMA will afford them, one that uses PGMs and Information Warfare to threaten a government's ability "to govern or command its armed forces."

Faced with such a threat, "Russia or similarly-oriented states" might indeed strike first or preemptively with nuclear systems even against purely conventional attacks. Nuclear weapons take on a renewed aura of usability, "as if they were just particularly lethal missiles," the line between nuclear and conventional is blurred and the threshold for nuclear is lowered. As Blank notes, as a result of the RMA, Russian "[n]uclear strategy and policy have become conventionalized." It is the prospect that the RMA may be at odds with the goals it is supposed to achieve and in the process undermine the evolving post-Cold War consensus, to the detriment of Russian and Western security, that has prompted arms control concerns about it.

At the same time in the case of Russia and, to a lesser extent, China, the continuing fear of nuclear attacks upon the United States itself will serve as a powerful deterrent to any military action and thus the existing strategic stability and arms control regimes may remain unaffected, although both countries may attempt to acquire RMA technologies.

More concern will focus on the potential of other states, such as Iran, which may strive for category one status, especially with regard to WMDs. The potential for crisis or conflict here may be greater and it is not at all clear that the application of RMA technologies can easily overcome large conventional forces where that state has the capacity to employ them skillfully and the numbers to fight a protracted struggle, particularly one involving land forces and the need to capture and hold large amounts of territory. If this state also deploys some RMA technologies, such as cruise missiles or a capacity to disrupt communications and intelligence links, then the United States will have less confidence in the kind of quick decisive victory which the RMA promises.

In the future the presence of an advanced WMD capacity in countries such as Iran would also raise the cost of any military action as it could place at serious risk not only deployed forces but the surrounding populations, including those in neighbouring countries which might be drawn into the conflict. This was the fear during the Gulf War.

In the most extreme case, where an Iran or Iraq had developed long-range missiles, the United States, or other allies participating in a coalition effort, would be at risk. In these circumstances, Washington might find itself deterred from taking any military action at all, especially if the issues at stake were not those of vital interest to the United States or its allies. In general, category-one states provide the United States and its allies with reasons to retain nuclear weapons as instruments of deterrence, further weakening general arms control efforts.

In order to provide protection for neighbouring countries which may be friendly to the West, Washington would rely upon political pressure backed-up by its general deterrent capabilities, including nuclear weapons. The United States could, as it is already doing, organize and support multilateral non-proliferation efforts, and if necessary call for sanctions and embargoes.

It could use its extensive NTM capabilities to monitor the situation and engage in unilateral counter-proliferation policies, all of which remain available with or without the RMA. But without a change in the political relationship, arms control efforts will be difficult and the cause of general arms control will not be much advanced.

In the case of states with less formidable conventional capabilities but an extensive WMD capacity, the RMA offers more potential for effectiveness since this state has fewer options in the event of a high-tech attack by the United States.

However, in this category the impact of RMA attacks will vary with the size of the country and the size, sophistication and deployment of its conventional forces. It will also depend upon the amount of damage its leaders are prepared to accept. An initial RMA attack may have to be followed up by an invasion in which case the costs to the United States will rise.

If a category-two states is unable to counter the RMA with its own conventional forces and lacked the numbers to sustain a protracted conflict, but was unwilling to surrender, such a state would face the problem of whether to cross the WMD threshold.

The resort to WMDs would be a last desperate measure likely to draw even more conventional attacks, if not a nuclear response. Moreover, with a weaker conventional capability, especially in the area of aerospace defence, WMD facilities would be subjected to concerted attack. Given the lack of a strong conventional capability, the uncertainties regarding the utility of WMDs, and the underdevelopment of WMDS, such a state may be more amenable, depending upon the political situation, to arms control measures.

With proper inducements, it might be persuaded to sign, or more closely adhere to, an existing WMD treaty or regime and more accepting of intrusive methods of verification. Here again though, some category two states, those with larger conventional capabilities and a leadership more hostile to the West, such as Iran or North Korea, may be less receptive to WMD arms control.

Category-three states with limited capabilities in both conventional forces and WMDs are in one sense the best targets for RMA technologies as they are the most vulnerable. In addition, as they are generally weaker militarily, their political influence is likely to be correspondingly less. In another sense, with a more rudimentary conventional force, one that depended less on fixed infrastructure and concentrated forces, and in a situation where governmental institutions and communications links were already weak, RMA technologies may find few suitable targets.

If these states were also prepared to accept high civilian casualties and engage in a protracted guerilla war, technological superiority may not yield a quick military victory and political settlement. A target state in this position may also make use of the new era of "globalization" Portraying itself as a helpless victim of aggression by the powerful they "have an unprecedented opportunity to manipulate the burgeoning global media to their advantage, whether by courting world opinion or undermining an adversary's domestic base of support.."

The category three state may have limited WMD capabilities without the kind of supporting facilities that could be easily attacked by conventional forces and thus may survive an RMA attack.

The willingness of the target state to engage the United States at high cost, could lower the threshold at which a limited number of WMDs were employed, especially against forwardly deployed American forces and bases. But if such a state were already able to raise the cost of intervention through conventional means, and in so doing keep the leadership in power, it is difficult to see the use of even limited WMD given the expected response.

In this case, as in the one above, external persuasion to accept limits on armaments may be possible. This will depend though on the extent to which the international community can provide security assurances, particularly if they face neighbouring states which have acquired greater conventional or WMD capabilities.

Ironically, one way of providing such assurances may be the RMA which in these instances would assume something of a post-Cold War mechanism for extended deterrence in the service of nonproliferation. At the same time category three state which had more rudimentary and limited WMD capabilities and whose political leadership wished to retain them as means of deterring an attack might be less receptive to becoming a party to international arms control regimes.

The United States is taking such scenarios seriously as indicated by the emphasis it is putting on both deterring and coping with WMD attacks on its forces and even the American homeland. The National Missile Defense (NMD) is justified on the grounds that it will allow the United States more freedom of action in terms of dealing with "rogue" states and providing protection if their leaders irrationally cross that threshold and use their "limited" WMD capabilities.

The deterrent dimension of this approach should not be underestimated. After all, "limited" is a relative term. A rudimentary chemical attack on American forces which resulted in scores of deaths, would be considered a national disaster for a country where the avoidance of casualties has become almost military doctrine.

At the same time, it should not be forgotten that there remains a large element of speculation in such scenarios, especially with regard to categories two and three. We have the record of the Gulf War, but it is inconclusive. The United States was not deterred from mounting a coalition against Iraq by the potential of WMD use against its forces. Was this because Washington was convinced that Iraq would not risk nuclear retaliation? Was Washington less sure of avoiding a WMD response if it had continued on to occupy Iraq and therefore was it deterred from doing so? In the case of the Kosovo campaign, would NATO have even mounted an attack if it knew or suspected that Yugoslavia had a limited number of WMDs? Yet how would they have been used and to what end?

The point here is that while the scenarios described above highlight some of the arms control implications of the RMA, they also draw attention to the uncertainties that remain as the United States grapples with the impact of the "revolution" it is bent on inciting.

WILL ARMS CONTROL SURVIVE THE RMA

Whether revolutionary or evolutionary, the new technologies, military organizations and doctrines of warfare as fielded by the West, especially the United States are already having an impact on the way in which force is applied. In general, this suggest a growing military imbalance between the United States and other countries. And the expectation that more rapid advances will be made which will further widen the gap. Indeed, thinking has already begun on "The RMA After Next" with the suggestion that the next technological breakthrough will be the application of the "biotech revolution" to warfare.

This is not surprising, since it is explicitly the goal of the American RMA effort to preserve a dominant military position and allow the United States to intervene quickly, effectively and at minimal cost overseas.

The RMA has not created new weapons or systems that are easily subjected to traditional arms control and verification. Regardless of RMA capability or not a state may still comply with or be subjected to arms control verification on WMD. Weapons that were subject to verification prior to RMA are still verifiable by the same means, even though those systems may have been altered or advanced as a result of RMA.

But what the RMA has done is make the international control of WMDs more difficult because it has introduced into the international security environment enhanced conventional weapons which appear to give the United States and the West even more relative military power then they already possess and which can be used to further their own vision for global stability as they interpret it.

To this extent, the RMA seems to foretell a continuation of trends in international security relations which began with the end of the Cold War and which are generally favourable to the United States and its major allies. The major concern is that the RMA, as an instrument of Western power, may persuade some countries to retain or expand WMD capabilities as potential asymmetric responses in the event of attack by a country using RMA capabilities. This in turn will cause difficulties in maintaining, enforcing and expanding those existing arms control regimes. Not only could the inequality of those regimes be perceived as being exacerbated, but the more advanced RMA surveillance technologies could be employed to monitor compliance by NTMs as the United States responds to potential asymmetric threats.

Yet the impact of the RMA on the future international security environment and hence on arms control and verification needs to be kept in perspective for a number of reasons. First of all, while the world has witnessed some impressive applications of the RMA, during the Gulf War and the conflicts in the Balkans, it is not at all evident that it will live up to its optimistic predictions. As noted in the discussion above, the circumstances of the Gulf War were in many ways unique and there has been no repeat of such large scale inter-state conflict involving massed forces since.

In Bosnia and Kosovo, the new technologies appeared to be effective in bringing about a temporary end to hostilities and compliance with NATO demands, but once the stand-off weapons did their job, more traditional forces had to be deployed, albeit with the support of new surveillance technologies. The conclusion of a permanent peace in the region seems to have little to do with the new technologies of warfare. Moreover, as Stephen Blank stresses, the promise of short decisive wars based upon technological superiority is not a certainty. States confronted with the RMA may utilize strategic surprise followed by attrition tactics.

Secondly, the international strategic environment is not just a function of weaponry and differences in relative military capabilities. The current and foreseeable future security setting will be one dominated by the United States. It will also be an environment marked by continued regional instability and ethnic conflict. The RMA is not so much a product of this environment as a response to it, in the sense that it is designed to afford America ability to intervene when it chooses.

But as critics of American "boosterism" and "unipolarism" such as Samuel Huntington caution, "However much foreign policy elites may ignore or deplore it, the United States lack the domestic political base to create a unipolar world." A recent poll taken by the Chicago Council on Foreign Relations found that seventy-two percent of respondents did not believe

American vital interests were at stake abroad, the lowest since 1978. This situation, combined with the fact that the vital interests of the United States are often not at risk in regional conflicts suggests that is not self-evident that the 1990s trend of U.S. interventionism will continue.

Here again, a protracted involvement in the Balkans, as well the confrontation with Iraq may well temper future enthusiasm for applying force, however technologically impressive, abroad. To the extent that the RMA is linked to America's willingness to harness this capability to continued regional interventions, its import may well be less than expected.

The third point is that the concern about rogue states, so much at the heart of the arguments in favour of the RMA, and the consequent worry and asymmetric WMD responses, may wane. After all, there really are only a handful of states in this position. As seems evident in the case of Iran, efforts are being made by Washington and other governments to keep open lines of engagement.

There is even some movement with regard to relations between North and South Korea. If this is the case, then any detrimental impact of the RMA on arms control efforts may well be moderated and the prospects for arms control under existing regimes and methods improved. As the lessons of the Cold War indicate, the efficacy of arms control depends on political factors. An international security environment in which rogue states become less of a preoccupation for the United States and its allies, and confrontation is moderated by a lowering of threat perceptions, is one more amenable to arms control.

Fourthly, while it may not be possible to implement measures specifically directed at controlling the spread of the new technologies associated with the RMA, there is much that is readily observable. This is especially the case with regard to changes in military organization and doctrine which might accompany the new technologies. But even in the case of the weapons themselves there is a great deal of information in the open sources. Combined with the kind of surveillance that goes on continuously, it its possible for the international community to monitor the RMA, even if is unable to create a regime to control it.

Finally the RMA will not be regarded as entirely morally neutral. As noted above, the destructive power of some of these weapons, in particular their ability to strike at the civilian infrastructures of states, will continue to impose a measure of caution on the part of the United States in how it applies unmatched military power.

That Americans may well be in favour of measures to reduce their own casualties, does not mean that they impose no limits on the amount of death and destruction their armed forces can inflict, especially in cases where vital interests are not at stake. In an era of a globalized media, the "roar" of the victim mice subjected to RMA attacks may arouse sympathy in the international community.

This leads to the conclusion that although the RMA has already had an impact on the international security environment and complicated arms control, there is no reason to abandon it and good grounds to continue current efforts. It is, to be sure, easy to be cynical about arms control in the face of the evolving technologies of warfare heralded by the RMA. Cynicism, though, is not always the same as realism.

Indeed it would be unrealistic to conclude that because the RMA has introduced new complications into multilateral arms control efforts that its adverse affects are so pervasive that any effort to mitigate them will be fruitless. Arms control and the methods put in place to verify it have always had to keep pace with technological advances in weaponry. Despite the inability to achieve major reductions in nuclear weapons until the end of the Cold War, real progress was made on arms control and verification with regard to other WMDs.

The future international security environment is likely to be one where *both* the RMA and arms control will present competing, but not always mutually exclusive, claims for the enhancement of international strategic and political stability. In this situation, the best that can be done is to continue to sustain existing regimes which seek to reduce and check the spread of WMDs. These efforts will be supported by the United States for reasons directly related to its own perceptions of national security.

Other countries can point out the links between proliferation and the RMA in continued efforts to curtail the spread of all weapons and steps can be taken to monitor the trade in advanced technologies. But mitigation of the adverse impact of the RMA is likely to be more a function of political trends rather than arms control considerations, even as the specific technologies advance.

The RMA, has indeed raised serious questions about the future of arms control. But it is just one of a number of dramatic political and military trends of the post-Cold War era, not all of them detrimental to global peace and security. Given the other factors that affect the international security environment, and the very uncertainties associated with the RMA, there is reason to conclude that arms control will survive the RMA.

CONCLUSION

This paper posits the following conclusions:

1. Whether the technologies associated with the RMA constitute a "revolution" in warfare as it has been understood in the past has not been conclusively resolved and indeed is unlikely to be in the absence of a major war, especially between states who have deliberately sought to implement the RMA. However, the RMA is more than just a new way of delivering weapons. It involves the application of the most advanced computer technologies to warfare and the implementation of changes in the organization and structure of armed forces. Led by the United States, the RMA has become integral to an American national security policy which, whether explicitly nationalistic or couched in the language of liberal internationalism, is designed to maintain American global dominance. The RMA has thus already had immediate impact on the international geostrategic environment.

2. If the RMA has fostered a measure of obscurity and uncertainty, rather than clarity, about the future of warfare, it has done no less when it comes to arms control. There are two related problems. First, is the susceptibility of the RMA itself to arms control and the second the adverse impact of the RMA on existing efforts to control WMD.
3. While there is much that is observable about the RMA, its weapons systems are not easily susceptible to our present arms control methodologies and technologies in manner that would allow for a credible arms control regime.
4. The RMA has made the international control of WMDs more difficult because it has introduced into the international security environment enhanced conventional weapons which appear to give the United States and the West even more relative military power than they already possess and which can be used to further their own vision for global stability as they interpret it.
5. The Western states who have pursued the RMA in the post-Cold War era have by no means rejected arms control as a means of fostering global stability. They are concerned about the proliferation of WMD and conventional weapons. However, there appears to be a reluctance to make a link between the RMA and the WMD proliferation problem. Because they use, "conventional," indeed civilian technologies, the weapons systems associated with the RMA are for the most part considered, particularly by the United States and its allies, as outside any arms control regimes. Yet, one of the major concerns with the RMA is the possibility of an asymmetrical response by states or groups against whom RMA technologies are to be used. This in turn has contributed to efforts by the United States and its allies to deal with the WMD threat through multilateral arms control measures, such as the Non-Proliferation Treaty and unilateral counterproliferation efforts. Amongst the latter is the retention by the United States

and NATO of the threat of nuclear response in the event that WMDs are used against them. Thus the West now has a new reason not to fully abandon nuclear deterrence, fear of asymmetrical responses to the RMA.

6. Nevertheless, concern about WMD is very much on the international agenda and much has been done to establish new norms. In some areas of arms control, such as with regard to conventional forces in Europe, major progress has been made.
7. What this suggests is that, despite the RMA, existing efforts to control WMD can and should be pursued while acknowledging that the future international security environment is likely to be one where *both* the RMA and arms control will present competing, but not always mutually exclusive, claims for the enhancement of international strategic and political stability.

6

THE FUTURE OF WAR AND PEACE

The 20th century was the most murderous in recorded history. The total number of deaths caused by or associated with its wars has been estimated at 187m, the equivalent of more than 10% of the world's population in 1913. Taken as having begun in 1914, it was a century of almost unbroken war, with few and brief periods without organised armed conflict somewhere. It was dominated by world wars: that is to say, by wars between territorial states or alliances of states.

The period from 1914 to 1945 can be regarded as a single "30 years' war" interrupted only by a pause in the 1920s - between the final withdrawal of the Japanese from the Soviet Far East in 1922 and the attack on Manchuria in 1931. This was followed, almost immediately, by some 40 years of cold war, which conformed to Hobbes's definition of war as consisting "not in battle only or the act of fighting, but in a tract of time wherein the will to contend by battle is sufficiently known". It is a matter for debate how far the actions in which US armed forces have been involved since the end of the cold war in various parts of the globe constitute a continuation of the era of world war. There can be no doubt, however, that the 1990s were filled with formal and informal military conflict in Europe, Africa and western and central Asia. The world as a whole has not been at peace since 1914, and is not at peace now.

Nevertheless, the century cannot be treated as a single block, either chronologically or geographically. Chronologically, it falls into three periods: the era of world war centred on

Germany (1914 to 1945), the era of confrontation between the two superpowers (1945 to 1989), and the era since the end of the classic international power system. We can call these periods I, II and III. Geographically, the impact of military operations has been highly unequal. With one exception (the Chaco war of 1932-35), there were no significant inter-state wars (as distinct from civil wars) in the western hemisphere (the Americas) in the 20th century. Enemy military operations have barely touched these territories: hence the shock of the bombing of the World Trade Centre and the Pentagon on September 11.

Since 1945 inter-state wars have also disappeared from Europe, which had until then been the main battlefield region. Although in period III, war returned to south-east Europe, it seems very unlikely to recur in the rest of the continent. On the other hand, during period II inter-state wars, not necessarily unconnected with the global confrontation, remained endemic in the Middle East and south Asia, and major wars directly springing from the global confrontation took place in east and south-east Asia (Korea, Indochina). At the same time, areas such as sub-Saharan Africa, which had been comparatively unaffected by war in period I (apart from Ethiopia, belatedly subject to colonial conquest by Italy in 1935-36), came to be theatres of armed conflict during period II, and witnessed major scenes of carnage and suffering in period III.

Two other characteristics of war in the 20th century stand out, the first less obviously than the second. At the start of the 21st century we find ourselves in a world where armed operations are no longer essentially in the hands of governments or their authorised agents, and where the contending parties have no common characteristics, status or objectives, except the willingness to use violence.

Inter-state wars dominated the image of war so much in periods I and II that civil wars or other armed conflicts within the territories of existing states or empires were somewhat obscured. Even the civil wars in the territories of the Russian empire after the October revolution, and those which took place after the collapse of the Chinese empire, could be fitted into the framework of international conflicts, insofar as they were inseparable from them. On the other hand, Latin America may not have seen armies crossing state frontiers in the 20th century, but it has been the scene of major civil conflicts: in Mexico after 1911, for instance, in Colombia since 1948, and in various central American countries during period II. It is not generally recognised that the number of international wars has declined fairly continuously since the mid-1960s, when internal conflicts became more common than those fought between states. The number of conflicts within state frontiers continued to rise steeply until it levelled off in the 1990s.

More familiar is the erosion of the distinction between combatants and non-combatants. The two world wars of the first half of the century involved the entire populations of belligerent countries; both combatants and non-combatants suffered. In the course of the century, however, the burden of war shifted increasingly from armed forces to civilians, who were not only its victims, but increasingly the object of military or military-political operations. The contrast between the first world war and the second is dramatic: only 5% of those who died in the first were civilians; in the second, the figure increased to 66%. It is generally supposed that 80 to 90% of those affected by war today are civilians. The proportion has increased since the end of the cold war because most military operations since then have been conducted not by conscript armies, but by small bodies of regular or irregular troops, in many cases operating high-technology weapons and protected against the risk of incurring casualties. There is no reason to doubt that the main victims of war will continue to be civilians.

It would be easier to write about war and peace in the 20th century if the difference between the two remained as clear-cut as it was supposed to be at the beginning of the century, in the days when the Hague conventions of 1899 and 1907 codified the rules of war. Conflicts were supposed to take place primarily between sovereign states or, if they occurred within the territory of one particular state, between parties sufficiently organised to be accorded belligerent status by other sovereign states. War was supposed to be sharply distinguished from peace, by a declaration of war at one end and a treaty of peace at the other. Military operations were supposed to distinguish clearly between combatants - marked as such by the uniforms they wore, or by other signs of belonging to an organised armed force - and non-combatant civilians. War was supposed to be between combatants. Non-combatants should, as far as possible, be protected in wartime.

It was always understood that these conventions did not cover all civil and international armed conflicts, and notably not those arising out of the imperial expansion of western states in regions not under the jurisdiction of internationally recognised sovereign states, even though some (but by no means all) of these conflicts were known as "wars". Nor did they cover large rebellions against established states, such as the so-called Indian mutiny; nor the recurrent armed activity in regions beyond the effective control of the states or imperial authorities nominally ruling them, such as the raiding and blood-feuding in the mountains of Afghanistan or Morocco. Nevertheless, the Hague conventions still served as guidelines in the first world war. In the course of the 20th century, this relative clarity was replaced by confusion.

First, the line between inter-state conflicts and conflicts within states - that is, between international and civil wars - became hazy, because the 20th century was characteristically a century not only of wars, but also of revolutions and the break-up of empires. Revolutions or liberation struggles within a state had implications for the international situation, particularly during the cold war. Conversely, after the Russian revolution, intervention by states in the internal affairs of other states of which they disapproved became common, at least where it seemed comparatively risk-free. This remains the case.

Second, the clear distinction between war and peace became obscure. Except here and there, the second world war neither began with declarations of war nor ended with treaties of peace. It was followed by a period so hard to classify as either war or peace in the old sense that the neologism "cold war" had to be invented to describe it. The sheer obscurity of the position since the cold war is illustrated by the current state of affairs in the Middle East. Neither "peace" nor "war" exactly describes the situation in Iraq since the formal end of the Gulf war - the country is still bombed almost daily by foreign powers - or the relations between Palestinians and Israelis, or those between Israel and its neighbours, Lebanon and Syria. All this is an unfortunate legacy of the 20th-century world wars, but also of war's increasingly powerful machinery of mass propaganda, and of a period of confrontation between incompatible and passion-laden ideologies which brought into wars a crusading element comparable to that seen in religious conflicts of the past.

These conflicts, unlike the traditional wars of the international power system, were increasingly waged for non-negotiable ends such as "unconditional surrender". Since both wars and victories were seen as total, any limitation on a belligerent's capacity to win that might be imposed by the accepted conventions of 18th- and 19th- century warfare - even formal declarations of war - was rejected. So was any limitation on the victors' power to assert their will. Experience had shown that agreements reached in peace treaties could easily be broken.

In recent years the situation has been further complicated by the tendency in public rhetoric for the term "war" to be used to refer to the deployment of organised force against various national or international activities regarded as anti-social - "the war against the Mafia", for example, or "the war against drug cartels". In these conflicts the actions of two types of armed force are confused. One - let's call them "soldiers" - is directed against other armed forces with the object of defeating them. The other - let's call them "police" - sets out to maintain or re-establish the required degree of law and public order within an existing political entity, typically a state. Victory, which has no necessary moral connotation, is the object of one force; the bringing to justice of offenders against the law, which does have a moral connotation, is the object of the other. Such a distinction is easier to draw in theory than in practice, however. Homicide by a soldier in battle is not, in itself, a breach of the law. But what if a member of the IRA regards himself as a belligerent, even though official UK law regards him as a murderer? Were the operations in Northern Ireland a war, as the IRA held, or an attempt in the face of law-breakers to maintain orderly government in one province of the UK? Since not only a formidable local police force but a national army was mobilised against the IRA for 30 years or so, we may conclude that it was a war, but one systematically run like a police operation, in a way that minimised casualties and the disruption of life in the province. Such are the complexities and confusions of the relations between peace and war at the start of the new century. They are well illustrated by the military and other operations in which the US and its allies are at present engaged.

There is now, as there was throughout the 20th century, a complete absence of any effective global authority capable of controlling or settling armed disputes. Globalisation has advanced in almost every respect - economically, technologically, culturally, even linguistically - except one: politically and militarily, territorial states remain the only effective authorities. There are officially about 200 states, but in practice only a handful count, of which the US is overwhelmingly the most powerful. However, no state or empire has ever been large, rich or powerful enough to maintain hegemony over the political world, let alone to establish political and military supremacy over the globe. A single superpower cannot compensate for the absence of global authorities, especially given the lack of conventions - relating to international disarmament, for instance, or weapons control - strong enough to be voluntarily accepted as binding by major states. Some such authorities exist, notably the UN, various technical and financial bodies such as the IMF, the World Bank and the WTO, and some international tribunals. But none has any effective power other than that granted to them by agreements between states, or thanks to the backing of powerful states, or voluntarily accepted by states. Regrettable as this may be, it isn't likely to change in the foreseeable future.

Since only states wield real power, the risk is that international institutions will be ineffective or lack universal legitimacy when they try to deal with offences such as "war crimes". Even when world courts are established by general agreement (for example, the International Criminal court set up by the UN Rome statute of July 17 1998), their judgments will not necessarily be accepted as legitimate and binding, so long as powerful states are in a position to disregard them. A consortium of powerful states may be strong enough to ensure that some offenders from weaker states are brought before these tribunals, perhaps curbing the cruelty of armed conflict in certain areas. This is an example, however, of the traditional exercise of power and influence within an international state system, not of the exercise of international law.

There is, however, a major difference between the 21st and the 20th century: the idea that war takes place in a world divided into territorial areas under the authority of effective governments which possess a monopoly of the means of public power and coercion has ceased to apply. It was never applicable to countries experiencing revolution, or to the fragments of disintegrated empires, but until recently most new revolutionary or post-colonial regimes - China between 1911 and 1949 is the main exception - emerged fairly quickly as more or less organised and functioning successor regimes and states. Over the past 30 years or so, however, the territorial state has, for various reasons, lost its traditional monopoly of armed force, much of its former stability and power, and, increasingly, the fundamental sense of legitimacy, or at least of accepted permanence, which allows governments to impose burdens such as taxes and conscription on willing citizens. The material equipment for warfare is now widely available to private bodies, as are the means of financing non-state warfare. In this way, the balance between state and non-state organisations has changed.

Armed conflicts within states have become more serious and can continue for decades without any serious prospect of victory or settlement: Kashmir, Angola, Sri Lanka, Chechnya, Colombia. In extreme cases, as in parts of Africa, the state may have virtually ceased to exist; or may, as in Colombia, no longer exercise power over part of its territory. Even in strong and stable states, it has been difficult to eliminate small, unofficial armed groups, such as the IRA in Britain and Eta in Spain.

The novelty of this situation is indicated by the fact that the most powerful state on the planet, having suffered a terrorist attack, feels obliged to launch a formal operation against a small, international, non-governmental organisation or network lacking both a territory and a recognisable army.

How do these changes affect the balance of war and peace in the coming century? I would rather not make predictions about the wars that are likely to take place or their possible outcomes. However, both the structure of armed conflict and the methods of settlement have been changed profoundly by the transformation of the world system of sovereign states.

The dissolution of the Soviet Union means that the Great Power system which governed international relations for almost two centuries and, with obvious exceptions, exercised some control over conflicts between states, no longer exists. Its disappearance has removed a major restraint on inter-state warfare and the armed intervention of states in the affairs of other states - foreign territorial borders were largely uncrossed by armed forces during the cold war. The international system was potentially unstable even then, however, as a result of the multiplication of small, sometimes quite weak states, which were nevertheless officially "sovereign" members of the UN.

The disintegration of the Soviet Union and the European communist regimes plainly increased this instability. Separatist tendencies of varying strength in hitherto stable nation-states such as Britain, Spain, Belgium and Italy might well increase it further. At the same time, the number of private actors on the world scene has multiplied. What mechanisms are there for controlling and settling such conflicts? The record is not promising. None of the armed conflicts of the 1990s ended with a stable settlement. The survival of cold war institutions, assumptions and rhetoric has kept old suspicions alive, exacerbating the post-communist disintegration of south-east Europe and making the settlement of the region once known as Yugoslavia more difficult.

These cold war assumptions, both ideological and power political, will have to be dispensed with if we are to develop some means of controlling armed conflict. It is also evident that the US has failed, and will inevitably fail, to impose a new world order (of any kind) by unilateral force, however much power relations are skewed in its favour at present, and even if it is backed by an (inevitably shortlived) alliance. The international system will remain multilateral and its regulation will depend on the ability of several major units to agree with one another, even though one of these states enjoys military predominance.

How far international military action taken by the US is dependent on the negotiated agreement of other states is already clear. It is also clear that the political settlement of wars, even those in which the US is involved, will be by negotiation and not by unilateral imposition. The era of wars ending in unconditional surrender will not return in the foreseeable future.

The role of existing international bodies, notably the UN, must also be rethought. Always present, and usually called upon, it has no defined role in the settlement of disputes. Its strategy and operation are always at the mercy of shifting power politics. The absence of an international intermediary genuinely considered neutral, and capable of taking action without prior authorisation by the Security Council, has been the most obvious gap in the system of dispute management.

Since the end of the cold war the management of peace and war has been improvised. At best, as in the Balkans, armed conflicts have been stopped by outside armed intervention, and the status quo at the end of hostilities maintained by the armies of third parties. Whether a general model for the future control of armed conflict can emerge from such interventions remains unclear.

The balance of war and peace in the 21st century will depend not on devising more effective mechanisms for negotiation and settlement but on internal stability and the avoidance of military conflict. With a few exceptions, the rivalries and frictions between existing states that led to armed conflict in the past are less likely to do so today. There are, for instance, comparatively few burning disputes between governments about international borders. On the other hand, internal conflicts can easily become violent: the main danger of war lies in the involvement of outside states or military actors in these conflicts.

States with thriving, stable economies and a relatively equitable distribution of goods among their inhabitants are likely to be less shaky - socially and politically - than poor, highly inegalitarian and economically unstable ones. The avoidance or control of internal armed violence depends even more immediately, however, on the powers and effective performance of national governments and their legitimacy in the eyes of the majority of their inhabitants. No government today can take for granted the existence of an unarmed civilian population or the degree of public order long familiar in large parts of Europe. No government today is in a position to overlook or eliminate internal armed minorities.

Yet the world is increasingly divided into states capable of administering their territories and citizens effectively and into a growing number of territories bounded by officially recognised international frontiers, with national governments ranging from the weak and corrupt to the non-existent. These zones produce bloody internal struggles and international conflicts, such as those we have seen in central Africa. There is, however, no immediate prospect for lasting improvement in such regions, and a further weakening of central government in unstable countries, or a further Balkanisation of the world map, would undoubtedly increase the dangers of armed conflict.

A tentative forecast: war in the 21st century is not likely to be as murderous as it was in the 20th. But armed violence, creating disproportionate suffering and loss, will remain omnipresent and endemic - occasionally epidemic - in a large part of the world. The prospect of a century of peace is remote.

7

PAKISTAN'S NUCLEAR FUTURE

Raise the issue of Pakistan's nuclear program before almost any group of Western security analysts, and they are likely to throw up their hands. What might happen if the current Pakistani government is taken over by radicalized political forces sympathetic to the Taliban? Such a government, they fear, might share Pakistan's nuclear weapons materials and know-how with others, including terrorist organizations. Then there is the possibility that a more radical government might pick a war again with India. Could Pakistan prevail against India's superior conventional forces without threatening to resort to nuclear arms? If not, what, if anything, might persuade Pakistan to stand its nuclear forces down? There are no good answers to these questions and even fewer near or mid-term fixes against such contingencies. This, in turn, encourages a kind of policy fatalism with regard to Pakistan. This book, which reflects research that the Nonproliferation Policy Education Centre commissioned over the last 2 years, takes a different tack.

Instead of asking questions that have few or no good answers, this volume tries to characterize specific nuclear problems that the ruling Pakistani government faces with the aim of establishing a base line set of challenges for remedial action. Its point of departure is to consider what nuclear challenges Pakistan will face if moderate forces remain in control of the government and no hot war breaks out against India. A second volume of commissioned research planned for publication in 2008 will consider how best to address these challenges.

What proliferation risks might the current government still be tempted to take? What is required of Pakistan to maintain nuclear deterrence with India? What new vulnerabilities will the expansion of Pakistan's civilian nuclear sector require Islamabad to attend to? Finally, how daunting a task might it be to keep Pakistan's nuclear weapons assets from being seized or to take them back after having been seized? Each of these questions is tackled in the chapters that follow.

Along the way, a number of interesting discoveries are made. First, from the historical analyses done by Bruno Tetrais and George Perkovich, we learn that despite the significant nuclear export control efforts of the current Pakistani government, it might well proliferate again. Why? The same reasons that previous Pakistani governments tolerated and, at times, even sanctioned the nuclear-rocket export-import activities of Dr. A. Q. Khan: Perceived strategic abandonment by the United States, lack of financing for its own strategic competition against India, insufficient civilian oversight of a politically influential military and intelligence services, and a perceived need to deflect negative international attention from Pakistan to third countries.

One or more of these factors were in play throughout the last 3 decades. Two still are. Certainly, the United States has done all it can to reassure Pakistani officials about Washington's commitment to Pakistan's security. Yet, there still is Pakistani cause for concern. Might Washington tie future security and economic assistance to Pakistani progress toward democratic elections and cracking down more severely against radical Islamic groups in Pakistan? As for the matter of being isolated, Pakistan now has to be concerned not just about maintaining good relations with Washington, but somehow fending off the encircling efforts of India. Most recently, these activities included formal military-to-military ties with Iran; the construction of a major naval port at Chahbahar near Pakistan's own new naval base at Gwador; the joint construction with Iran of roads to Afghanistan (and Indian aid efforts to Afghanistan); the stationing of Indian intelligence officers at Zahedan, Iran close to Baluchistan rebel activities in Pakistan; the creation of an

Indian air base in Tajikistan; Indian energy investments and commerce with Iran and countries in the Gulf; and continued Indian military, nuclear, and rocket enhancements. All of these developments have put Pakistan's military and political officials on edge.

As for oversight of the military and intelligence services, this remains an open question. The elections may give some indication of things to come, but for now the military and intelligence arms of the government are still in clear control of much of Pakistan's political, military, and economic activities. A new president may try to reduce the amount of power the military and intelligence sectors have over Pakistan but this is a long-term undertaking.

This, then, brings us to an enduring nuclear challenge Pakistan faces no matter who is running the government: What must Pakistan's military do to deter nuclear war against India? Greg Jones of RAND, Peter Lavoy, and Zia Mian and his coauthors all have different takes on what will be required. Mr. Jones takes a somewhat optimistic view. Pakistan and India currently have roughly the right level of forces and are unlikely to increase them dramatically for the next 20 years. Pakistan's nuclear force requirements would have to grow dramatically, Mr. Jones notes, merely to destroy just 5 percent of India's population (This would require a five-fold increase in Pakistan's current nuclear force.) or only a relatively small portion of India's conventional forces (a task which would require a doubling of Pakistan's current nuclear forces). Enlarging Pakistan's forces to these levels, he argues, would be quite costly. Using history as a guide, Mr. Jones argues that India, meanwhile, seems unlikely to press Pakistan by building up its nuclear forces. Perhaps, but others are not so certain. In his chapter, "Islamabad's Nuclear Posture: Its Premises and Implementation," Dr. Peter Lavoy notes that the prospect of the U.S. and Indian strategic partnership "shifting" the "strategic balance" announced in 2005 set off a series of nuclear alarms in Islamabad. The first of these fears is that India, with U.S. high-technology targeting and intelligence assistance, might knock out Pakistan's nuclear assets in a "preventative" attack.

This, in turn, has already prompted Pakistan's National Command Authority to announce that if the nuclear deal alters the nuclear balance, the command would have to reevaluate Pakistan's commitment to minimum deterrence and to review its nuclear force requirements. This, in turn, will require making Pakistan's nuclear weapons assets even more survivable through increased mobility, hardening, and numbers.

The second Pakistani worry is much more basic: The U.S.-India nuclear deal could enable India to outstrip Pakistan's capacity to make nuclear weapons. How likely is this? The short answer is very. A much more detailed analysis can be found in the chapter by Zia Mian, A. H. Nayyar, R. Rajaraman, and M. V. Ramana entitled, "Fissile Materials in South Asia and the Implications of the U.S.-India Nuclear Deal." Here the authors detail how critical the import of additional uranium fuel might be to expand India's ability to make more nuclear weapons while expanding its nuclear power industry. The authors also cite one Indian expert who suggests that India will attempt to build roughly 400 nuclear warheads % at least four times what the Pakistanis currently possess. Matching this number and controlling the nuclear system deployments that might be made would demand a good deal of Pakistan's government and nuclear establishment. So far, the Pakistani government has hedged its bets against this contingency by beginning construction of a new plutonium production reactor and a new reprocessing plant.

Beyond this, Pakistan has announced plans to expand its own civilian nuclear power sector roughly 20-fold by the year 2030 to 8.8 gigawatts generating capacity. The idea would be to have a nuclear weaponsmaking mobilization base that could be used to make power if India did not make more weapons. This hedging strategy seems to be reasonably cautious. It, however, cannot be implemented without running several important attendant risks.

Besides being uncompetitive against non-nuclear energy alternatives, such a nuclear buildup is likely to increase the vulnerability of Pakistan's civilian reactor sector to sabotage and attack. The good news is that the Pakistani government understands this point. In his detailed analysis, "Preventing Nuclear Terrorism in Pakistan," Abdul Mannan, a senior official serving in Pakistan's nuclear regulatory agency, details the ramifications of a terrorist attack against Pakistan's civilian nuclear sector. Mr. Mannan believes attacks against Pakistan's nuclear facilities are far less likely to inflict damage than a possible attack against spent fuel that is likely to be shipped from Pakistan's power reactors to Pakistan's reprocessing plant. Fortunately, such attacks, even in or near Karachi, are unlikely to produce many fatalities. Unfortunately, they could contaminate a considerable amount of property, and will require the decontamination and quarantining of large numbers of people. To cope with these contingencies, Mr. Mannan calls for the establishment of an extensive list of civil defense measures to be taken.

He is optimistic that Pakistan can take these steps to assure nuclear power's safe expansion.

Dr. Chaim Braun of Stanford's Centre for International Security and Cooperation, though, is not so sure. In his analysis, "Security Issues Related to Pakistan's Future Nuclear Power Program," Dr. Braun examines Pakistan's nuclear reactor operating history, its ability to license new reactors and regulate their operation properly, to train sufficient numbers of new qualified nuclear operators and regulators for the planned expansion of Pakistan's nuclear power sector, and to screen this new staff to assure none have terrorist organization ties. His final assessment is troubling. Pakistan, he fears, will have great difficulty avoiding a major nuclear accident or terrorist-induced sabotage, as well as defending the planned number of civilian facilities against military attacks. Among his key concerns is Pakistan's current lack of qualified and security-screened nuclear personnel. To staff up for the planned nuclear reactor expansion, he estimates that Pakistan will need to find and train 1,000 qualified nuclear regulators and operators per year over the next 20 years. Dr. Braun also believes that Pakistan's nuclear expansion will create a large number of tempting terrorist targets-spent fuel ponds-all of which could be vulnerable to terrorist or military attacks.

This, then, suggests one of the most sensitive challenges an expanded nuclear program in Pakistan presents-the possible seizure of the plants by subnational groups and the need to take them back by force, if necessary. Thomas Donnelly examines this issue in his analysis, "Bad Options." What we learn is that even in the case where the Pakistani government invites U.S. forces to help it to retake the most sensitive Pakistani nuclear facilities at Kahuta, the logistics and military challenges facing U.S. and Pakistani forces are extremely daunting. Besides the logistical challenges of landing a large enough force to retake the city-sized complex at Kahuta, the expeditionary force would have to be prepared to fight its way through a single access road and move quickly enough to assure no material was passed off to terrorist organizations or other opposing groups.

Assuming success and taking control of the facility, many questions would remain. Is all the nuclear material that could be fashioned into bombs accounted for? How could we know? Would the United States hand the material it had secured back to the Pakistani government immediately or hold in trust until the dust of civil disorder had settled? If so, would we render it "safe" and what might this mean? To get the answers to these questions, Mr. Donnelly strongly recommends that the government of Pakistan and the United States work together closely on these issues now.

What is the upshot of all of this analysis? One bottom line is that the government of Pakistan has its hands full with more than enough nuclear issues even if it never goes to war against India, is attacked by Indian forces, or is overthrown by radical Islamic parties. Certainly, to deal with all of the nuclear issues these analyses have raised, one would need to have a fairly robust and active national government capable of mastering nuclear regulation, nuclear physical security, emergency preparedness, peacetime military strategic planning, energy research and development, and electrical system planning. It is most unlikely that such a government would be the kind that could be overthrown or destabilized very easily.

This insight brings us to the second series of studies to be commissioned on Pakistan's nuclear future. These will focus on what can be done to reduce Pakistan's need to expand its civilian nuclear sector. On the one hand, what can be done with India and China to reduce Pakistan's justified fears that India will expand its own nuclear stockpile? Could more be done to address Pakistan's energy needs in a more cost effective manner without building additional nuclear generators? How might India and Pakistan cooperate in promoting less nuclear powered futures for both their countries and one in which the nuclear physical security threats are kept to a minimum for both countries? More generally, what can be done to reduce Pakistani fears of being encircled or overwhelmed by Indian conventional forces (the key propellants for possible future proliferation, nuclear buildups, and war)? What might be done to reduce the most likely escalation threats? Finally, what might be done to pacify Pakistani politics so that greater mutual confidence could be built with India?

PAKISTAN'S NUCLEAR ARSENAL

Pakistan's current nuclear arsenal appears to rely almost exclusively on mobile land-based ballistic missile delivery systems. Pakistan has three deployed missile systems. These are the 350 km range *Ghaznavi*/ M-11, the 750 km range *Shaheen 1*, and the 1,300-1,500 km range *Ghauri*. The first two missiles are solid-fueled; the last utilizes storable liquid fuels. The *Ghaznavi*/M- 11 is deployed in a complex of dispersed garages near Sargodha. The deployment areas of the other two missiles are unknown. The *Shaheen 1* reportedly uses the same TEL as does the *Ghaznavi*/M-11; and, since they are both solid-fueled, they could be deployed at the same locations. However, the liquid-fueled *Ghauri* would need a completely separate deployment location. Not only would it require a different supporting infrastructure, but its fuel (in particular, its concentrated nitric acid oxidizer) would be extremely dangerous to handle around solid-fueled missiles. As is related in the next section, Pakistan initially imported 34 M-11 missiles from China in 1993. The *Ghaznavi* appears to be an indigenously manufactured version of the M-11. Presumably, as the Chinese versions of the missile have aged, they have required remanufacture. Having tested the missile four times since 2002,

Pakistan appears to be serious about maintaining this missile in its arsenal.

This is somewhat surprising since with the longer-range *Shaheen 1* now available, one might expect Pakistan to shift its production to this missile. Clearly, this is not the case and it appears that the *Ghaznavi*/M- 11 will be an important part of Pakistan's arsenal for many years to come. The *Military Balance* gives the size of Pakistan's missile force as 50 *Ghaznavi*/ M-11, 15-20 *Ghauri*, and 6 *Shaheen 1*.23 Though it is likely that Pakistan relies mainly on its ballistic missile force for its nuclear weapons delivery capability, its force of 34 F-16s also could be used in this role. Before 2003 when the *Shaheen 1* and *Ghauri* were deployed, these aircraft would have been the only means to attack targets that are beyond the range of the *Ghazavi*/M-11. However, given the growing strength on India's air defenses and the importance of the F-16s in the conventional air balance, these longerrange ballistic missile have likely taken over the deep nuclear strike role. Currently, the main utility of these aircraft in a nuclear strike role would be to attack mobile tactical targets that would be difficult to target with ballistic missiles.

Pakistan produces both highly enriched uranium and plutonium for its weapons program. The highly enriched uranium is produced by the use of centrifuges. The first facility was at Kahuta and additional plants of various sorts are also at Sihala, Golra, and Wah. In the mid-1990s, Pakistan's total enrichment capacity was estimated to be around 5,000 separative work units (SWU) per year, which would produce about 25 kg of heavy enriched uranium (HEU) per year. Since its 1998 nuclear tests, its total enrichment capacity appears to have expanded to around 10,000 SWU per year (50 kg of HEU per year). Also since 1998, Pakistan has had a 50 MWth plutonium production reactor in operation at Khushab. Its production rate will depend on the reactor's capacity factor, but is probably around 10 kg of plutonium per year.

The ISIS has produced a set of reasonable estimates for Pakistan's total fissile material production as of the end of 2003.25 Pakistan's total HEU inventory was estimated to be between 1,000 and 1,250 kg and its total plutonium inventory was estimated to be between 20 and 60 kg. Assuming 20 kg of HEU or 5 kg of plutonium is required for each weapon, there would be a possible nuclear inventory at the end of 2003 of about 50 to 70 weapons. Taking into account fissile material production in 2004 and 2005 would lead to an estimate of about 60 to 80 weapons. These estimates are similar to many other that have been made for Pakistan. Note that while estimates such as these have been useful for sizing Pakistan's nuclear arsenal in the past, at some point in the future, fissile material inventories will not be the limiting factor in producing a nuclear arsenal.

With regard to the weapons themselves, presumably Pakistan possesses two weapon types: The first, a weapon produced at the beginning of Pakistan's program, is designed to be delivered by an F-16; and the second, a smaller lighter weight weapon, is suitable for ballistic missile delivery. As to the possible yield of these weapons, the 1998 nuclear tests provide the only insight available. These tests probably did not serve the purpose for which nuclear tests are usually conducted, namely to provide information about the characteristics of the nuclear devices being tested.

Such information would have already been supplied to Pakistan from China. Rather, the purpose of the tests appears to have been political, to respond to India's tests and to declare Pakistan an overt nuclear weapons state. Therefore Pakistan's main purpose would have been to conduct tests as quickly as possible after India's, and it would have likely used weapons from its existing arsenal for this purpose. And since India claimed that it had tested four weapons simultaneously on May 11, Pakistan claimed that it tested five weapons on May 28. However, again, this seems to have been for political effect. Based on the small overall magnitude of the seismic signal on this date, it is far more likely that only one weapon was tested. The seismic signal on May 28 had a body-wave magnitude of 4.9, which is equivalent to a yield of 6 to 13 kt. Pakistan also conducted a single nuclear test on May 30. Its seismic signal had a bodywave magnitude of 4.3, which is equivalent to a yield of 2 to 8 kt. Both weapons then appear to have been simple fission devices, the first with a yield of around 10 kt and the second 5 kt. The difference in yield between the two tests might represent the difference between the aircraft-delivered design and the missiledelivered one, or it could have been the same weapon using different fissile cores. Also, since the uncertainty bounds overlap, it is possible that it was the same weapon tested twice. At any rate, it seems that the yield of Pakistan's nuclear weapons is likely in the range of 5 to 10 kt and probably no more than 15 to 20 kt.

As to the readiness of the Pakistani nuclear force, President Musharraf has indicated that the weapons are kept in an unready state. He has stated, "Missiles and warheads are not permitted together. There is a geographical separation between them." At a minimum what this probably means is that the fissile cores are stored separately from the missiles and their warheads. Though some observers have contrasted this practice with the Superpower experience, actually the United States handled its weapons in the same way for the first decade or so of its weapons program. In the U.S. case, the fissile cores were kept separately from the high explosive parts of the warhead, not only for security reasons but for safety reasons as well. Indeed, given the technology of the era, the high explosive components could not be maintained at high levels of readiness for any great period of time.

Since 2000 Pakistan has had a formal command and control arrangement for its nuclear forces. This is the "National Command and Control Authority" jointly headed by President Musharraf and Pakistan's Prime Minister.

PAKISTAN'S NUCLEAR WEAPONS PROGRAM

It is widely accepted that Pakistan's formal nuclear weapons program began in the aftermath of its defeat in the December 1971 Indo-Pakistan War. In January 1972, Prime Minister Zulfikar Ali Bhutto convened a meeting with Pakistan's top scientists in the city of Multan where he announced that Pakistan would develop nuclear weapons. Like all nuclear weapons efforts, the main barrier to the production of weapons was the need to procure the special nuclear material (plutonium or highly enriched uranium) required for any such weapon.

Initially, Pakistan concentrated its efforts on acquiring plutonium. In December 1972, Pakistan's first nuclear power reactor (Kanupp), which had been supplied by Canada, began sustained operation. It would produce tens of kilograms of plutonium per year. Utilizing this material would require diverting it from IAEA safeguards, but this apparently was not considered a problem. However, Pakistan needed a reprocessing plant to separate the plutonium from the spent reactor fuel. Pakistan began negotiations with France for the purchase of a large reprocessing plant, which would be located at Chashma. In October 1974, a deal was signed to build the plant. U.S. opposition to this facility would eventually lead France to cancel the deal. Pakistan managed to build a smaller reprocessing facility known as the New Labs, with the help of Belgian and French companies. New Labs facility was probably completed sometime in the early to mid 1980s. By that time, Pakistan had shifted its main effort to the production of highly enriched uranium and New Labs would not operate for many years, as Pakistan decided not to face the political controversy that would result from violating the IAEA safeguards at Kanupp, and there was no other source of spent fuel available.

As is now well-known, Pakistan acquired enrichment technology through the efforts of Dr. Abdul Qadeer Khan. He began work in 1972 at the Almelo facility in the Netherlands, which is part of the Urenco centrifuge enrichment project. Due to lax security, Khan was able to gain information about much of the centrifuge enrichment technology. When Khan returned to Pakistan for a visit in 1974, he was able to convince the Pakistani government to begin its own centrifuge enrichment project. In 1975 Khan returned to Pakistan permanently to head the centrifuge development effort. Key to this endeavor was Pakistan's ability to procure many centrifuge components from Urenco suppliers, as well as to purchase other facilities needed for the centrifuge effort. For example, in the late 1970s, Pakistan was able to buy an entire facility for the production of uranium hexafluoride (the chemical form required for the enrichment plant) from companies in West Germany. Construction of an enrichment facility at Kahuta began in 1978. By 1984 the plant was in operation producing low enriched uranium. By 1987 it was producing the highly enriched material needed for weapons production.

In the late 1970s, in response to Pakistan's nuclear weapons development efforts, the United States cut off aid to Pakistan. However, the Soviet invasion of Afghanistan at the end of 1979, led the United States to reverse course and strengthen ties with Pakistan. In 1981, the United States agreed to sell 40 F-16 fighters to Pakistan. The aircraft were delivered to Pakistan between 1983 and 1987. Of these aircraft, 32 are thought to be still operational today.

In the mid-1980s, China supplied Pakistan with a nuclear weapon design suitable for tactical aircraft delivery. In addition it provided Pakistan with important components required to detonate a nuclear weapon.

A 1985 U.S. law known as the Pressler Amendment required the president to annually certify that Pakistan did not possess a nuclear device for U.S. aid to Pakistan to continue. With Pakistan's production of highly enriched uranium and its having both a viable nuclear weapon design and F-16s to deliver the weapons, providing the certification became increasingly difficult. But as long as the war in Afghanistan continued, the certification was provided. However, with the end of this war, there was no longer any need for such close ties with Pakistan. In October 1990, the president failed to provide the certification and aid to Pakistan was again cut off. This date should be considered the latest that Pakistan had become a de facto nuclear weapons state with an arsenal based on F-16 delivered highly enriched uranium weapons.

With the imposition of sanctions against Pakistan, it could not obtain spare parts for the F-16s or additional aircraft that had been ordered. This threatened to undermine the long-term viability of Pakistan's nuclear force. In 1993 China supplied Pakistan with 34 M-11 missiles. These utilize solid fuel and were reported to have a range of 300 km. The public reporting of this transfer was delayed until 1996. Even then it did not appear to be particularly significant since, with a range of only 300 km, the missiles could not be used to hit major Indian cities, if launched from Pakistan. However, more recent reporting assigns the missile a range of 350 km, which would allow the missile to reach New Delhi when launched from Pakistan. Unclassified satellite photographs taken in early 2000 show a dispersed complex of 12 storage garages where these missiles and their TELs are deployed near Sargodha. Equipping these missiles with nuclear warheads would require the use of a warhead somewhat smaller and lighter than the one developed for F-16 delivery, but there is no reason to suppose that China would not have supplied Pakistan with such a warhead design.

In April 1998, Pakistan tested the *Ghauri* missile. It appears to be an unmodified imported North Korean *No Dong* missile. The *No Dong* is reported to have a range of 1,300 km, though the *Ghauri* is usually reported to have a range of 1,500 km. The importation of this missile appears to represent bureaucratic rivalry between A. Q. Khan's research organization (which was responsible for the importation of the *Ghauri*) and Pakistan's National Development Complex (which is developing Pakistan's solid-fueled missiles). This missile has been tested five additional times: April 1999, May 2002, May 2004, June 2004, and October 2004. The missile was officially handed over to the Pakistani military in January 2003.

Also in April 1998, Pakistan started sustained operation of its 50 MWth heavy-water plutonium production reactor at Khushab. The Chinese reportedly provide assistance in the construction of this reactor.

In early 2000, unclassified satellite photos of this site showed what appears to be a heavy water production plant only a few miles south of the reactor.

On May 28 and May 30, 1998, Pakistan conducted nuclear tests in response to the ones conducted by India earlier in the month. These tests marked the transition from Pakistan as a de facto nuclear weapons state to that of an openly declared nuclear weapons state.

In April 1999, Pakistan tested the *Shaheen 1* ballistic missile. It utilizes solid fuel and has a range of 750 km. The missile was tested twice in October 2002, twice more in October 2003, and again in December 2004. The missile was officially handed over to the Pakistani military in March 2003.

In February 2000, Pakistan established a National Command Authority. Though little is known about it publicly, it is believed to be responsible for nuclear doctrine, as well as nuclear research and development, wartime command and control, and advice to President Musharraf about the development and employment of nuclear weapons.

Twice in 2002, Pakistan tested the *Ghaznavi*. It is believed to be a domestically produced copy of the Chinese M-11 ballistic missile. The missile was also tested in October 2003 and November 2004. The missile was formally inducted into service with the Pakistani military in February 2004.

In March 2004, Pakistan tested the *Shaheen 2* ballistic missile. This is Pakistan's first two-stage missile, with both stages using solid fuel. It has a range of about 2,000 km, which will allow it to hit almost any target in India. The missile was tested again in March 2005 and April 2006, but it has yet to be inducted into the military.

In August 2005, Pakistan tested the *Babur* cruise missile with a range of 500 km. It was tested again in March 2006 and may be deployed by the end of the decade.

In December 2005, the United States supplied Pakistan with two F-16s.30

8

POST-COLD WAR MILITARY CONFLICTS

EXECUTIVE SUMMARY

The attack on the United States and the war that has been visited upon us highlights a fundamental condition of our circumstances: we cannot and will not know precisely where and when America's interests will be threatened, when America will come under attack, or when Americans might die as the result of aggression. We can be clear about trends, but uncertain about events.

This chapter examines the performance of U.S. armed forces in three major post-Cold War military conflicts (Iraq in 1991, Kosovo in 1999, and Afghanistan in 2001) to identify commonalities and associated trends that may have implications for the conduct of warfare in the early 21st century. Skeptics on the value of "lessons learned" from the three wars typically emphasize the unique characteristics of each war and the unlikely prospects that such conditions will apply in the future. In contrast, we believe that disparities in the size, scope, and overall prosecution of each conflict strengthen the likelihood that trends in common areas across all three wars will characterize future conflicts.

Our methodology is similar to that employed by long-range planners—looking for significant areas of commonality (and leverage) across widely different future scenarios. However, instead of speculating on alternative futures, we searched for commonalties and associated trends in three wars that have already occurred. Our selected scenarios are not hypothetical but rooted in factual evidence. Accordingly, they should be valuable in discerning trends that have emerged in the American way of war over the last decade. We examined three main areas for trends: the security environment, military capabilities, and key technologies. Dividing our work into these three categories introduces some complications, as some issues overlap and the categories themselves are broadly defined. But the approach taken in this study provides a useful framing edifice from which to analyze trends likely to characterize U.S. involvement in early 21st century warfare. They are:

Political-Military Shifts in the Security Environment

The migration of conflict toward Asia.

Connect the dots representing the geographic areas of armed conflict in Kosovo, Iraq and Afghanistan, and the locus of those points suggests a shift from the European region that dominated U.S. Cold War military planning toward Asia, a region of vast economic import and diverse security challenges. One astute observer of military affairs recently observed: "For nearly half a century, the American military organized itself to fight a short, extremely intense battle in Europe from large fixed bases dispersed over relatively short distances. Whatever a future war in Asia might look like, that will not be it."

The primacy of ad hoc military coalitions. In the Cold War, the United States relied heavily on formal alliances, such as NATO, for collective security. In the Gulf and Afghanistan conflicts, the coalitions formed to defeat aggression resulted from an ad hoc approach to secure international support for U.S.-led military operations. Thus, rather than the long-term "marriages" that typified Cold War alliance formation, future coalitions will be characterized as a series of temporary liaisons—with some partners proving more faithful than others.

A new political currency measuring the contributions of coalition partners. Again, in contrast to the Cold War, allied contributions have come, for the most part, in the form of political support and access to facilities rather than combat firepower. Trends in coalition capabilities indicate that widening disparities in military capabilities will cause future allies to fall further behind the United States, although specialized intelligence and military niche capabilities (such as special operations forces) will remain valuable.

An amplification of the anti-access/area denial problem. Evidence from the three conflicts underscores the potential for military "showstoppers" arising from political issues, the tyranny of distance, and infrastructure constraints. The need to conduct offensive operations could entangle efforts to obtain political access while the vast reaches of Asia feature a much lower base density and less developed infrastructure compared with Europe and the Middle East. Although military anti-access threats were minimal in these conflicts, improved adversary capabilities could further complicate future U.S. power projection.

The ability of adversaries to undermine the threat and use of force. In each of the three conflicts, adversaries sought to deter attack with threats calculated to heighten perceived U.S. sensitivities to casualties and to exploit instances of collateral damage to evoke international condemnation and weaken coalition resolve. Failing that, they sought to reduce their vulnerability to coalition military actions through a variety of means (air defenses, camouflage, concealment, deception, dispersal, mobility, and hardened and deeply buried facilities). Weapons of mass destruction (WMD) also cast a shadow in all three conflicts. The consistency of these adversarial approaches suggests that the United States will face similar challenges in the future.

MILITARY CAPABILITIES ENABLING NEW WAYS OF WARFARE

An "order of magnitude" increase in battlefield situational awareness. Two prominent consequences of increased situational awareness and their implications for time-critical strike operations in the future warrant particular mention: (1) the rapidly improving speed at which targets can be generated and prosecuted by a combination of battle management, sensor, and strike platforms, compressing what has become known as the "kill chain"; and (2) the blurred distinction between command and control and the execution of military operations, resulting from real time operational snapshots of the battlefield and the intervention of senior leaders (both civilian and military) in issuing targeting guidance. The latter trend is resulting in the creeping centralization of both command and execution, as command echelons in the rear reach forward to the battlefield in near-real time. Owing to the enhanced political content of armed conflict in a world of high-speed information, evidence from these conflicts indicates that centralized execution will now accompany centralized control.

A move from deliberate to adaptive planning, and the concomitant execution of dynamic military operations. A legacy of the Cold War, the deliberate planning process instills an institutional predilection for scripted as opposed to dynamic military operations. However, the nonlinear and fluid operating environments that will characterize future battlefields necessitate renewed emphasis on both adaptive planning and dynamic military operations. The combined experiences of planners and operators in Desert Storm, Allied Force, and Enduring Freedom underscore this point. In the Gulf War, for example, 20% of targets were selected after aircraft launch, whereas over Kosovo, 43% of the targets were selected once the aircraft were airborne. In Afghanistan, 80% of the carrierbased sorties were launched without pre-designated targets.

A dramatic decline in U.S. casualties compared with previous conflicts. Throughout the three conflicts, U.S. combat losses were statistically insignificant, despite adversary objectives to cause high casualty rates as a means to achieve conflict termination. The reasons for this lie in a combination of new operational capabilities, highly survivable combat platforms, and guidance to limit the vulnerability of U.S. forces.

An increasing emphasis on extended range operations. This is an outgrowth of the access problem and the migration of conflict to distant and remote regions of the world. Throughout the Cold War, U.S. planners developed concepts of operation based on the premise that forward operating bases would be available to launch and sustain combat operations. From the Gulf War to Afghanistan, trends suggest that premise to be increasingly risky and, as such, must be hedged against to guarantee U.S. abilities to project firepower over long distances.

The diminishing role of heavy ground forces. Whereas rapidly deployable, highly maneuverable ground forces that can leverage the effects of modern precision weaponry are integral to dynamic military operations against elusive enemies—as witnessed most recently in Afghanistan—there is a mismatch between the capabilities of slow-moving and late-deploying heavy ground forces and the demands of the future operating environment. Moreover, the ways in which the United States delivers firepower to the battlefield have fundamentally changed. On this point, Secretary Rumsfeld observed in October 2002: "Looking at what was overwhelming force a decade or two decades ago, today you can have overwhelming force, conceivably, with lesser numbers because the lethality is equal to or greater than before."

TECHNOLOGIES ENHANCING U.S. MILITARY ADVANTAGES

The increasing dominance of precision weapons. Precision-guided munitions (PGMs) emerged as the centerpiece of a revolutionary style of modern warfare. The clear trend since the Gulf War is that precision-guided weapons represent a steadily increasing percentage of munitions delivered: about 8% in Iraq, 30% in Kosovo, and 60% in Afghanistan. Other trends are the increasing number of PGMs delivered per sortie and the increasing percentage of PGMs that can be delivered in adverse weather (from 13% in the Gulf War to almost 90% in Afghanistan). Notably, all three conflicts witnessed strained inventories of precision weapons, particularly long-range standoff weapons. Finally, the trends suggest the promise of new capabilities stemming from increased payload fractionation (larger loads of smaller guided weapons) and mass precision (rapid delivery of large numbers of PGMs in short time periods).

The increasing quantity and quality of sensors and their integration into systems and networks. The shift toward "network-centric warfare" is pushed by the promise of information dominance and battlefield situational awareness. Underpinning this promise are technologies to create network-centric architectures consisting of high-quality sensors and rapidly transmitted data streams that will be fused and integrated at command and control centres. Conflicts since the Gulf War witnessed modest forms of integration of command and control, intelligence, surveillance, and reconnaissance (C2ISR) assets. In the future, trends in sensor technology toward less expensive, more capable, and lighter sensors will support intelligence-quality sensors networked around the battlefield. Assuming that data streams from multiple sources can be integrated in a timely fashion—a tall order— future commanders will enjoy even greater situational awareness to employ their forces more effectively.

The increasing importance of stealth aircraft and electronic countermeasures. From the Gulf to Kosovo and, to a lesser degree, in Afghanistan, low observable aircraft were employed with remarkable success and revolutionary impact. Low observable technologies applied to combat aircraft have allowed them to operate with relative impunity against sophisticated air defense systems. The ability of stealth aircraft to operate independently has reduced, to some extent, the requirement for large strike packages laden with supporting escort aircraft. Electronic warfare assets were critical in enabling non-stealthy aircraft—the mainstay of the current force structure—to survive in non-permissive threat environments. Continued emphasis on air powercentric campaign plans will ultimately demand renewed investment in stealth and electronic countermeasures.

The increasing use and utility of unmanned aerial vehicles (UAVs). Since the 1950s, the U.S. has invested over $25 billion (in FY98 dollars) developing and fielding UAVs, primarily for intelligence, surveillance, and reconnaissance missions. This sizeable investment has resulted in unmanned systems that demonstrated their operational utility over the battlefield, enabled by advances in satellite guidance and communications, computerized flight control systems, and sensor technologies. Indeed, in each of the three conflicts examined, unmanned systems assumed new roles, due in large part to improvements in range, endurance, on-board sensors, and data transmission. Used initially as decoys during the Gulf War, by 2001 UAVs had evolved into sophisticated, air-breathing, hunter-killer platforms.

In summary, the U.S. has fielded impressive capabilities to meet the military challenges of the immediate post-Cold War era, up to and including the war on terrorism. However, the road ahead appears ever more challenging, both in terms of the diversity of our future adversaries and the military capabilities they will acquire. Our trend analysis suggests strongly that, to better prepare for uncertain events in a hostile security environment, the U.S. will need to invest in concepts, capabilities, and technologies to sustain its competitive advantages on the future battlefield. These trends were demonstrated to varying degrees in the Gulf War, over the former Yugoslavia, and most recently in Afghanistan. What will ultimately be required, we believe, is an agile, access-insensitive military force that can project sustained, precise, and survivable military power across great distances, with little preparation or reliance on external political or military support.

INTRODUCTION

Since the end of the Cold War, the United States has engaged in three substantial armed conflicts. In 1991, the U.S. led a coalition of powers to force the Iraqi army to retreat from occupied Kuwait and to restore that country's independence. In 1999, the U.S. and NATO conducted an air campaign to halt the ethnic cleansing of Kosovar Albanians by the Serbian government, eventually toppling Slobodan Milosevic's regime. In 2001, responding to the terrorist attacks on the World Trade Centre and the Pentagon, the U.S. and its coalition partners defeated Afghanistan's terrorist-sponsoring Taliban regime and destroyed the al Qaeda infrastructure in that country.

These military interventions have not brought about a lasting peace. Indeed, the U.S. remains militarily committed in Iraq, the former Yugoslavia, and Afghanistan, and will remain engaged for many years to come. The war on terrorism, moreover, is expected to require a sustained effort, consisting of sporadic but intense combat operations against transnational terrorist organizations. Consequently, it is ever more likely that the U.S. will employ military force in additional contingencies over the next decade or two. While no one can accurately predict where U.S. forces will be deployed in the future, there is considerable interest in what future warfare might entail and, more importantly, how state and nonstate actors will fight one another on the battlefields of the early 21st century. Traditionally, this has been left for futurists to ponder in provocative far-reaching studies. Other scholars have emphasized the import of factual evidence, rooted in military history, in their descriptions of future warfare.

Of these two approaches, we believe a retrospective look at recent military conflicts can be valuable in describing and explaining trends likely to be evident on future battlefields. With this in mind, we examined the performance of U.S. armed forces during three major post-Cold War military conflicts (Iraq in 1991, Kosovo in 1999, and Afghanistan in 2001) with an aim toward identifying commonalities and associated trends that may have implications for the conduct of warfare in the early 21st century. In particular, we set out to answer the following questions: • What political-military trends have significantly impacted the use of U.S. military force?

- What trends in U.S. force employment have emerged over the last decade?
- What trends in technology have contributed to U.S. dominance on the post-Cold War battlefield?

We recognize that looking backward is not universally seen as a useful technique to develop observations on the conduct of future warfare. There is, after all, the overused adage that the military continually prepares to fight the last war. A corollary to that aphorism might be phrased,

"Little can be learned from past conflicts owing to their unique nature." We would be the first to agree that the three conflicts examined here are quite unique, but our research leads us to take issue with the premise that comparative historical experience is of marginal utility in thinking about future warfare.

In particular, we disagree with the two fundamental arguments often cited to support the claim that little can be learned from Desert Storm, Allied Force, and Enduring Freedom:

(1) that the conflicts were sui generis owing to a range of variables such as climate, terrain, adversary capabilities, warning and build-up time; or (2) that each conflict did not exercise or test the range of military concepts and capabilities existing in the current force that might be critical in other conflicts. In the case of Desert Storm, for example, Jeffrey Record concluded that the conflict possessed an exceptional character, describing it as "a set of circumstances so fortuitous that it is highly unlikely it will ever be duplicated again." A similar theme was echoed in a General Accounting Office (GAO) report on the Gulf War air campaign.

It concluded that "Desert Storm's lessons are limited in some regard because the environmental and military operating conditions for aircraft and weapons system performance are unlikely to be repeated outside Southwest Asia..." And a Department of the Navy report included this observation: "Lessons should be interpreted in light of the Desert Shield/ Desert Storm scenario and in some cases may be less applicable generally. For example, we did not test our open ocean concepts."

Skeptics also judged that the other two conflicts offered minimal guidance for the future. Operation Allied Force, as the NATO war in the Balkans was titled, clearly demonstrated unique characteristics. It represented NATO's first extended use of military force, and was the first major armed conflict conducted by a coalition for humanitarian purposes against a state persecuting its own citizens within its borders. The use of air power alone to prosecute the war, combined with the declaration that ground forces would not be introduced, added to the singular nature of the war over Kosovo. Pundits criticized this apparent imbalance before, during, and after the air campaign. In a June 2002 interview, for example, Deputy Secretary of Defense Paul Wolfowitz asserted that "you don't win wars just from the air. I would have to say I was astonished that we accomplished as much as we did in Kosovo without ground forces, and I think that was a fluke."

More recently, the overwhelming success of Enduring Freedom is frequently tempered with admonitions that the conflict presented unique challenges to U.S. forces that will not be replicated in the future. The conflict featured extended range air operations, special operations forces, proxy ground forces, and air mobile light infantry to overthrow the Taliban regime and dismantle the al Qaeda organization in Afghanistan. The lack of friendly forward air bases in the region from which to launch Air Force tactical fighters also resulted in the majority of the sorties taking off from aircraft carriers, and the bulk of the weapons being dropped by long-range bombers.

Unsurprisingly, Air Force leadership concluded that the campaign in Afghanistan, in which ground-based fighters played a minor role, could not serve as a paradigm for future conflicts. "First of all," stated Air Force Secretary Jim Roche, "[Chief of Staff General] Johnny Jumper and I both agree, and we've reaffirmed: this is not like any other, and the next one isn't going to be like it."

No doubt about it, these were three very different wars. They were fought for different objectives with dissimilar forces against disparate enemies that varied markedly in size, power, organization, training, equipment, and morale, in strikingly different terrain, and in significantly varied climates. Nonetheless, when we look at these conflicts and variables across the board, their very diversity supports our argument that commonalities and associated trends do have explanatory value in studies of future warfare.

Objective and Methodology

This paper examines the performance of U.S. armed forces in the three major post-Cold War military conflicts to identify common areas and associated trends that have implications for future warfare. To accomplish this objective in a reasonable amount of time and space, we established some artificial boundaries and limited the scope of our work. Of these, the most important to emphasize is our focus on relatively high-intensity combat operations, as we considered U.S.-led military campaigns in Iraq, over Kosovo, and in Afghanistan. Although at times we refer to U.S. military experiences in the 1990s that span the conflict spectrum, our mandate is to examine trends in military contingencies approximating the "major theatre wars" that served as illustrative force planning scenarios over the last decade. In discussing the issue of invading Iraq, Deputy Secretary Wolfowitz observed in December 2002:

"You've got to be prepared for the worst case... It would be a terrible mistake for anyone to predict with confidence what the course of a war is going to be".

As Wolfowitz pointed out—and history has illustrated so painfully—predicting the future is not a high-confidence enterprise. Since the end of the Cold War, the Northrop Grumman Analysis Centre has conducted various studies of future warfare to advise our company and our customers of what the future might hold in state-of-the-art warfare. But predicting any future is approached with low confidence. Such speculative endeavors involve significant degrees of uncertainty, so much so that long range visions of future warfare prove increasingly less actionable as errors are magnified over time. Therefore, we chose to restrict our future vision here to a relatively modest timeframe—we suspect the trends demonstrated over the last 10 years are probably good for another 10—relying on methods of description and explanation rather than prediction.

With this in mind, we employed a scenario-based methodology to facilitate our short-term snapshot of the future battlefield. From the standpoint of business planning, the decision-scenario approach articulated by Peter Schwartz in his 1991 book, The Art of the Long View, has proven a useful technique. This method employs building alternative future scenarios to help senior managers learn about outcomes they might otherwise fail to consider, while providing an appreciation for the future value of present decisions.

The U.S. Air Force Innovation Task Force used an alternative futures approach in the mid-1980s, constructed four plausible visions of global conflict, and selected capabilities that appeared valuable for future investment in each of the contrasting scenarios. In the 1990s, the force-sizing approach adopted in the Pentagon also relied on the generation of two nearly-simultaneous major regional wars to codify threat assumptions against which the adequacy of the planned force could be validated.

The methodology utilized here is similar to that adopted by long-range planners. However, rather than generating plausible alternative scenarios, we are looking to past conflicts in our search for insights into what combat operations will look like in the early 21st century. Our selected contingencies are not hypothetical but rooted in factual evidence. Accordingly, they should prove valuable not only in discerning trends that have emerged in the American way of war over the last decade, but also in underscoring strategic realities, military capabilities, and enabling technologies that have relevance for the near future.

Finally, our analysis was informed using a mix of primary and secondary sources. To the extent possible, we reviewed available official unclassified literature and supplemented it with memoirs, analyses, and media reports to identify common areas and define a list of candidate trends. To winnow the list further, we rehearsed our hypotheses during a series of interviews and briefings with subject matter experts in the Army, Air Force, Navy, Marine Corps, Office of the Secretary of Defense, defense industry, and policy research organizations. Using their feedback, we selected the most salient trends and proceeded with supporting research and analysis. While there is a fair degree of subjectivity to this process, we believe that what follows provides a useful framing edifice to analyze the evolving American way of warfare in the early years of this century.

Assumptions

From the outset, we need to make our assumptions transparent. The most obvious is that U.S. military forces are likely to be engaged in armed conflict over the next decade or more. The fact that we are examining three major conflicts occurring over the last decade is evidence enough that the near-term security environment will not likely be a peaceful one. Our previous studies have convinced us that armed conflicts will occur with uncertain frequency, and predictions as to where, when, and against whom U.S. forces will be engaged are speculative at best. Currently, U.S. military forces are prosecuting a global war on terrorism, and President Bush has made it clear that the war will be a lengthy one. Finally, at this writing, there are increasing signs that the U.S. will initiate military operations to remove the current regime in Iraq, possibly in early 2003.

Second, we assume that revolutionary technologies will not outdate the trends evident in the conflicts examined here, at least not within the next 10 years. Prior Analysis Centre work that examined the complex connections between technological advance and fundamental change in combat dynamics also confirmed the difficulties involved in forecasting whether specific technological advances would revolutionize combat interactions. For example, Barry Watts documented that even in relatively mature combat areas, such as air-to-air engagements, hardware and software advances that appeared revolutionary when initially fielded often had surprisingly little effect on combat outcomes. On the other hand, precision-guided munitions have had a dramatic impact on combat operations. However, their revolutionary potential was largely ignored after the first widespread use of such weapons in Vietnam. The full implications of PGMs were not realized until two decades later during the Gulf War.

Moreover, scholars examining the "revolution in military affairs" with an historical frame of reference argue that technical breakthroughs are not sufficient in themselves to bring about an entirely different way of warfighting. This view of military transformation is based largely on events during the interwar period, when it was observed that "revolutions" took hold only when new concepts of operation were developed and new organizations formed to exploit technological breakthroughs. Ultimately, these organizational and doctrinal changes combine to form a new way of warfare which takes time to evolve and mature—perhaps 20 or 30 years. Our nearterm look into the future of war does not, therefore, envision a technology-driven revolution. Third, we assume that the trends revealed here have applicability across the conflict spectrum. An overarching feature of all three wars is that they were waged against relatively small state and non-state actors. Although U.S. ground troops deployed to the Gulf and fighter squadrons employed against Serbia approximated forces sized to fight a major theatre war, the adversary's capabilities, particularly in Afghanistan, were clearly less than that of a first-rate military power.

Therefore, doubts could be reasonably expressed regarding the value of a study that discerns trends from conflicts with second- or third-rate militaries. At first glance, these capabilities may imply that further preparations are needed for conflicts at the lower end of the conflict spectrum, but how useful will they be in confronting an emerging regional near-peer competitor? For that matter, how do we account for the war on terrorism and the capabilities needed to prosecute it successfully? Our answers to these legitimate queries point to the scalability of the trends described. We focus on strategic shifts, military capabilities, and enabling technologies that appear useful across the conflict spectrum and against a range of adversaries. For example, the exponential improvement in situational awareness witnessed in command and control centres, from the "Black Hole" in the Gulf War to the Combined Air Operations Centre (CAOC) directing the war in Afghanistan, should be applicable in the battlefield management of U.S. military forces against any foe. Indeed, the diversity of the three conflicts examined here, as well as those we anticipate in the future, argues for capabilities suitable to both high-intensity conflicts and smaller-scale contingencies.

Fourth, we assume a favorable imbalance between U.S. military capabilities and the lesser capabilities of future adversaries, and that the imbalance will encourage adversaries to seek asymmetric approaches (as force multipliers) to offset it. In the aftermath of the Gulf War, U.S. rivals were cautioned not to fight the U.S. on its terms, but to find, attack, and exploit an "Achilles' heel." Therefore, the United States must prepare itself for an enemy unlikely to confront its strengths head-on, but one inclined to pursue indirect approaches against perceived weaknesses. As examined in Section II, all three adversaries acted to undermine both the credibility of the threat of conventional military force and its utility. Despite the popularity of "asymmetry" as a Washington buzzword, we agree with Colin Gray's observation that all of America's wars have been "asymmetrical": "[T]here are no identical belligerents, with identical forces, who behave identically."

Given the asymmetry inherent in future warfare, our task is to search for trends in recent military conflicts describing those adversarial actions, and point to areas in which the United States can increase its competitive advantage.

Finally, we assume a degree of subjectivity in adjudicating what constituted a noteworthy trend and what did not. In the process, we uncovered some trends that, while they were not significant factors in the conflicts we examined, should not be discounted. For example, planners would be wise not to undervalue the importance of air-toair capabilities in future warfare based on the few air-to-air engagements that transpired during operations Desert Storm, Allied Force, and Enduring Freedom.

One might make similar conclusions about the import of theatre ballistic missile defense that was important militarily and politically in the Gulf War but absent in Kosovo and Afghanistan. We were also unable to document the increasing dependence of air, ground, and sea-based military operations on space-based assets—although tracking the use of global positioning systems from ground forces in the Gulf War to direct attack munitions in Afghanistan may serve as a useful surrogate. Nor does the absence of urban warfare in post-Cold War military conflicts absolve planners from considering urban combat in future operating environments.

Presumably there are other "dogs that did not bark" during these wars that did not make it into our trend analysis. These issues deserve further study.

Organization

This monograph explores key trends in three broad areas: the security environment, military force employment, and technologies that enable new forms of warfare. Dividing our work into these categories introduces some complications, as some issues overlap and the categories themselves are broadly defined, but organizing the study in this fashion provides a useful framework for analyzing key trends in modern warfare.

The first section focuses on political-military shifts in the post-Cold War security environment that will impact the planning and conduct of U.S. military operations in the future. Highlighted trends include: the migration of conflict toward Asia; the primacy of ad hoc military coalitions; a new political currency to measure the contributions of allies to military coalitions; an amplification of the anti-access/area denial problem; and the promise of adversarial actions to undermine the threat and use of force. The second section then identifies important trends in military force employment. Identified as salient trends here are: the great increase in situational battlefield awareness; the move from deliberate to adaptive planning, and the concomitant execution of dynamic military operations; the dramatic decline in U.S. casualties compared with previous conflicts; an increasing emphasis on extended range operations; and the diminishing role of heavy ground forces. Finally, the third section will highlight key technology trends that will enable new forms of warfare, with particular emphasis on the increasing utility of precision weapons; the increasing quantity and quality of sensors and integrated sensor networks; the increasing importance of stealth aircraft and electronic countermeasures; and the growing use and utility of unmanned aerial vehicles.

POLITICAL-MILITARY SHIFTS IN THE SECURITY ENVIRONMENT

The end of the Cold War in 1989 did not meet with universal agreement on what it meant for the international security environment or what it implied for U.S. foreign and defense policy. Looking back, however, the strategic shifts in the security environment affecting past U.S. military engagements and influencing future wars are more transparent. This section highlights four political-military trends that our analysis suggests will significantly impact the planning and execution of U.S. military operations in the future:

- The migration of conflict toward Asia;
- The primacy of ad hoc military coalitions and the consequent role of coalition partners in military operations;

- An amplification of the anti-access/area denial problem; and
- The ability of adversaries to undermine the threat and use of force.

The Migration of Military Conflict Toward Asia

Connect the dots representing the geographic areas of armed conflict in the former Yugoslavia, Iraq, and Afghanistan and the locus of those points denotes a shift away from the European region that dominated military planning before the Cold War. To be sure, the United States had global interests during its competition with the Soviet Union, fought two proxy wars on the Asian periphery against Soviet-supported North Korea and Vietnam, and gradually expanded its strategic vision to encompass the oil-rich Persian Gulf. But with the threat removed from central Europe, the U.S. focus has now moved unequivocally to the East, as articulated most recently in the 2001 Quadrennial Defense Review Report (QDR):

> In particular, Asia is gradually emerging as a region susceptible to large-scale military competition. Along a broad arc of instability that stretches from the Middle East to Northeast Asia, the region contains a volatile mix of rising and declining regional powers. The governments of some of these states are vulnerable to overthrow by radical or extremist internal political forces or movements. Many of these states field large militaries and possess the potential to develop or acquire weapons of mass destruction. Maintaining a stable balance in Asia will be a complex task. The possibility exists that a military competitor with a formidable resource base will emerge in the region. The East Asian littoral—from the Bay of Bengal to the Sea of Japan—represents a particularly challenging area.

In essence, the QDR simply recognized a consensus echoed in various geographic, political, and economic analyses of the post-Cold War international environment: the course of the twentieth century was determined primarily in Europe, whereas the 21st century will be the "Pacific Century." Validating such a thesis is beyond the scope of this paper, but common comparisons emphasize the growing economic and military importance of the Asian region. Overall, U.S. trade with Asia is twice that of Europe and, despite trade deficits, foreign trade with Asia continues to be increasingly robust. China is now the fourth largest economy in the world and continues to expand. With expanding trade, investment, telecommunications, and travel, the interdependence between the U.S. and Asia will continue to increase. In the meantime, potential military flash points such as the Koreas, the Spratly islands, Taiwan, the Philippines, and Indonesia all point to the need for flexible U.S. military options in the event that forceful intervention is required in defense of those interests and objectives.

But flexible military options demand a robust basing infrastructure that may not be attainable in Asia and which, for geographical reasons alone, will look much different from the integrated infrastructure of Europe. "For nearly half a century," Eliot Cohen noted, "the American military organized itself to fight a short, extremely intense battle in Europe from large fixed bases dispersed over relatively short distances. Whatever a future war in Asia might look like, that will not be it." Similarly, the QDR acknowledges the necessity of pursuing basing and infrastructure agreements with partners in the region:

> The density of U.S. basing and en route infrastructure is lower than in other critical regions.
>
> The United States also has less assurance of access to facilities in the region. This places a premium on securing additional access and infrastructure agreements and on developing systems capable of sustained operations at great distances with minimal theatre-based support.

The QDR is silent on when, where, and to what extent U.S. forces will be forward based in Asia, but future alignments will be part of an emerging global posture with the goal to "render forward forces capable of swiftly defeating an adversary's military and political objectives with only modest reinforcement." Should U.S. intervention become necessary in this regard, the enabling force will draw from capabilities both in and out of the theatre. According to the QDR, these capabilities will include a "new combination of immediately employable forward stationed and deployed forces; globally available reconnaissance, strike, and command and control assets; information operations capabilities; and rapidly deployable, highly lethal and sustainable forces." Also key to this new global posture, the QDR explains, are capabilities and forces located in the continental United States and in space, including long-range strike aircraft and special operations forces to leverage forward forces, strengthen conventional deterrence, and support pre-emptive strikes.

The Primacy of AD HOC Military Coalitions

The role played by America's political and military allies has shifted quite dramatically since the end of the Cold War. Allies in Europe were united by membership in the NATO alliance.

Pledged to a common cause, they trained and equipped to interoperable standards, and viewed their homeland and the battlefield to be one and the same. Although initial post-Cold War formulations of military strategy and force planning failed to account for allied contributions and warfighting capabilities—the Bottom Up Review in 1993, for example, does not mention them— increased attention was paid to what the allies could bring to the fight during the last three armed conflicts.

However, allied military contributions have declined significantly from those planned for Cold War battlefields. Indeed, their contributions today are, for the most part, better measured in terms of political support and access to facilities rather than firepower. Whereas during the Cold War, the U.S. and its European NATO partners were united in common cause against the Soviet Union, the often mercurial relationship between America and its military allies now seems better characterized as a series of temporary partnerships—with some of its partners proving more reliable than others.

When President George H. Bush articulated his views on the use of military force in support of U.S. foreign policy in 1993, he posited that, in the post-Cold War world, multilateral support was desirable but not essential. This was a dramatic departure from the past. Although the U.S. had occasionally acted unilaterally during the Cold War—for example, the 1986 air attack on Libya—by and large the U.S. conducted itself as a staunch advocate of collective security and multilateralism. Since the end of the Cold War, however, two noticeable patterns have emerged in managing coalition warfare: (1) the ad hoc approach to coalition-building for contingency operations; and (2) the U.S. need for diplomatic or economic, rather than military support from its allies. Both patterns are clearly reflected in allied contributions to coalition military operations in Iraq, Kosovo, and, most recently, Afghanistan.

Before the Iraqi invasion of Kuwait in August 1990, only the United Arab Emirates (UAE) asked the U.S. to demonstrate its military commitment to the region. The other Persian Gulf states feared that such a move might provoke the conflict. After the invasion, when the U.S. announced it would act militarily to reverse Iraqi aggression, assembling a broad ad hoc coalition to legitimize the intervention became essential. In a series of demarches, the U.S. engaged key countries in the Middle East including Egypt, Syria, Saudi Arabia, and Turkey. Equally important was obtaining access to Saudi Arabia to prepare for and launch the attack to expel Iraqi forces from Kuwait. Although troops from other countries, particularly France and the United Kingdom, participated in the ensuing air and ground operations, the bulk of the heavy lifting was conducted by U.S. military forces.

In Kosovo, the United States did not face the task of putting together an ad hoc coalition but, rather, keeping it together. Engaged in the Balkans since the end of the Cold War, NATO had become increasingly frustrated in dealing with Slobodan Milosevic and the genocidal violence in Bosnia and Croatia. When diplomatic negotiations failed to bring peace to Kosovo, NATO members resolved in March 1999 to use force to compel the Milosevic regime to cease the repression in Kosovo. That is not to say, however, that the alliance remained steadfast in its resolve throughout the conflict. Certainly the German, Italian, and Greek governments had serious reservations about the military option, and might have vetoed the entire operation had they envisioned a 78-day air bombardment and the prospect of a ground invasion. Throughout the campaign, NATO's cohesion hung in the balance, inviting repeated Serbian efforts to divide the member states.

With NATO's credibility at risk, maintaining the coalition throughout the air campaign became an objective unto itself. Yet trepidation over alliance maintenance was driven far more by the need to preserve the political legitimacy of the air campaign than the useful but modest resources that NATO countries brought to the air war over the former Yugoslavia. For example, out of the total 28,018 weapons delivered against targets in Kosovo, Montenegro, and Serbia, the total non- U.S. allied contribution was a meager 17%. As it turned out, this was perhaps a desirable outcome, as there were transaction costs in managing the allied air campaign. The coalition provided the legitimacy perceived as necessary for the U.S. and its partners to intervene in the internal affairs of a sovereign state (even if it was ruled by a despotic regime). But the premium paid for this imprimatur came in the form of constraints on the conduct of the air campaign. Gen. Wesley Clark, who at the time was NATO's Supreme Allied Commander Europe (SACEUR), described specifically how differences in campaign objectives can impact the prosecution of the war and the selection of specific targets:

On this issue we were exposing what I came to understand as a fundamental difference within the alliance on the nature of the campaign. The United States was increasingly committed to the idea of strategic strikes, going after the heart of Milosovic's power. The Europeans, or at least the French and a few others, were more interested in limiting the strikes to Kosovo, trying to hit ground forces, and avoid actions that might antagonize or damage Serbia further.

Perhaps in recognition of this experience, the U.S. did not seek out coalition partners to fight alongside American forces in Afghanistan, but instead seized on securing an ad hoc international mandate to prosecute a global war on terrorism. To this end, by March 2002, the United States received 46 declarations of support; NATO invoked Article V of the

Washington Treaty for the first time in its history, declaring that an attack on any NATO member equated to an attack on them all; and over 136 countries offered some sort of military assistance.

Once again, however, the support the United States needed from its allies was not military, but economic and diplomatic. Financial actions freezing the assets of suspected terrorist organizations were important, as were increased law enforcement cooperation and financial assistance to Afghanistan. Military contributions from other nations, such as the U.K.'s commandos, and special operations forces from Australia and New Zealand, provided needed specialized capabilities, but in the main were eclipsed by the U.S. commitment in manpower and firepower. Operating in one of the world's most remote regions, U.S. and allied forces were also aided considerably by the establishment of forward bases in Uzbekistan, Kyrgyzstan, and Tajikistan. The addition of these Central Asian states to the expanding list of America's ad hoc allies reaffirmed the emerging trend in U.S. efforts to manage allied contributions to coalition military campaigns: seek international support and access to facilities while selectively inviting allies to participate in planning and conducting U.S.-led military operations.

This need for selectivity is due largely to a widening disparity between U.S. military capabilities and those of its principal allies. Simply put, many prospective partners have relatively little to offer militarily. This trend in relative U.S. military superiority appears to be accelerating, with little prospect that the allies will fund the modernization programs to narrow the gap. The Gulf War provided the first glimpse of this capabilities gap, with the U.S. demonstrating the dividends resulting from investments in information technology, systems integration, stealth technologies, and precision weapons. While U.S. capabilities continued to improve in the 1990s, NATO forces remained incapable of performing the type of operations American forces conducted in 1991. For example, NATO leaders acknowledged that the European members of the alliance could not have undertaken the mission in Kosovo without U.S. participation. In the wake of Afghanistan, where the U.S.

conducted the air war almost unilaterally, the United States urged its allies to emphasize priorities such as special forces and low density, high demand (LD/HD) systems, or to pool their forces and develop national specializations.

The factors that have caused this gap to develop are not easily ameliorated. The United States spends over 60% more on defense than its European allies, and that spread is widening. In investment accounts, the gap is even wider—the U.S. outspends Europe in procurement and R&D by a two-to-one margin. The European position is worsened further by the fractionation of its investment among multiple nations. Meanwhile, the United States is transforming its military into an information-intensive, manpowerlean force, while European investments in similar transformational initiatives remain quite modest. With few opportunities available to close this gap, it is likely that the United States will depend on its European allies less and less for military contributions during a future war.

An Amplification of the Anti-Access/Area Denial Problem

Although the Cold War ended more than a decade ago, many of the plans, concepts, and forces that underpinned U.S. power projection are still with us. Among them is planning based on lengthy deployment schedules, as well as dispatching forces to forward bases with robust infrastructure, akin to the main operating bases that characterized Western Europe. Indeed, this is exactly how the United States prepared for the Gulf War when, over approximately six months, great quantities of warmaking materiel were transported to launch Desert Storm. But adversaries draw lessons from combat too, and the post-Gulf War consensus was that a future opponent would take every conceivable measure to deny U.S. abilities to build up a regional presence in preparation for a counter-offensive. As such, this "anti-access" capability—using political and military means to thwart the deployment of U.S. military forces into a region—has emerged as a critical area in current Pentagon planning.

In 1997, Congress commissioned a distinguished group of strategists and retired senior military officers known as the

National Defense Panel (NDP) to review U.S. military strategy in conjunction with the ongoing Quadrennial Defense Review. The NDP formally laid out what would become known as the "anti-access" challenge:

The cornerstone of America's continued military preeminence is our ability to project combat power rapidly and virtually unimpeded to widespread areas of the world. Much of our power projection capability depends on sustained access to regions of concern. Any number of circumstances might compromise our forward presence (both bases and forward operating forces) and therefore diminish our ability to apply military power, reducing our military and political influence in key regions of the world. For political (domestic or regional) reasons, allies might be coerced not to grant the United States access to their sovereign territory. Hostile forces might threaten punitive strikes (perhaps using weapons of mass destruction) against nations considering an alliance with the United States...

Even if we retain the necessary bases and port infrastructure to support forward-deployed forces, they will be vulnerable to strikes that could reduce or neutralize their utility. Precision strikes, weapons of mass destruction, and cruise and ballistic missiles all present threats to our forward presence, particularly as standoff ranges increase.

Debate over the NDP's conclusions has dominated defense policy discussions ever since. In the first QDR, completed in 1997, defense planners warned that adversaries would probably employ weapons of mass destruction against deploying U.S. forces: "In particular, the threat or use of chemical and biological weapons (CBW) is a likely condition of future warfare, including in the early stages of war to disrupt U.S. operations and logistics." The most recent QDR elevated concern for future anti-access strategies even further, emphasizing that "projecting and sustaining U.S. forces in distant anti-access or area-denial environments and defeating anti-access and areadenial threats" would be a high priority operational objective in wartime.

Given this emphasis, what do the three wars considered here tell us about anti-access trends? For analytic purposes, we reduced the access problem to three critical focus areas: politics, geography and infrastructure, and enemy military threats to forward bases.

The Political Dimension of Anti-Access

Whether American forces are based overseas or in the continental United States, the U.S. needs to gain political approval from foreign nations to use their territory and airspace during conflict. Foreign bases from which U.S. forces operate in peacetime are also subject to continuing constraints and pressures, even from close allies, and access rights can constitute a pressure point in negotiations. Now, more than ever, U.S. policy is to develop strong relations with host countries to minimize the threat of political access problems. Political access constraints typically depend on the type of mission the U.S. plans to conduct from host nation bases. Airlift, refueling, surveillance missions, covert special forces assistance, and naval port visits gain approval from a host country far more easily than deploying ground forces or conducting strike operations. The host country's level of perceived threat also plays an important role in determining whether or not to grant access.

During the Gulf War, various nations previously reluctant to permit a large scale U.S. presence on their soil reversed that policy following Iraq's invasion of Kuwait. Still, the United States encountered several political access difficulties in deploying its forces to the Gulf. Throughout the deployment, Spain required individual clearance requests for each flight. For a time, France allowed only two aircraft per hour through its airspace. Portuguese, Italian, and German actions also slowed airlift flows. Saudi Arabia initially refused to allow the Army and Marine Corps to conduct gunnery training or permit B-52 basing. But overall, political access problems did not have a major impact on the conduct of the war.

In subsequent crises in the Gulf, however, political problems have surfaced on a recurring basis:

In the September 1996 Irbil crisis, when Iraqi forces attacked the Kurds in northern Iraq, Saudi Arabia and Turkey refused permission to conduct offensive operations from their soil with the 100 USAF fighters based in those nations. Jordan refused to permit the United States to deploy 30 fighters to that nation. Because the target was located beyond the range of carrier-based aircraft, the U.S. was forced to use cruise missiles launched from bombers and ships to strike unrelated air defense sites in southern Iraq. Access problems continued to bedevil the U.S. in the aftermath of the crisis. Kuwait agreed to host eight F-117 strike aircraft but delayed in permitting U.S. Army force deployments, causing additional diplomatic embarrassment.

In the December 1998 Desert Fox strikes against Iraq, half of the forward-based USAF fighters in the Gulf—about 60—could not be employed because Saudi Arabia and the United Arab Emirates objected. Combat aircraft operating from Kuwait and Oman took part in the operation. However, Saudi Arabia and the UAE did allow support operations, such as tanker refueling sorties.

Political access issues were equally present in the Kosovo conflict and, to some degree, influenced how NATO air operations were actually conducted. Indeed, the linkage between access and airpower employment in the Balkans first surfaced in October 1995 when the Italians, apparently irritated by their limited political influence over air strikes against Bosnia, attempted to improve their negotiating position by refusing base access to U.S. F-117s. Later, in 1999, there was concern that Italian domestic opposition would prevent the use of the crucial NATO air base at Aviano. Five days after the start of operations, Italian authorities insisted to Gen. Clark that unless the coalition focused its air power efforts against the Serbian forces committing atrocities in Kosovo, Italy would deny access to its facilities. As one might expect, Clark acceded to Italian demands and focused the air campaign on Serbian ground forces. France also denied use of its air space for UK-based B-52s carrying cruise missiles, forcing the bombers to fly around Spain and across the Mediterranean to deliver their weapons.

Although the United States had not developed formal basing arrangements in countries neighbouring Afghanistan prior to Enduring Freedom, the commander of USAF forces in Europe (USAFE), Gen. Gregory Martin, observed that many nations supporting U.S. combat operations in Afghanistan had participated in U.S. training conferences and operations, greatly facilitating access to airspace and bases. Following the Washington D.C. and New York attacks in September 2001, the United States made multiple requests to Pakistan, including unrestricted access to Pakistani airspace and bases. Approval was granted almost immediately. In return, the United States pledged $800 million in aid, assistance in eliminating Pakistan's foreign debt, and reconsideration of the previously blocked F-16 sale. The U.S. also eliminated economic sanctions related to the Pakistani nuclear program that blocked the provision of credits, military sales, economic assistance, and loans to Pakistan.

To support Enduring Freedom, the United States successfully obtained access to other Central Asian nations and developed 13 bases in and around Afghanistan; associated costs have not been revealed.

Political access difficulties were also encountered elsewhere. In the buildup to combat operations, Saudi Arabia signaled that it might not permit the United States to employ its new command and control centre at Prince Sultan Air Base to direct offensive air operations. A few months later, the Saudi government floated rumors that Riyadh might ask the United States to remove its forces and personnel, and the United States has built a similar facility in Qatar to reduce dependence on the uncertain Saudi position. The long-term viability of U.S. bases in central Asia has also raised concerns. Because Osama bin Laden's terrorist tactics were prompted in part by the presence of U.S. forces in Saudi Arabia, U.S. forces concentrated at bases in Central Asia might also be subjected to attacks by Islamic and nationalist forces.

Although political access issues were resolved successfully in all three conflicts, they loom large over U.S. war planning for a future attack on Iraq. In November 2002, Saudi Arabia's apparent unwillingness to provide access to bases in the Kingdom was such that initial U.S. war plans presumed that fighters based there would be unavailable for combat. Instead, the war plan was tailored around a U.S. deployment of five divisions and five aircraft carriers to the region, showcasing again the impact of political access constraints on force employment options.

The Geographical and Infrastructure Dimension of Anti-Access

The emerging strategic focus on Asia, with its vast distances and lack of suitable infrastructure, magnifies the importance of "access insensitive" forces, such as aircraft carriers and long-range bombers that do not require close-in regional basing. Past U.S. military operations in Asia illustrate this point. In the early stages of the Vietnam conflict, for example, carrier-based naval forces provided about half the strike sorties flown in both North and South Vietnam until the base infrastructure was sufficiently developed to handle a larger quantity of land-based fighters. The same held true for more recent operations in Afghanistan. Because of the lack of basing infrastructure within effective fighter range of Afghanistan targets, the United States relied primarily on carrier-based naval forces and bombers to provide striking power during offensive operations. Overall, the bomber force delivered 70% of total weapons, carrier-based fighters about 20%, and land-based fighters about 10%.

Future operations will likely continue to confront the tyranny of distance and infrastructure constraints encountered in Afghanistan. The airfield database maintained by the National Imagery and Mapping Agency (NIMA) provides some insights into Asia's infrastructure. Asia contains 14% of the world's airfields (excluding Russia, China, and North Korea). In comparison, the North American continent—a substantially smaller geographical area, particularly when considering the oceans separating many areas in Asia—contains 32% of the world's airfields, while Western Europe—an even smaller area—contains 18%.

Constructing a network of facilities in Western Europe and the Gulf sufficient to support U.S. power projection forces took decades of sustained effort. Developing a similar infrastructure in Asia could take even longer. Moreover, Asia's vast size suggests that pre-positioned assets and facilities may not be in the right spot to provide the support needed for future conflicts. Given these huge distances, the United States could expend enormous resources on developing regional infrastructure and still "get it wrong."

The high cost of developing basing infrastructure is also a significant complicating factor. A single USAF air base in Europe was conservatively estimated to cost roughly $1.5 billion in current year dollars. Base structure development in Saudi Arabia—a single country with a much smaller land mass than Asia—was estimated to cost about $30 billion. Constructing bases in multiple Asian locations could cost several times that amount. Moreover, Saudi Arabia and NATO had the resources to fund most of this base development, but few countries in South, Central, and East Asia possess such wealth. Obtaining approval to invest U.S. resources for overseas base development would also confront domestic political opposition, as Congress is typically more supportive of investment in local, rather than overseas, bases. Overall, distance and infrastructure constraints will place new emphasis on "access insensitive" forces in future Asian conflicts.

The Military Anti-Access Dimension

Anti-access military threats consist of air defense systems to deny access to regional air space; mines, submarines, and naval combatants to interdict shipping lanes, disrupt sealift, and generally threaten friendly naval and amphibious forces and operations; and deep-strike systems and weapons of mass destruction to hold forward bases and forces at risk while intimidating regional U.S. allies. As Deputy Secretary of Defense Wolfowitz remarked in November 2001 regarding operations in Afghanistan:

Although our access to Afghanistan has improved steadily and most recently spectacularly, we have been forced by circumstances to operate from very great distances, and this against an enemy whose active efforts to deny us access have met so far with little success. It's only a shadow of what a more determined, more advanced enemy could do. In none of the three conflicts did adversaries succeed in preventing U.S. force deployments. Therefore, we cannot document a trend that hostile military capabilities might deny access to U.S. military forces in the future. The worldwide proliferation of military capabilities, however, including sophisticated air defense systems and deep-strike weapons, suggests that the minimal military opposition the U.S. and its allies have faced in the last three major campaigns will grow in quantity and quality in the future.

In sum, the experiences of U.S. forces deployed overseas in the last three major conflicts suggest that the trend of anti-access/area denial needs to be considered seriously. Since the Gulf War, the United States has encountered a series of political and geographic constraints on its ability to position and employ its forces with maximum effect.

At the least, such constraints have added cost, risk, and inconvenience; at worst, access denial has caused the U.S. to abandon prudent courses of military action and to pursue less effective substitutes. That these constraints, to include an emerging array of military anti-access capabilities, will continue to plague U.S. forces in the future is a certainty. Their ultimate effect on achieving warfighting aims may depend considerably on how successful the U.S. is in developing forces and operational concepts that can overcome these hurdles.

Increasing Adversarial Action to Undermine the Threat and use of Military Force

Iraq suffered a shattering defeat in the Gulf War. Its vaunted air defense system was degraded and dismantled. Its air force was forced to flee piecemeal to Iran and its small navy was destroyed. And its demoralized ground forces either surrendered en masse or fled the battle area. But Iraq's defeat was not total. Iraqi Scud missiles rained on targets in Saudi Arabia and Israel, mines laid in the northern Persian Gulf nearly sank two U.S. Navy ships, and low-level air defenses inside Iraq proved particularly persistent.

During the culminating phase of allied military operations, many of the elite Republican Guard divisions managed to escape from Kuwait with their equipment. Finally, and perhaps most ominously, Iraq succeeded in shielding its vast clandestine network of facilities for WMD research and development.

That Iraq managed to accomplish this in spite of U.S. military actions ultimately spurred professional military thought—even cooperation between states—on how to undermine the threatened use of U.S. conventional force in future conflicts. In one prominent example, Yugoslav defense specialists in 1998 met with Iraqi military officers in Baghdad seeking to learn more about ways to degrade the effectiveness of U.S. air operations. More recently, in 2002, Yugoslav air defense officers traveled to Iraq to assist in defending against a potential U.S. attack. Analysis of the three conflicts indicates that some Iraqi successes were evident in enemy strategies adopted in both the Serbian and Afghanistan conflicts. In this section, we review attempts by Iraq, Serbia, and the Taliban regime in Afghanistan to weaken U.S. domestic support for combat operations, to fracture alliances, and to degrade the effectiveness of military operations.

Overall, the three adversaries consistently sought to deflect attack with threats calculated to heighten perceived U.S. sensitivities to casualties; to exploit instances of collateral damage to evoke international condemnation and weaken coalition resolve; to reduce their vulnerability to offensive strikes through a variety of means (air defenses, camouflage, concealment, deception, dispersal, mobility, and hard and deeply buried facilities); and to stoke the fear of escalation and use of weapons of mass destruction. Given the wide differences in the characteristics of these three wars, the consistencies in adversary strategies and concepts lend credence to the notion that these same issues may recur in future conflicts.

Perceived U.S. Sensitivity to Casualties

All three adversaries believed that the United States was sensitive to combat losses and attempted either to deter U.S. actions or limit force employment options by emphasizing the prospect for significant American casualties. In part, this perception grew out of assessments of the Vietnam War, when mounting U.S. casualties proved crucial in turning American public opinion against the conflict. More recently, lessons drawn from the U.S. withdrawal from Beirut following the bombing of the Marine barracks in 1983, and from Somalia following the loss of U.S. troops in 1993, were often cited by opponents as testaments to their efforts to weaken American domestic support for military operations abroad. For example, in reference to the Somali operation, Osama bin Laden stated in a 1998 interview:

> *They [Islamic soldiers] had thought the Americans were like the Russians, so they trained and prepared. They were stunned when they discovered how low was the morale of the American soldier. America had entered with 30,000 soldiers in addition to thousands of soldiers from different countries around the world.... As I said our boys were shocked by the low morale of the American soldier and they realized that the American soldier was a paper tiger. He was unable to endure the strikes that were dealt to his army, so he fled, and America had to stop all its bragging.... After a few blows, it forgot all about those titles and rushed out of Somalia in shame and disgrace, dragging the bodies of its soldiers.... I was in Sudan when this happened. I was very happy to learn of that great defeat that America suffered, so was every Muslim.87*

Citing U.S. experiences in Vietnam, Saddam Hussein's objective was to foster images of massive U.S. casualties in the act of dislodging Iraqi forces from Kuwait. As one captured Iraqi general revealed, Hussein believed that "Americans would not be able to stand the loss of even hundreds of soldiers, that Iraqis were prepared to sacrifice thousands." To do this, Hussein's forces constructed elaborate defensive lines, consisting of belts of barbed wire, mines, and fire trenches filled with crude oil, fortified with 150 battalions of tube and rocket artillery. The Iraqi plan envisioned saturating coalition ground forces stalled in front of the belts with shell and rocket fire to inflict heavy casualties.

Similarly, Yugoslav strategy since World War II had been to draw an adversary into its territory and then inflict significant losses through hitand- run partisan/guerrilla operations. In the absence of a ground threat, however, Serb forces dispersed and hid from air attack to outlast the political will of the fractious NATO alliance. U.S. commanders clearly recognized that alliance cohesion was NATO's most vulnerable area and was constantly threatened by casualties, attrition, and collateral damage. Moreover, combat losses could enable Serbia to wait out the alliance.

Gen. Clark warned his commanders that "[t]he first measure of merit is not to lose aircraft, minimize the loss of aircraft." Clark later explained in his wartime memoirs: I was motivated by a larger political-military rationale: if we wanted to keep this campaign going indefinitely, we had to protect our air fleet. Nothing would hurt us more with public opinion than headlines that screamed: 'NATO LOSES TEN AIRPLANES IN TWO DAYS.' Take losses like that, divide it into the total number of aircraft committed, and the time limits on the campaign would be clear. Milosevic could wait us out.

Finally, the Taliban "hide and wait" strategy was similar to that pursued by both Iraq and Serbia— inflict as many casualties as possible on U.S. forces. The strategy was to camouflage, conceal, and disperse Taliban military units as a prelude to inflicting high casualties on arriving U.S. ground forces—a strategy similar to that employed successfully by the Mujahedin against the Soviets.

Taliban commanders would taunt their Northern Alliance opponents with predictions of death when the Americans attacked. But the lethal combination of air power, precision weapons, and special operations forces laid waste this strategy. One analyst observed later that "[t]hey were fighting an air force they could not see." Precision weapons proved effective against Taliban hiding places, preventing them from riding out the bombing and, in the end, Taliban and al Qaeda forces suffered far more casualties than the United States.

Collateral Damage

Adversaries attempted to exploit collateral damage and civilian deaths in all three conflicts to gain sympathy, separate the United States from its allies, and reduce the effectiveness of U.S. and allied/coalition air operations. In the process, senior U.S. decision-makers (both military and civilian) were encouraged to assume greater roles in the target selection and approval process. The implications of this "reach forward" are discussed in more detail in Section III.

During the Iraq conflict, the United States attempted to minimize collateral damage for humane reasons and political concerns. One Arab official noted, "If the United States attacks civilian targets, you will lose the war. It will be seen as the infidels slaughtering Arabs. Saddam can get away with it, but you can't." The potential that civilian deaths would fracture the coalition was foremost in the minds of U.S. officials.

A ten-page "no fire" list forbade any damage to mosques, hospitals, schools, and cultural sites. Statements from U.S. officials during combat reflected the painstaking tasks American planners assumed in selecting targets, weapons, and attack routes. President George H. Bush declared: "I'd like to emphasize that we are going to extraordinary, and I would venture unprecedented, lengths to avoid damage to civilians and holy places.... We are doing everything possible and with great success to minimize collateral damage...."

The Iraqi government worked hard to exploit mistakes or unintended casualties, publicizing civilian deaths, and exaggerating death tolls. And mistakes occurred. In Najaf, 50 houses were damaged and reporters were called in to view the dead. In Al Dour, 23 houses were flattened and many civilians killed. A bridge attack in Nasiriyan killed 50 noncombatants, and an errant bomb hit a hospital in Kuwait City, killing several foreign medical personnel. Basra neighbourhoods were hit several times, killing several hundred Iraqis. The Iraqi government consistently exploited these attacks, providing video of those killed and allowing the wounded to be interviewed. Radio Baghdad broadcasts proclaimed that the coalition had bombed scientific, economic, cultural, medical, civilian, and holy sites. While Human Rights Watch estimated that between 2,000-3,000 Iraqi civilians were killed during the conflict, Iraq claimed that allied bombing had taken 7,000 innocent lives. For the first four weeks of operations, U.S. air targeteers managed to avoid major collateral damage.

But on 13 February, an F-117 struck the Al Firdos bunker in Baghdad, which U.S. planners believed was sheltering Iraqi Intelligence Service personnel. The penetrating precision weapon not only killed some Iraqi intelligence personnel, but also hundreds of civilians who had taken shelter in the bunker. The Iraqi government sensationally exploited this incident, leading the White House and Joint Chiefs to rein in the air campaign and demand high-level approval of any proposed air attack on Baghdad. Thus, the political fallout from the attack managed to achieve what Iraqi air defenses could not: curtailing air strikes on Baghdad. From Gen. Colin Powell's viewpoint, a few more events like Al Firdos and the coalition would have come apart.

Concern over inflicting excessive casualties in strikes against the retreating Iraqi army also played a role in the U.S decision to halt operations before destroying the fleeing Republican Guard.

Collateral damage constraints played an even more dominant role in the Serbian operation owing to similar concerns about alliance cohesion. A fundamental difference of opinion led to immediate friction in the alliance. The United States wanted to conduct strategic strikes to go after the heart of Milosevic's power, while many European leaders wanted to avoid attacks that would severely damage Serbia. Obviously, civilian deaths could inflame world opinion and lead to additional pressure on the United States to curtail bombing. A RAND study of the air campaign concluded that "pressures to avoid civilian casualties and unintended damage to nonmilitary structures were greater in Allied Force than in any previous campaign involving U.S. forces."

The issue of collateral damage preoccupied Gen. Clark, the Allied Force military commander. He remembered the attack on the Al Firdos bunker and how it had impacted the air campaign. He accordingly sought to avoid such a problem in Serbia. Once past the pre-designated target set, almost every proposed target proved controversial for one reason or another. For the U.S. approval chain, each target needed to be individually analyzed for its military value and the possibility for collateral damage. Using overhead imagery and computer modeling of each weapon type against various physical target characteristics, planners attempted to predict infrastructure damage and risks of unanticipated civilian casualties. The target then underwent additional review in Washington and finally ended up on President Clinton's desk for approval. NATO executed a similar process.

Collateral damage concerns exerted a powerful influence over the conflict. For example, early in the campaign, Washington disapproved NATO plans to strike eight bridges, apparently because the Joint Staff believed that too many civilians would be killed. Ben Lambeth observes in his book that a "nontrivial" number of sorties were cancelled before launch or disappproved before weapons release out of concern for collateral damage. Some U.S. officers referred to these targets as "morally hardened."

Despite these attempts, civilians were killed and Yugoslav authorities, like the Iraqis in 1991, attempted to drive wedges within the NATO alliance and curtail air operations by exploiting civilian deaths and exaggerating losses. Although it backfired psychologically at home, the Serbs publicized almost every incident, attempting to make the front pages of the Western press. Commander of Allied Forces in Southern Europe, Adm. James Ellis, observed that NATO public affairs efforts were "not a shining moment for the U.S. or NATO. The enemy was better at this than we were...and far more nimble."

NATO typically proved unable to respond quickly to Serb attempts to exploit collateral damage or U.S. targeting errors. The most famous example of the latter was the bombing of the Chinese embassy, which for a time severely strained U.S.-Sino relations. Meanwhile, concerns over collateral damage also resulted in a White House decision to stop using cluster weapons to avoid negative publicity. For the entire conflict, Serb officials claimed a civilian death toll ranging from 1,200 to 5,000. After extensive on-scene investigations, Human Rights Watch concluded that about 500 civilians were killed—on average about six per day.

The Taliban government employed similar propaganda strategies during Enduring Freedom. According to Afghan reporters, the Taliban routinely altered media reports to inflate civilian casualties (and minimize their own losses). For example, just over three weeks into the campaign, the Taliban claimed

1,500 to 1,600 civilians had been killed. Western media frequently published Taliban casualty reports with the caveat that the loss totals were unconfirmed, but the Arab and Muslim media reported them as fact. An Afghan reporter noted, "Our bosses called this the war against the Christian crusaders. They thought that if the people were told that the Americans were deliberately bombing civilians, they would rise up and kill the invaders."

To some degree, the Taliban succeeded in these efforts. In Pakistan, tens of thousands of protestors stormed through Quetta and Karachi. Thousands of Pakistanis also joined Taliban ground forces. U.S. officials noted in press briefings that the same sorts of procedures employed in Allied Force to minimize collateral damage were also employed in Enduring Freedom. President George W. Bush made low collateral damage a key criterion to avoid inflaming public opinion in the Islamic world. This led to delays in decisionmaking— not only weapon selection but also fuse-settings were subject to high-level review— and apparent reductions in effectiveness. According to the press, this resulted in missed opportunities during the first six weeks to kill senior Taliban and al Qaeda officials, including Mullah Omar. As one Air Force officer commented, "We knew we had some of the big boys.

The process is so slow that by the time we got the clearances, and everybody had put in their two cents, we called it off." Additionally, the Taliban deliberately mixed in with civilians to avoid being targeted. One U.S. official noted:

"Our mores in America are, we don't kill innocent people. We have extreme sensitivity to that. For people to say we missed opportunities, that to me oversimplifies the situation." The Taliban moved soldiers and military hardware into civilian neighbourhoods, mosques, and cultural sites. Whole villages were employed as human shields. "They've gotten smarter every day. They know what we say we're not going to hit—and they go there," observed another U.S. official.

Given this consistent pattern, future opponents will attempt to increase the chances of collateral damage by commingling military and civilian assets while exploiting civilian deaths in the same manner as the Iraqi, Serbian, and Taliban governments. In recent years, for example, Iraq has constructed civilian housing over several of its bunker complexes to increase the probability of civilian deaths in the event of U.S. strikes against these facilities.

Efforts to Degrade Military Effectiveness

Dispersal, Camouflage, Concealment, Deception, and Mobility. In the Gulf War, Iraq employed dispersal, camouflage, concealment, deception, and mobility to reduce the effectiveness of U.S. and coalition air power. Before the onset of coalition military operations, Iraq moved key instrumentation from air defense command posts and removed computer equipment from oil refineries for post-conflict recovery and reconstitution. Iraqi engineers also emptied water reservoirs and filled them with oil to maintain POL supplies. At the same time, Iraq successfully applied camouflage, deception, mobility, and dispersal to preserve its ballistic missile force; coalition forces reportedly did not succeed in destroying a single mobile missile launcher.

Furthermore, Iraq concealed the true scale and nature of its WMD development facilities. Although U.S. intelligence before the conflict concluded that Iraq possessed 23 such facilities, post-war UN inspections revealed 252 sites.

Iraqi air defense forces opposing operations Northern and Southern Watch over the past decade further refined mobility, deception, and concealment techniques to blunt U.S air power. An Air Force pilot assessed that the Iraqis were "getting really smooth. They can pick up and move in an hour or so. They can fire a missile, break down and leave before we can get in and drop a bomb."

During Allied Force, Serbian forces also successfully employed camouflage, concealment, deception, dispersal, and mobility to reduce their vulnerability to allied air attack. While prosecuting the Serb assault into Kosovo, Serb forces dispersed and concealed their tanks and vehicles in villages and forests. Digging in and hiding had constituted the heart of Yugoslav doctrine since World War II, and Serb forces proved masters at blending into the terrain. Elements of the Serbian air defense system, such as radars and surface-to-air missile launchers, were moved routinely to frustrate allied targeting, thereby allowing the Serbs to maintain air defenses sufficient to continuously complicate and threaten allied air operations.

To further compound allied targeting problems, the Serbs made tank decoys out of tetra-pak milk cartons and artillery pieces out of stovepipes (complete with infrared signatures), used smoke to hide targets, and employed camouflage materials to hide military equipment from NATO air forces. Post-conflict analyses indicated that many tanks believed destroyed were most likely decoys.

Worst case estimates suggest that coalition air power may have destroyed only 58 pieces of equipment in contrast to the 744 pieces NATO claimed soon after the conflict. Of Serbia's 25 known mobile SA-6 batteries, NATO spokesmen confirmed that only three had been destroyed. The official USAF account of the air war over Serbia concluded: "The Air Force must continue to investigate new technologies and techniques for locating hidden or dispersed ground force elements with targeting quality accuracy, and rapidly passing that data to the 'shooters.'"

The Taliban and al Qaeda employed similar techniques in Afghanistan with varying degrees of success. The Taliban adopted a strategy similar to the one the Mujahedin had used so successfully against the Soviets: hide in the terrain and then wait to inflict losses on the invader. The strategy enjoyed mixed results, as Taliban fielded forces proved increasingly vulnerable to precision weapons: "We couldn't gather in large groups because that made a target. We were waiting for our comrades to tell us what to do, but there was nothing to do but hide."

However, much of the Taliban and al Qaeda leadership evaded capture and remains at large. In addition, some experts speculate that the terrorist organization may have learned from their Afghanistan experience, realizing the perils of centralizing the majority of its organization and training facilities in a single country. Future terrorist organizations dispersed throughout multiple nations may be far more difficult to hunt down and destroy.

Clearly, these sorts of techniques will be adopted in the future. For example, ballistic and cruise missile systems can be fired from mobile launchers, thereby enhancing survivability through dispersal and mobility. Other examples of deception abound. Preparing for their surprise nuclear tests in May 1998, for example, the Indians reportedly utilized their knowledge of U.S. reconnaissance satellites, in combination with a period of frequent sandstorms, to conceal their activity. An Indian nuclear researcher subsequently stated, "It's not a failure of the CIA. It's a matter of their intelligence being good, our deception being better."

Hardened and Deeply Buried Facilities. Hardened and deeply buried facilities aid in deception campaigns by concealing activities from surveillance systems while simultaneously affording protection from air strikes. Such facilities are particularly useful for resources that cannot be effectively dispersed or concealed, such as command and control sites or weapons production facilities. Following the Israeli air strike against the Osirak nuclear facility in 1981, Iraqi engineers built a series of deep underground bunkers that exceeded Warsaw Pact standards for surviving nuclear bursts. Iraq contracted out much of this work. Yugoslav engineers built a series of special "bomb proof" bunkers—nicknamed "Yugos" by U.S. targeteers—for the Iraqi air force. Yugoslavia also constructed hardened shelters for the air defense command posts. Overall, Iraq hardened much of the country's military facilities to reduce its vulnerability to air attack.

Some Iraqi installations were buried at a sufficient depth to be invulnerable to U.S. "hardcase" penetrating weapons. One prominent example was the 12 room bunker constructed 50 feet beneath the guesthouse of the presidential palace in Baghdad. The main entrance was a three-ton steel door, the walls were made of leadlined concrete six feet thick, and the design allowed 25 people to survive in the bunker for a year without resupply. After the war started, the USAF developed and fielded a 4,700 lb. penetrating weapon that became known as the GBU-28. Consisting of an artillery barrel filled with explosives and fitted with laser guidance, the GBU-28 was developed, tested, and deployed in about six weeks. Two GBU-28s were airlifted into theatre and delivered by F-111 fighters in the closing stages of the Gulf War. One may have penetrated a similar bunker and killed many Iraqi senior military officials. In recent years, Iraq has reportedly constructed additional underground complexes in and around Baghdad, presumably of strength sufficient to withstand large U.S. penetrating weapons.

At the behest of Marshall Josip Tito after World War II, Yugoslavia built an extensive series of bunkers designed to shelter military forces if the country came under nuclear attack. Yugoslav planners also envisioned using the bunkers as command centres to direct partisan/guerrilla operations against enemy invaders. In the following decades, Yugoslavia built dozens of deeply buried, hardened bunkers around the nation, particularly in mountainous Bosnia-Herzegovina.

These bunkers had multiple backup systems for communications and power. The Mount Avila bunker, located a few miles southeast of Belgrade, was a multi-story facility buried 100 feet deep. It was capable of supplying the entire Yugoslav general staff with communication equipment, medical facilities, living quarters, and sufficient food to last for months.

Yugoslavia also built huge shelters on the Dalmatian coast to protect naval vessels, although these were judged to be vulnerable to modern precision-guided weapons. Similar hardening efforts were applied to aircraft bases. For example, USAF aircraft repeatedly attacked a bunker facility at the Pristina airfield in Kosovo. Yet, following the conflict, the Serbs towed 11 MiG-21s out from the bunker (which had obviously not been penetrated) and flew the aircraft back to Serbia. In addition, Serb hardening of air defense systems—underground command sites and buried landlines—frustrated NATO efforts to disrupt the Serb air defense network.

Most recently, Taliban and al Qaeda forces employed a large set of caves and bunkers developed following the 1979 Soviet invasion of Afghanistan. At Tora Bora, enemy forces took shelter in approximately 200 separate caves. The Zhawar Kili cave complex near the Pakistan border covered nine square miles with 70 interconnected caves and tunnels, providing miles of protected space.

Similar facilities are proliferating around the world. Following the Gulf War, Libya began building the massive Tarhuna complex 60 km southeast of Tripoli, apparently to produce and store chemical weapons. This nine-square mile facility is buried in the side of a mountain; internal blast doors shield its three tunnel entrances; and 100 feet of sandstone and reinforced concrete protect its six miles of tunnels. Iran has constructed a series of tunnels on its southeast coast to protect its force of ballistic missiles and, working around the clock, is rapidly building other underground shelters. Officials from U.S. Central Command (CENTCOM) described the purpose of the tunnels as "storage or forward deployment facilities for missiles or missile related equipment." The Russians, who constructed vast shelter complexes during the Cold War, continue to build an underground city complex in the Urals. China has constructed underground shelters to protect its mobile ballistic missile forces threatening Taiwan. North Korea (which has a long tradition of burying key complexes) has reportedly excavated up to 22 facilities beneath its numerous mountains to house its nuclear weapons industry.

As indicated by U.S. combat experience in all three conflicts, it is very difficult to estimate the purpose or size of underground facilities. For example, U.S. forces were stunned at the extent of the Zhawar Kili cave complex near Khost and the Pakistan border when ground forces began exploring the area. In addition, the effects of strikes against such facilities often remain unknown. Based on the evidence from these three conflicts and activity worldwide, the presence of hardened and deeply buried facilities will continue to characterize future conflicts. Persistent Low-Level Air Defenses. All three conflicts featured adversary attempts to protect their air space from U.S. and allied/coalition aircraft. In the Iraq and Serbian conflicts, the lethal combination of airborne early warning aircraft (the E-3A and E-2C), advanced air superiority fighters (F-14, F-15, F-16, and F/A-18), and modern airto- air missiles quickly eliminated any fixed-wing interceptor threat. The Taliban launched no fighters.

Trends in ground-based air defenses appear more worrisome. Iraqi air defenses capable of threatening aircraft at medium and high levels were disrupted and eliminated within a few days by coalition tactics, stealth aircraft, and air defense suppression assets. Yet, as has been the case historically, U.S. and allied forces were unable to eliminate low-altitude air defenses such as antiaircraft artillery (AAA) and man-portable SAMs.

During the Soviet invasion of Afghanistan, Stinger missiles are reported to have downed 269 Soviet helicopters and aircraft with only 340 missiles (though such reports may be exaggerated). And more recently in Chechnya, man-portable SAMs are estimated to have caused 66% of Soviet aircraft losses. Although U.S. countermeasures appear to have gained the upper hand against older models, modern infrared (IR) man-portable missiles have greatly increased lethality with the development of advanced seekers resistant to traditional counter-measures such as flares.

Overall, the large number and dispersed nature of these systems made it impossible to eliminate these threats in the Gulf War, leading military commanders to direct flights at medium and high altitudes to minimize vulnerability. This, in turn, greatly reduced the effectiveness of aircraft armed with unguided ordnance—the vast majority of U.S. and allied aircraft in the Gulf War—by greatly reducing their bombing accuracy.

Quite possibly, meetings between Iraqi air defense experts and their Serbian counterparts before Allied Force also provided Serb planners insight into maintaining more effective air defenses. Overall, Serbian air defense systems, of 1960s vintage, were no more capable than Iraq's. In terms of radar-directed SAMs, Serbia possessed about 40 single-rail SA-2 launchers, about 50 four-rail launchers for SA-3s, and 25 SA-6 launchers. As to low-level air defenses, Serbian forces possessed about 850 IR-guided SAMs and thousands of anti-aircraft guns. But Serbian air defense forces, learning lessons derived from Iraqi experience, employed these forces far more effectively to maintain a "threat in being." Elements of the Serbian air defense system, such as radars and SAM launchers, adopted Iraqi tactics employed against Northern and Southern Watch air operations. The Serbs moved to frustrate allied targeting, allowing them to maintain a significant air defense threat and requiring allied commanders to devote a considerable percentage of sorties to defense suppression. The Serbs also fused radar data from disparate locations to reduce vulnerability, using radars in the northern part of the country to detect in-bound NATO aircraft, and to cue air defenses in the south.

The cumulative effect of these operations is evident in the burgeoning demand for electronic warfare platforms to provide tactical jamming for strike aircraft. In the Gulf War, approximately 4% of total combat sorties were electronic warfare missions, flown by EA-6Bs and EF-111s.

In contrast, USAF and USN combat aircraft flew nearly 12,000 sorties in Allied Force, of which roughly 1,318 (11%) were EA-6B electronic warfare sorties. Also instructive here is a comparison of the quantities of EW aircraft deployed in SEAD (Suppression of Enemy Air Defense) operations during Desert Storm and Allied Force.

In the case of the former, the U.S. deployed 88 SEAD/EW aircraft out of a total U.S. fighter/ bomber force of 1,078—about 8% of the force. Data on the total U.S. air combat force for Serbia is not publicly available, but the USAF alone deployed 64 F-16CJs (the current version of the Wild Weasel) out of a total fighter/bomber force of 232—about 27% of the force. Overall, in the Gulf War, 10% of coalition sorties (both electronic warfare and missile shooters) were devoted to suppressing and destroying enemy air defenses. In comparison, the most comprehensive overview of the Serbian air war states that 35% of total allied combat sorties in Serbia were directed against enemy air defenses.

This increased effort did manage to minimize aircraft loss rates, with the U.S. loss rate calculated at .02% in Serbia compared with .05% in Iraq. But again, allied aircraft chose to operate at medium altitudes to minimize the threat posed by Serbian low-altitude air defenses. UAV loss rates, however, were a sobering 250 times higher than manned aircraft, in part because these systems operated within range of the low-level air defenses. The Serbs, having learned from previous allied UAV operations in the mid-1990s, also appeared to employ special tactics to shoot down these aircraft. In Afghanistan, Taliban missile defenses were quickly eliminated, although lowlevel threats persisted and U.S. aircraft were compelled to fly at medium altitudes throughout most of the campaign. When U.S. helicopters operated at low level within range of enemy forces, such as in operation Anaconda, they suffered battle damage and losses from enemy fire.

A key issue for the future is whether the pervasive threat posed in low altitude environments can be extended to medium and higher altitudes with the proliferation of advanced SAM systems such as the SA-10. Compared with previous generation SAMs, the SA-10's radar suite is more powerful and resistant to jamming; the system is equipped with multiple missiles and is easier to relocate; and the missiles themselves feature longer-range, higher speed, and greater agility. Lt. Gen. Michael Short, Allied Force air component commander, admitted:

> I can tell you what I worried about every day and I can tell you what General Clark worried about every day—that somehow Mr. Milosevic would find a way to float an SA-10 or SA-12 up the Danube River, put it together and bring it to bear as a part of this conflict. If that had happened, it would have profoundly changed the balance of the threat and our ability to maintain air superiority.

To put this threat in perspective, USAF Gen. Richard Hawley, the commander of Air Combat Command during Allied Force, noted that B-1Bs (and other non-stealthy aircraft) could not operate survivably in the face of "double digit SAMs," even when employing advanced decoys and other countermeasures. Fortunately, to date, the proliferation of such systems has been limited, largely owing to their high cost. Finally, we should note that this trend is evident in Iraqi preparations for another confrontation with the U.S. and its allies. As noted previously, teams of Iraqi intelligence officers visited Yugoslavia in the aftermath of Allied Force to understand and assess methods the Serbs used to overcome NATO's superior weaponry and protect its military forces from air attack. According to Gen.

Clark, the most significant of these measures "was the ability of Yugoslavia's air defenses to foil NATO electronics by using different radar frequencies and profiles, and by using 'passive tracking' systems that do not give off radiation." We should therefore expect future adversaries to attempt to draw lessons from past conflicts as they seek to identify and exploit weaknesses in the application of U.S. military power.

Weapons of Mass Destruction

Weapons of mass destruction—nuclear, chemical, and biological—were present in all three conflicts to varying degrees and, as expected, emerged as a critical issue of concern for both U.S. policymakers and potential opponents. WMD accordingly will likely form a focal point in future conflicts. These weapons are regarded as force multipliers for weaker nations when dealing with American conventional superiority. As was widely reported, a top Indian military official noted in the aftermath of the Gulf War: "[T]he lesson of Desert Storm is don't mess with the United States without nuclear weapons."

Such weapons have the potential to destroy or disrupt forward deployed U.S. conventional forces, strike at the American homeland, increase the power and prestige of possessing nations, and deter U.S. intervention and the willingness of neighbouring nations to provide basing for American forces—all at a low relative cost compared with conventional forces. This combination of attributes has stimulated proliferation of these weapons around the world. As Serbian president Slobodan Milosevic noted in May 1999: "I think your strategic thinkers are also beginning to understand that missiles and other sophisticated weapons will not always be the monopoly of high-tech societies. And with the example it is now setting, we can see the day when lesser nations will be able to retaliate. The development of these weapons is taking place so fast there is not a single spot on the planet that cannot be reached. America can be reached from this part of the world."

Before the Gulf War, Iraq possessed an array of chemical and biological agents and had been actively seeking nuclear weapons for several decades. It possessed or experimented with multiple delivery means: ballistic missiles, the longrange "super gun," and even unmanned aerial vehicles. Serbian forces also possessed chemical weapons. Fortunately, in both cases, Iraqi and Serbian leadership proved unwilling to escalate. In Afghanistan, concerns about WMD were heightened over evidence of collaboration between Pakistani nuclear scientists and reported al Qaeda attempts to purchase nuclear weapons for terrorist strikes against the United States. Post-war intelligence revealed al Qaeda efforts to develop chemical and biological weapons as well.

Vice President Cheney soberly noted in 2002 that "(d)eliverable weapons of mass destruction in the hands of a terror network, or a murderous dictator, or the two working together, constitute as grave a threat as can be imagined." As was seen in the Gulf War and Afghanistan, the U.S. attempted to destroy weapons, WMD research facilities, and means of delivery to reduce the threat to coalition forces. Unfortunately, successfully prosecuting such attacks offers enormous challenges. As noted earlier, the U.S. discovered after the Gulf War that Iraq's network of facilities proved much larger than initially estimated. Similar problems confronted U.S. operations in Afghanistan. The extent of al Qaeda development of WMD remained a mystery until coalition ground forces entered the country. These significant problems will continue to confront U.S. forces in conflicts against adversaries armed with WMD. Attacks against an adversary's WMD, if only partially successful, also run the risk of driving an enemy to employ such weapons before losing them. It therefore appears that the mere specter of WMD employment will continue to influence U.S. decision-making and policy.

MILITARY CAPABILITIES ENABLING NEW WAYS OF WARFARE

Looking retrospectively at selected U.S. military operations in the immediate post-Cold War era, we identified four political-military trends that will most significantly impact U.S. force applications in combating future forms of aggression and terror in the first decade of the 21st century and, quite possibly, beyond. With the conflict spectrum becoming increasingly diverse, both in terms of the sources and nature of emerging threats, the clashes that will ensue between the U.S. and future adversaries also will be characterized by how the U.S. might employ its military capabilities.

Hence, the purpose of this section is to focus more specifically on identifying salient trends in force employment. As was the case in the prior chapter, we base our observations on a comparative view of U.S.-led military operations in Iraq, Kosovo, and Afghanistan, under the assumption that the trends highlighted will prove valuable to predictive assessments of future warfare.

Our analysis revealed five key trends in force employment that will shape the future conduct of U.S. military campaigns:

- An order of magnitude increase in battlefield situational awareness;
- A move from deliberate to adaptive planning, and the concomitant execution of dynamic military operations;
- A dramatic decline in U.S. casualties compared with previous conflicts;
- An increasing emphasis on extended range operations; and
- The diminishing role of heavy ground forces.

Persistent Situational Awareness over the Battlefield

Of all the categories of military capability considered over the last three major engagements, the partly fulfilled promise of technological omniscience in the battlespace has dramatically transformed the command and control of U.S. forces in combat. Although we remain cognizant of Clausewitzian logic and acknowledge the timeless trends of fog and friction inherent in warfare, we nevertheless remain impressed by marked increases in battlefield situational awareness possessed by commanders at the strategic, operational and tactical levels. Indeed, a key participant in the command and control of allied air forces over Afghanistan cited an "order of magnitude" increase in overall battlespace awareness between operations Desert Storm and Enduring Freedom.

More specifically, we view two related trends with particular interest, as both pertain to the consequences of increased situational awareness over the battlefield:

- The rapidly increasing speed at which targets can be generated and prosecuted by a combination of battle management, sensor, and strike systems, compressing what has become known in the air operations community as the "kill chain"; and
- A blurred distinction between command and control and the execution of military operations, a trend resulting from real time operational snapshots of the battlefield and the intervention of senior leaders in issuing targeting guidance.

Progress Toward Increased Compression of the Kill Chain

During the Cold War, prescient military thinkers in the Soviet Union laid the conceptual groundwork for a "reconnaissance-strike complex" and of a "military-technical revolution," both of which inspired American interests in a "revolution in military affairs." In theory, the concept argued for intelligence, surveillance, and reconnaissance (ISR) systems to find, identify, and track military targets, aided by command and control assets to bring the weapons to bear effectively against those targets. But, in practice, the concept depended on enabling information technologies to facilitate collecting and quickly disseminating data essential to long-range target acquisition and attack—an area in which the U.S. enjoyed an enormous advantage over the Soviet Union. In the words of Eliot Cohen: "If the key to future warfare would be the rapid processing of electronically acquired information, how could a society that was virtually incapable of manufacturing a simple personal computer keep up in the technological race?"

Quite clearly, the Soviet Union could not keep pace with U.S. progress in establishing and exploiting these electronic linkages, as demonstrated by the overwhelming U.S. competitive advantage against Soviet tactics and technologies employed by the Iraqis during the Gulf War. Enabling this advantage is an overarching and constantly improving command and control architecture (if not yet truly integrated, joint, or interoperable), complete with information technology solutions to facilitate near-real time decision making. This architecture is, in turn, supported by a constellation of space-based assets, manned and unmanned air-breathing platforms, and ground sensors. As discussed in more detail in Section IV, trends observed in the three conflicts examined here highlight the promise of increased numbers and improved quality of intelligence-gathering sensors (particularly allweather, high resolution radars), and dramatic improvements in collecting, processing and disseminating "precision information" to achieve "precision effects" on the battlefield.

However, progress toward increased kill chain compression was uneven in the 1990s. For example, it took days, even weeks, to provide Desert Storm targeteers with mensurated coordinates (latitude, longitude, and altitude) for cruise missile targeting. Considerable time also elapsed between target generation, attack execution, and bomb damage assessment (BDA).

Quite often, air commanders in the theatre relied on CNN or other public media for information about the timing and success of their air strikes. On the first day of the air campaign, USAF Lt. Gen. Charles Horner had one of his planners watch television to judge the results of the opening attacks. When the Iraqi station went off the air, Horner confirmed that the strikes against the telecommunications centre had been successful.

But one could hardly place such methods of judging results in the category of reliable battle damage assessment. As one F-15E pilot complained, "I got more information and more specific mission results from listening to radio broadcasts from the BBC than what I got through CENTAF channels."

Shortfalls in tactical reconnaissance exacerbated the problem of battlefield awareness, with Air Force RF-4Cs in limited supply and Marine Corps RF-4Cs squadrons already disbanded. To circumvent the cumbersome procedures and rigid hierarchies that slowed the information flow to battlefield commanders, workarounds were devised. The "Black Hole" planning cell in Riyadh used the STU-III secure phone/fax to receive target development and damage assessment from Washington-based intelligence organizations, and at one point resorted to reviewing F-117 and F-111 strike videos to extract timesensitive intelligence. But even then, target damage data would be received, at best, a day later, while interpreting it at the operational level prompted frequent debates and caused further delays. Meanwhile, in-theatre intelligence organizations were left unaware of these workarounds.

Adequate coordination with tanker, electronic countermeasures, and reconnaissance aircraft was virtually non-existent, resulting in a loss in sorties and combat effectiveness. Years later, in 1999, situation awareness was only modestly improved for commanders directing Allied Force, moving beyond what was once characterized as "BDA by commercial television" during the Gulf War to "swivel-chair integration," in which battle managers sought to integrate by themselves the various streams of data fed from stove-piped means and modes of transfer. An incremental improvement at best, it was certainly better than the situation commanders confronted in the Gulf War, when data streams from sensors typically could be sent only to line-of-sight ground stations. In the case of Joint STARS— the prototype airborne ground surveillance system—the theatre air commander had to leave his headquarters and travel to the ground station to view the radar display. In contrast, during air operations over Kosovo, satellite links allowed data streams from Predator, Joint STARS, RC-135s, and U-2s to be transmitted directly to command centres.

During Allied Force, what was later described as an "inefficient targeting process" also hampered kill chain compression. Because NATO planners had anticipated a short-lived bombing campaign, a well-organized target generation and review process was not established beforehand. What sufficed instead during the first six weeks proved extraordinarily time consuming and was subject to review and veto by NATO member states, thereby limiting the number of targets that could be struck and resulting in what some critics later termed "ad hoc targeting." Also evident was the absence of critical command and control functions, which might have facilitated prosecuting fleeting targets of opportunity. In his analysis of the campaign, Ben Lambeth of RAND observed that, on the first night of the war, "there was no assigned strategy cell, no flexible targeting cell, no established guidance, apportionment and targeting process, and no BDA team in place." The end result was a kill chain cycle that, in the words of one official, "three to four hours is the best we can do" from identifying the target to delivering a weapon. As Lambeth points out, there was no data link to transmit near-real time information to strike assets for time-sensitive targeting missions.

Although platforms such as Joint STARS, Predator, U-2, and the RC-135 could transmit data directly to controllers in the Combined Air Operations Centre (CAOC) in Vincenza, Italy, battle managers were often unable to utilize these data streams in a timely fashion. Despite these obstacles, the kill chain cycle was significantly compressed during Allied Force. Whereas in Desert Storm, the targeting cycle for the Tomahawk Land Attack Cruise Missile (TLAM) took days, in Allied Force the cycle was reduced to 101 minutes, and to double-digit minute response times during Enduring Freedom.

There are numerous reasons to explain this feat, including streamlined shipboard launch procedures and reduced mission planning requirements owing to improved guidance systems on the Tomahawk. But airborne platforms were also able to respond more quickly, due to technology improvements that beamed actionable sensor data directly to the cockpit. One such technology improvement is called "RainDrop," a precise positioning tool allowing targeteers to relate an image provided by a sensor (U-2, satellite, Global Hawk, and Predator) to a NIMA (National Imagery and Mapping Agency) data base, generating a mensurated set of threedimensional coordinates within minutes. Data can then be relayed to a ship or an aircraft to deliver a precision weapon guided by the spacebased global positioning system (GPS). In many cases, the response time was less than 20 minutes from target generation to target destruction, resulting in significant improvements in sortie effectiveness. Ironically, the problem with situation awareness in Afghanistan was, perhaps, that too many people were aware of battlefield developments— leading to layers of decision-making that extended, rather than compressed, the kill chain. For example, one report noted that U.S. forces had top Taliban and al Qaeda leaders in its gun sights many times, but was unable to get clearance from higher headquarters to attack them before they dispersed. On one documented occasion, the decision to attack a target positively identified by real time imagery from a Predator UAV was overturned by CENTCOM officials in Tampa, who wanted a second source of target verification. Similar tensions between command staffs and operators in the field are likely to occur in future conflicts as well, particularly as data flows and real time imagery provide senior leaders (both civilian and military) with an incentive to increase their participation in both the control and execution of military operations.

Increased Centralization in Control and Execution

The amount of data travelling over communication networks during Enduring Freedom— perhaps 10 times greater than during the Gulf War—clearly gave commanders and warfighters more real time surveillance, intelligence, and targeting information than in any previous military conflict. Although at times there were gaps in the aggregate operational picture of the battlefield, advances in computers and secure satellite communications since the Gulf War have made it increasingly possible to manage military conflict from a great distance.

Therein lies an important trend—the increased centralization of the control and execution of U.S. military operations. Centralized control bordering on centralized execution has been an issue in modern U.S. civilmilitary relations since the Vietnam War, when civilian leaders at the highest levels insisted on approving, and in some cases actually selecting targets in North Vietnam for attack. Largely in reaction to this experience, American authorities increasingly empowered the combatant commander in the field with operational command and control of U.S. military forces in theatre.

Despite this delegation of authority, chain-ofcommand issues encountered during the Gulf War simply underscored the increased reliance of forward-deployed commanders on rearward military staffs and organizations for battle management guidance and support. Hence the need for technologies, such as the STU-III secure telephone and video teleconferencing, to enable the exchange of critical information between organizations. This migration of data represented the origins of a trend toward increased centralization in control and execution. Indeed, the Gulf War Air Power Survey (GWAPS) notes: "[T]he dependence of modern military organizations on vast amounts of information, and the relative ease with which communications technology could disseminate that information, meant that supporting authority would, in some measure, trickle out of the theatre."

Because the command staff in Riyadh relied so heavily upon large staff organizations thousands of miles away to generate key inputs to battle management, the GWAPS team concluded that the prevalence of such distant influence might be part of a broader trend. The past two wars suggest that they were right.

Supporting this trend are heightened sensitivities to the laws of war, and in particular legal guidance as to what constitutes a legitimate military target. Thus, whether it is the law or technology that drives increased centralization in command and control, incentives still exist for senior political and military leaders to increase their involvement in operational and tactical planning and execution. In his study of Allied Force, Lambeth observed that Gen. Clark had the option to delegate controlling authority of the air campaign to his Joint Task Force Commander, Adm. Ellis in Naples, or his air component commander, Lt. Gen. Michael Short, in Aviano. "Instead," Lambeth writes, "Clark elected not only to shoulder his diplomatic burdens as NATO's supreme commander, but also to conduct the air war himself from Brussels...." As coalition politics and legal rules of engagement imposed constraints on the conduct of air operations, frequent video teleconferencing among senior leaders encouraged them to expand their influence.

Gen. Short believed the use of video conferencing "improperly allowed senior leadership to reach down to levels they did not need to be involved in." Similarly, Adm. James Ellis observed that videoconferencing invited "senior leadership to sink to past comfort levels...discipline is required to remain at the appropriate level of engagement and command."

Not surprisingly, videoconferencing and other real time communications links only increased interactions between commanders and planners located at CENTCOM headquarters in Tampa, in the Pentagon, and at forward locations in Southwest Asia. Indeed, Gen. Tommy Franks, CENTCOM combatant commander, never felt compelled to deploy forward into the theatre, observing that "[t]he technology available to us here allows us to do things we never have been able to do, and we wouldn't necessarily have that if we moved the headquarters forward."

Even more impressive is the fact that Franks enjoyed access to more information, more quickly, than perhaps any other military commander in history. Electronic map displays updated him by the minute, tracking the positions of every military unit, ship and aircraft involved in the war. Also available were live video from Predator drones (some controlled from CONUS), moving target indications from Joint STARS radar, and a variety of multi-intelligence, multi-integrated displays. In short, while there were complaints that it was difficult to coordinate operations in remote locations in Afghanistan—some 7,000 miles and nine time zones away—this was due more to the circadian nature of human decision-making cycles than to the technology of near-real time situation awareness that defies human endurance. Owing to the high political content of armed conflict in a world of high-speed information and the capability to transmit information over global distances in the blink of an eye, there is a high probability that centralized execution—a key military trend in these three conflicts—may be here to stay.

Increased Emphasis on Adaptive Planning and Flexible Force Employment

The order of magnitude leap in situational awareness has encouraged a second major trend, characterized here and in defense planning documents (most recently in the 2002 Defense Planning Guidance) as a move from deliberate to adaptive planning and from rigid to increasingly flexible force employment. While defense planners have for years argued for a move away from "offthe- shelf " plans to a more adaptive process emphasizing the fast-paced nature of crisis action planning, the information revolution is accelerating this shift, not only in pre-conflict planning but also in the execution of combat missions. The legacy of deliberate planning is proving difficult to discard.

Throughout the Cold War, and even for most of the 1990s, U.S. defense policy was shaped largely by hypothetical conflict scenarios, which in turn were used to size the force structure. Between 1953 and 1989, the plausible invasions of Western Europe and South Korea preoccupied U.S. defense planners. Later, following the demise of the USSR and the Persian Gulf War in 1991, notional conflicts with Iraq and North Korea served as "illustrative planning scenarios" to guide U.S. force planning. These scenarios, enormously detailed and focused on operational planning factors such as the enemy order of battle and the time-phased deployment of U.S. forces, became powerful force-sizing constructs.

To be sure, the U.S. military conducted a number of successful combat operations in the 1990s that fell outside of the canonical scenarios. But even then, little progress was made in overcoming the rigidity that made it increasingly difficult for the military to adapt quickly to non-standard contingencies. This was evident most recently in the wake of the terrorist attacks on 11, September 2001, when the Bush administration was pressed to formulate a strategy for military operations in Afghanistan. According to Bob Woodward:

The military, which seemed to have contingency plans for the most inconceivable scenarios, had no plans for Afghanistan, the sanctuary of bin Laden and his network. There was nothing on the shelf that could be pulled down to provide at least an outline. This was not a surprise for the secretary of defense. Now [Rumsfeld] turned to [General Richard] Myers with a message: When I've asked to see various plans, I've not been happy with what I've seen. They are neither imaginative or creative. Clearly the plans are old and have been on the shelf for too long.

We would be remiss in not acknowledging the utility of deliberate planning, as the process of developing operational plans in advance of contingencies normally include useful discussions of campaign objectives, the sequence in which these objectives are to be met, and the forces required to meet them—at least in theory. As the quote above suggests, however, the deliberate planning process also instills an institutional predilection for scripted military operations at the expense of dynamic military operations. A RAND study conducted in 1994 supports this observation and links the absence of planning adaptiveness—particularly profound during the Cold War—to a strong institutional reluctance to use military force without first exhausting all other policy options and then reconciling political with military objectives when armed conflict is unavoidable.

The view that military force should only be used overwhelmingly to defeat aggression further complicated matters, as planning for contingencies that fell short of major theatre warfare were largely resisted. Of additional concern was the political feasibility of deploying light and flexible "tripwire" units to demonstrate U.S. resolve without repeating the Task Force Smith debacle during the first stages of the Korean War. Ironically, it was the Iraqi invasion of Kuwait which reinforced the need for the U.S. military to begin to move beyond canonical Cold War scenarios and embrace more adaptive approaches to military planning.

In the minds of U.S. planners, Iraq did not conform to Cold War images of the enemy, that of a Soviet-style military mobilizing for a blitzkrieg. The experience, as a result, inspired a trend in military policy circles toward treating each conflict as so unique that it requires ad hoc planning. In this vein, the Gulf War was a "prototypical example of a nonstandard scenario." Indeed, the surprise attack and the lack of warning time for Desert Shield/Desert Storm are among the reasons that war has been considered unique. Nevertheless, U.S. Central

Command was able to use an off-the-shelf planning document—Operations Plan 90-1002—to prepare for and execute a concept of operations to oust Iraqi forces from Kuwait. With nearly six months to deploy overwhelming combat power and train its forces for the counteroffensive, there was plenty of time to adjust the plan to reality. Yet, once the air war started, it became apparent that the Air Tasking Order (ATO), as a scripted plan for servicing targets, was not flexible enough to cope with a changing battlefield and support dynamic military operations.

The ATO...was effective in managing the volume of sorties generated to concentrate coalition air power against Iraq, especially during the preplanned structured stages of the campaign.... After the first two days, late completion of the ATO impacted operations. As hostilities progressed and key targets had been struck (with delayed BDA) the ATO proved increasingly unresponsive to rapidly moving events.... The 'kill box' concept was an improvement, as it allowed decentralized target selection and coordination with airborne assets for real time target priorities... The Air Force might disagree with this contention, arguing that the ATO facilitated a scheduled flow of sorties, some of which were retargeted either before or after takeoff. Nevertheless, in Desert Storm, approximately 80% of the targets attacked were selected before the aircraft left their base or ship. The remaining 20% included time-sensitive targeting priorities, the most famous of which later became known as "the great Scud hunt." Owing to the political significance of Iraqi missiles launched at Saudi Arabia and Israel, considerable effort was dedicated to attacking Iraqi mobile Scud launchers, but enemy deception and "shoot-and-scoot" tactics negated these strikes. The fact that 20% of all F-15E sorties flown during the war were apportioned to Scud hunting, all to negligible military effect, brought the killing of mobile targets to the forefront of desired future capabilities.

While the Air Force pursued these capabilities in the 1990s, air operations over Kosovo enjoyed little success when it came to destroying elusive targets. Allied Force further revealed a systemic weakness in the dynamic command and control of air operations against time-critical targets, a situation aggravated when NATO emphasized the "flex targeting" of Serbian fielded forces in Kosovo. And, to make matters even worse, NATO failed to establish a smooth mechanism to develop, review, and approve an expanding target list throughout the various levels of NATO command and responsibility. The subsequent scramble to streamline the planning and targeting process, when it became apparent that the air war would be a lengthy one, led USAFE commander (and future USAF Chief of Staff) Gen. John Jumper to argue that the Air Force needed to start thinking of the air operations centre as a "weapons system," with an aim to improve the planning and managing of an air campaign.

Gen. Jumper understood the need for flex targeting for all strike platforms in general but particularly for the B-2 bomber, which launched its combat missions over Serbia from Whiteman AFB, Missouri—a 14-hour flight. The B-2 could plan an attack on a SAM position known hours earlier but adjust its sights on the movable target before weapons release using its radar to update the GPS-guided bomb. Gen. Jumper visited the B-2 crews to discuss the requirements of flex targeting and was pleased with the result. "On the first night, these guys, with the new process at work, knocked out two SA-3 sites that we had given them only a couple of hours out from the targets."

In Allied Force, the USAF estimates that 43% of aimpoints were targeted after aircraft launched. Air operations in Afghanistan again confirmed the strategic, operational, and tactical advantages of dynamic command and control. Approximately 80% of U.S. Navy sorties were provided with targets after launch, almost doubling the percentage rate from Allied Force. Indeed, the need for "flexibility" in conducting dynamic military operations was underscored by Secretary Rumsfeld in his testimony before Congress in May 2002:

I'd like to mention a couple of lessons from Operation Enduring Freedom.... First is flexibility.

The war in Afghanistan was not a war that the U.S. forces had planned to fight. There was no war plan on the shelf. There were no prepositioned stocks of equipment or basing agreements with neighbouring countries.... U.S. forces will be confronted with future surprises, for which they will also require flexibility.

U.S. forces must not only have a flexible mindset, they will also need capabilities that are more flexible and capable of adapting to a wide variety of circumstances.

A Dramatic Decline in U.S. Casualties

A third major trend evidenced in the three conflicts is the dramatic decline in U.S. casualties as compared with previous large-scale U.S. military operations. The United States suffered 34,000 dead during the three years of the Korean War, with 58,158 killed in Indochina between 1961 through 1975. In contrast, U.S. forces suffered 146 killed over 45 days of combat during the Gulf War, or a fatality rate of 3.2 per day. With simple extrapolation, the 146 killed in the Gulf equates to roughly 17,760 dead over a 15-year span, or about 30% of the combat losses suffered in Vietnam. In Allied Force, U.S. forces suffered no losses; in Enduring Freedom, 16 U.S. personnel were killed between October 2001 and August 2002.[206] Combat losses on the part of adversaries, however, remain unverified. The most comprehensive public analysis of Iraqi losses in Desert Storm concluded that a total of 1,500 Iraqi soldiers were killed and about 3,000 wounded (with civilian casualties reaching 2,500-3,000 at the maximum).

Serbian military losses have not been revealed, but civilian deaths were estimated at 500. Taliban and al Qaeda military losses are unknown (some estimates claim 5,000 dead); civilian casualties are estimated at 500. Overall, U.S.-led forces achieved remarkable military results with very few friendly casualties. Indeed, one needs to go back far in history (such as the Battle of Omdurman in 1899 or the Spanish campaigns against the Incas and the Aztecs in the sixteenth century) to find such favorable exchange ratios.

The U.S. military has a long tradition of substituting firepower for manpower but, even with such efforts, casualty counts in Korea and Vietnam numbered in the tens of thousands. Are these declining U.S. casualties indicative of a trend? The reasons for such low loss rates lie in the emergence of new operational capabilities, superior and survivable military platforms, and guidance from U.S. political and military leaders to limit the exposure of U.S. forces to hostile fire.

The Impact of New Operational Capabilities

In all three conflicts, the U.S. engaged the enemy from relatively safe distances and with its unparalleled comparative advantage: the overwhelming use of air power to coerce and/or destroy the enemy. This, in turn, resulted in lopsided victories on the ground, to the point where conventional ground forces are now viewed as more valuable for their ability to maneuver and fix targets on a non-linear battlefield than for their organic firepower. Indeed, with the exception of a 100-hour ground operation in Desert Storm and the limited counterinsurgency operations against remnant Taliban and al Qaeda forces in Afghanistan, the U.S. did not commit significant ground forces to engage the enemy, whereas in both Korea and Vietnam, ground forces were in constant engagement (or the threat of engagement) for years.

Hence, throughout the three wars considered here, the U.S. relied more heavily on aircraft to deliver firepower which, in the case of Serbia and Afghanistan, reduced the number of personnel exposed to enemy fire. To employ aircraft survivably, the United States used tactics to minimize the threat. Aircraft flew at medium and higher altitudes to reduce exposure to pervasive and persistent low-level threats. Precision weapons in growing numbers allowed properly equipped aircraft to strike effectively from these safer altitudes. Stealth aircraft and cruise missiles also allowed commanders to strike targets in heavily defended areas with reduced risk to personnel. Finally, expanded roles for UAVs provided commanders with capabilities to acquire battlefield intelligence and, in the case of Afghanistan, deliver ordnance at lower altitudes without exposing personnel to risk. U.S. forces also succeeded in engaging adversaries outside the range of many of their weapons, denying the adversary the ability to bring firepower to bear on American forces.

In the Gulf War, U.S. air forces largely flew above the effective range of Iraqi air defense units that had not been destroyed or suppressed, inducing rampant fear and psychosis among surviving units. On the ground, U.S. tanks engaged at night with systems outranging Iraqi armour. Later, in operations over Kosovo and Serbia, air power centric military campaigns reduced the number of American systems and personnel at risk, while operating aircraft at higher altitudes reduced the number and scale of potential threats. Finally, in Afghanistan, Taliban and al Qaeda forces were simply incapable of engaging U.S. aircraft delivering precision weapons (referred to once by a Taliban supporter as "an infidel army perched up in the skies"). U.S. Special Forces, typically operating outside effective enemy engagement ranges, targeted many of these weapons.

Highly Survivable Combat Platforms

Stealth technology employed in all three wars greatly reduced adversary capabilities to detect, track, and engage U.S. aircraft. Meanwhile, nonstealthy aircraft were equipped with threat-warning receivers and countermeasures (flares, chaff, and jammers) to react to threats. Supporting aircraft were also on hand to enable choreographed combat missions in non-permissive threat environments, with electronic warfare aircraft and anti-radiation missiles suppressing SAM and AAA threats to strike packages. Similarly, on the ground, lightweight composite body armour saved many lives. M-1A1 Abrams tanks were equipped with composite ceramic and steel "Chobham" armour, the capability to identify and engage enemy armour at night over extended ranges while on the move (Iraqi tank crews were typically reduced to firing at muzzle flashes), and key survivability features such as compartmentation to reduce the chances that armour penetration would kill the crew. In Desert Storm (the only one of these wars to feature a tank battle), there were instances where U.S. tanks suffered direct hits with minimal or no casualties.

Guidance to Limit the Vulnerability of U.S. Forces

Finally—and a factor that should not be underestimated—U.S. decision-makers deliberately sought to avoid casualties. This was due primarily to the widespread perception held among U.S. political and military leaders, as well as by our adversaries, of the impact that American casualties could have on public support for conflict. A legacy of the Vietnam era, when mounting U.S. casualties combined with the lack of clear objectives resulted in gradually eroding public support for the war, casualty rates have a demonstrated impact on public opinion. One study indicated that the perceived stakes involved in the conflict at hand often are most important in weighing friendly losses. Conflicts for limited ends or unclear objectives can quickly lose support if casualties are incurred (as was the case of Somalia in 1993) and the political leadership cannot credibly explain the reasons for those losses.

Edward Luttwak has observed that, following the Vietnam War, "when senior Pentagon officials and military officers discuss how the United States might intervene...the likelihood of combat and the probable magnitude of U.S. casualties are invariably dominant in their deliberations." The "Vietnam syndrome," as it is still called today, quickly surfaced following Iraq's invasion of Kuwait. Saddam Hussein's promise of a "Mother of all Battles" engendered a debate in Washington about whether and how to pursue a war. Given the prospect of high U.S. casualty rates during the ground offensive and Saddam's perceived insensitivity to Iraqi casualties, the first Bush Administration undertook a public relations campaign to convince Americans of the value of driving Iraq from Kuwait—even if it cost thousands of American lives.

Similarly, casualty concerns factored into military preparations for the war. Before hostilities commenced, USAF Brig. Gen. Buster Glosson, who ran the "Black Hole" air operations centre, told aircrews: "The outcome of the war is not in question. The only issue is how many body bags we're going to send back across the Atlantic. The bottom line is that there's not a damn thing worth dying for in Iraq. Nothing." The "Vietnam syndrome" was also evident in wartime planning, when the air campaign in Iraq was extended beyond original plans to maximize the combat degradation of heavily entrenched Iraqi forces in Kuwait. This decision was due in no small part to the potential for high U.S. casualty rates in conducting offensive operations against the Iraqi ground force.

In the end, casualty considerations did inhibit the conduct of the air campaign. In the aftermath of a large daylight raid of 90 aircraft (Attack Package Q) over Baghdad, which encountered heavy enemy opposition and resulted in the downing of two U.S. F-16s, coalition planners chose to limit future strikes on Baghdad. Package Q's losses, as well as related collateral damage, caused Lt. Gen. Horner to rely on stealth and smaller strike packages escorted by jammers and defense suppression assets to attack targets in Baghdad. Since stealthy F-117s comprised only about 2.5% of the force and electronic warfare aircraft were in short supply, this decision greatly reduced the coalition's military and political effectiveness.

Concerns over casualties also determined how the U.S. military would fight in Allied Force. In his remarks to the American public at the outset of the air operation, President Clinton placed clear boundaries on the U.S. contribution to NATO's military campaign: "I do not intend to put our troops into Kosovo to fight a war." With this statement, Clinton declared that Kosovo did not merit the death of American servicemen and women. To some extent, the Serbs capitalized on this hesitancy, continuing ethnic cleansing operations while concealing and dispersing ground forces in Kosovo. Without a credible ground threat, Serbian units were not compelled to mass forces defensively to repel an invasion.

As one might expect, the tragic events of September 11, 2001 have dampened casualty sensitivity among political and military decisionmakers, at least to some extent. Referring to the 1993 Mogadishu debacle, Gen. Peter Pace, USMC, the current Vice Chairman of the Joint Chiefs of Staff, revealed that "[w]e were told to circle the wagons and not get Americans hurt.... If people think you're going to sit there and you're afraid to attack, they're going to pick at you. 9/11 changed the American mind-set.... We're going to take the war to the enemy." Thus far in Afghanistan, casualty rates have been remarkably low during what has amounted to a high-technology manhunt for remnant Taliban and al Qaeda forces.

Throughout these three conflicts, U.S. combat losses remained very low, an achievement all the more remarkable in light of adversary objectives to kill as many Americans as possible. Will this trend continue into the future? The answer depends on U.S. guidance and/or reluctance to place its forces in harm's way; the use and availability of U.S. and proxy ground forces; success in protecting aircraft; and how adversaries respond to U.S. force deployments (such as fielding and delivering weapons of mass destruction).

EXTENDED RANGE OPERATIONS

The fourth military trend—the increasing emphasis on extended range operations—stems from the anti-access/area denial challenge and the migration of conflict to distant and remote regions of the globe. For many years, the United States planned its tactical air forces assuming the availability—and relative invulnerability—of forward operating bases. From the Gulf War to Afghanistan, trends suggest those assumptions are no longer assured and must be hedged against to guarantee U.S abilities to project firepower over long distances.

During the Cold War, the U.S. concentrated primarily on two theaters: Europe and Korea. The resulting global basing architecture had a powerful influence on the design and limits of U.S. power projection capabilities. The relatively short distances from U.S. forward bases to likely engagement zones resulted in an emphasis on tactical fighter/attack aircraft with unrefueled operating ranges of 350-500 nautical miles (NM).

From bases in Western Europe and Korea, these ranges placed most Warsaw Pact and Korean military targets within striking distance. Following the Soviet invasion of Afghanistan and the 1979 Iranian revolution, the U.S. developed contingency plans to defend Persian Gulf oil fields from a potential Soviet drive through Iran. Such plans stimulated a renewed search for bases, host nation support, and access to facilities among Gulf allies such as Oman and Saudi Arabia. But it also introduced a new emphasis on range, owing to the geography of the region. Aside from geography, access and force protection issues have also led to a surge in extended range operations. In the Gulf War, F-117s and F-111s routinely flew 900-1000 NM sorties from their bases in southwest Saudi Arabia to Iraq.

B-52s flew about 2400 NM from Diego Garcia to the Straits of Hormuz (and in the first day of the air campaign, from CONUS) to deliver conventional cruise missiles. Carrier aircraft in the Red Sea mounted 600 NM sorties against Iraq. F-15s flew lengthy, 10-hour missions to conduct combat air patrols on the Iraq/Iran border to intercept fleeing Iraqi aircraft. Although, at first glance, distances would appear shorter in Europe, operations against Serbia witnessed even longer average mission radii than in Iraq. Aircraft based in Italy had to cover distances of only 300-350 nautical miles, but F-15Es operating from the UK routinely flew missions of 1000 NM radii. UK-based B-52s flew combat missions of 2500 NM radii or more because France denied them overflight rights.

B-2s originating from the U.S. mainland mounted the first sustained intercontinental bombardment campaign in history, routinely flying 33-hour, 9300 NM roundtrip missions from Whiteman AFB in Missouri to targets in Serbia. Aircrews were subjected to even longer missions to reach Afghanistan during Enduring Freedom's initial months. B-2s flew six 44-hour missions from Whiteman to Afghanistan (with recovery in Diego Garcia), the longest bombing missions in history. B-1Bs and B-52s flew from Diego Garcia to Afghanistan, routinely delivering precision weapons over distances of 2500 NM. Air Force F-15Es flew from Kuwait to Afghanistan and back—a distance of 3000 NM. And carrierbased aircraft routinely flew 700 NM radii sorties. In addition to area denial and access issues, requirements for time-sensitive targeting and combat patrol missions have also encouraged longer sortie duration and a greater need for loiter endurance, particularly for air crews operating short-range aircraft. In Desert Storm and Allied Force, U.S. fighters often orbited for hours waiting for a fleeting target to appear. Bombers armed with the Joint Direct Attack Munition (JDAM) did much of the same in Enduring Freedom. These new stressful demands— on both aircrews and aircraft—will likely characterize future air operations, particularly as enemies employ increased mobility and deception to minimize their vulnerability to U.S. air power.

Larger long-range aircraft can reduce some of the pressure on the future tanker force. Simple physical principles dictate that larger aircraft are inherently more efficient than smaller aircraft. For example, a B-2 stealth bomber is approximately three times more efficient than an F-15E when measuring the amount of fuel required to carry a single JDAM one mile.

Similar ratios hold for other large aircraft compared with fighters. The trend in long-range operations should, therefore, increase the value of long-range, large-payload aircraft. Data from the three conflicts bear this out. In the Afghan conflict, the inherent efficiency of larger aircraft is most starkly revealed: land-based and sea-based fighter aircraft flew 90% of the sorties, but accounted for 30% of total weapons expended.

The Diminishing Role of Heavy Ground Forces

A final, somewhat controversial, military trend is the diminishing role of heavy ground forces in the three wars examined here. Whereas deployable, highly maneuverable ground forces that can leverage the effects of modern precision weaponry are integral to dynamic military operations against elusive enemies—as witnessed most recently in Afghanistan—there is a mismatch between the capabilities of slower-deploying heavy ground forces and the demands of the future operating environment. This is not to say, however, that we cannot envision roles for heavy ground formations against similarly equipped adversaries over favorable terrain and when sufficient time and lift is available for deployment, as might transpire in a future confrontation with Iraq. Already, in preparation for such a conflict, the battle staffs of the U.S. Army V Corps (consisting of the 1st Armored Division and the 1st Infantry Division) have been deployed to Kuwait. Yet, while heavy ground units will inevitably be part of another attack on Iraq, trends suggest their role on the future battlefield will decline as the U.S. relies on other, more deployable means to import heavy and sustained firepower. Secretary Rumsfeld recently noted: "Looking at what was overwhelming force a decade or two decades ago, today you can have overwhelming force, conceivably, with lesser numbers because the lethality is equal to or greater than before."

In view of the migration of future conflict to distant and remote areas, these graphs suggest strongly that maritime and air expeditionary forces, more so than ground forces, will form the mainstay of future U.S. power projection capabilities. The reasons for this appear relatively straightforward: maritime forces are less dependent on forward basing than either land-based air or ground forces. Moreover, both maritime and land-based air forces typically can bring combat power to bear more quickly than ground forces, have a much smaller logistical footprint in theatre, and will incur lower casualty rates than conventional ground force options. Although heavy ground forces have been deployed to Southwest Asia for possible military operations against Iraq in early 2003, the strategic responsiveness of these combat units will remain an open question in evaluating deployment options for future conflicts.

TECHNOLOGIES ENHANCING U.S. MILITARY ADVANTAGES

This section identifies four key technology trends that impacted the conduct of military operations in the three conflicts examined here and, more importantly, lend to our understanding of U.S. force applications in future conflicts. Advances in precision weaponry are perhaps the most dominant trend and, to be sure, will be featured along with related trends in munitions development and modes of delivery. Equally important are trends in sensor development and integration (between platforms and systems) expected to enable network-centric warfare, an emerging operational concept that relies on high quality sensors and increased automation in the speed, distribution, and integration of data. Also noteworthy here is the combination of stealth and electronic warfare, first showcased in the Gulf War, that increases the survival and effectiveness of U.S. airpower in high-threat environments. Finally, the three conflicts underscore the potential of unmanned aerial vehicles and their military utility above future battlefields.

The Increasing Utility of Precision Weapons

It is no exaggeration to observe that the increased use of air-delivered precision weaponry, as seen in the three conflicts, heralded a new chapter in the American way of war. That is not to say, however, that the technological push for such weapons is a recent phenomenon. Indeed, military history is filled with attempts to develop increasingly accurate weapons as a means to exploit a comparative firepower advantage on the battlefield. For examples, one might think of the English longbowmen at the Battle of Agincourt, or perhaps the advances in naval gunnery prior to World War I, which enabled capital ships at the Battle of Jutland to strike at long ranges and with increasing accuracy.

However, these were not "smart" weapons, in that the capabilities of the launch platform determined their accuracy; their flight paths could not be changed once fired. When the German Luftwaffe sank the Italian battleship Roma using FX1400 guided bombs in 1943, the ability to guide weapons during flight opened up the potential for aircraft to deliver weapons with much greater accuracy. Hence, any target within range of aircraft could presumably be attacked with a much higher probability of hitting the target. Ultimately, the U.S. would deploy aircraft-delivered guided weapons during World War II. Army Air Forces delivered radiocontrolled weapons against bridges in Burma during that conflict, and improved versions were used in the Korean War. Later, in Vietnam, the USAF and USN used laser designators and other aids to guide aircraft-delivered ordnance to their targets, with an exponential increase in accuracy.

Equipped with these new precision guided munitions (PGMs), between 1968 and 1972, the USAF delivered 28,000 laser and electro-optical guided weapons. However, in spite of PGM performance in Vietnam, the implications of precision weaponry did not become fully apparent until the 1991 Gulf War. Indeed, from Vietnam through the end of the Cold War, American air planners relied on a concept of operations where aircraft penetrated at very low altitudes (under the radar) to deliver unguided ordnance accurately using on-board electronics and visual cues. Advocates of this approach, which enjoyed broad support in both the USAF and USN, argued that such a policy was far more cost effective than outfitting tactical aircraft with expensive precision weapons, as cheap general purpose bombs were thought to produce equivalent effects at much lower costs. This logic—that it was better and cheaper to use smart airplanes and dumb bombs—prevailed until the outbreak of the Gulf War.

Given this preference, it is not surprising that only a very small percentage (roughly 3%) of the USAF's total combat force available at the time of the Gulf War was capable of delivering laserguided bombs. Compared with the Air Force, the U.S. Navy deployed roughly the same number of PGM-capable aircraft, but did not procure enough laser guidance kits to conduct sustained operations.

Nevertheless, the contrast between precision and unguided weapons was a stark one. GWAPS concluded that precision-capable aircraft were at least 13 times more effective in the number of targets attacked, and analysis concluded that precision weapons delivered by stealthy aircraft (F-117s) were 26 times more effective. If a single aircraft with PGMs was equal to or more capable than about 20 aircraft with unguided ordnance, then the 100+ aircraft delivering PGMs during the opening phase of the Gulf War were much more effective than the other 1100 combat aircraft deployed throughout the conflict.

As one might expect given this performance, investments in precision weapons (as well as in the delivery systems needed to employ them) since Desert Storm have led to their increased usage, as evident later in operations Allied Force and Enduring Freedom.

The steady rise in the average number of PGMs delivered per sortie also underscores the fact that precision guided weapons have intensified modern air campaigns. Figure 5 reveals that air operations over Kosovo and Afghanistan were much more significant, in terms of intensity, than commonly believed. In Allied Force, strike aircraft delivered approximately 0.73 PGMs per sortie, as opposed to 0.32 PGMs per sortie in Desert Storm, an increase of over 128%. Similarly, strike aircraft delivered, on average, 1.66 PGMs per sortie in Enduring Freedom, or more than double the amount delivered two years earlier in Allied Force.

These impressive increases are due in large part to four key factors: (1) larger inventories of PGMs; (2) more PGM-capable aircraft; (3) increased demand to employ PGMs out of concern for accuracy and effectiveness; and (4) the employment of large-payload bombers capable of mass precision strikes. Indeed, during Allied Force, B-2 stealth bombers accounted for roughly 10% of the precision guided munitions delivered on targets in

Serbia; in Afghanistan that percentage rises to an astonishing 46% when JDAM strikes by B-52s and B-1Bs are included. To further appreciate how PGMs have radically transformed modern air warfare since 1991, three supporting trends require specific mention: (1) the emergence of an all-weather capability enabled by satellite-aided navigation; (2) the rise of precision standoff weapons such as TLAM; and (3) advances in payload fractionation resulting from the miniaturization of munition bodies.

Developing an All-Weather Capability

One reason the U.S. military did not embrace PGMs in the wake of Vietnam was that laserguided and electro-optical weapons required a clear line-of-sight to the target and, as such, its acquisition could be disrupted by cloud cover or smoke. The only all-weather strike weapons available in the late 1970s and early 1980s used elaborate terrain mapping data for targeting that required time-consuming flight planning. Soon after the Gulf War, however, the U.S. military accelerated the deployment of two GPS-guided weapons—the Joint Direct Attack Munition (JDAM) and the Joint Standoff Weapon (JSOW). Although these weapons could not provide the same accuracy as laser and electrooptically guided munitions, they were characterized as "near-precision" and could be employed in any weather.

The B-2 stealth bomber delivered the first generation of GPS-guided weapons during Allied Force, and the value of all-weather delivery capability proved especially critical. During the first eight weeks of operations, the B-2s flew only 3% of the strike sorties, but struck 33% of the targets because poor weather prevented other aircraft with line-of-sight dependent weapons from being employed. What is striking is the rapid acceleration of this new technology's employment. The percentage of all-weather weapons used in Afghanistan more than tripled compared with Allied Force only two years earlier.

The Impact of Precision Standoff Weapons

Another trend in precision weapons is the steady emphasis on standoff weapons, and in particular, conventionally armed unmanned cruise missiles for long-range strike. The origin of the cruise missile can be traced to World War II, when Germany became the first nation to employ them in combat. But their poor accuracy greatly limited their military utility. In the 1950s, the U.S. developed a wide array of sea-based and landbased land-attack cruise missiles, primarily to support nuclear deterrence. It was not until the late 1970s, however, that terrain-mapping guidance technology provided sufficient accuracy to open the prospect of employing conventionally armed cruise missiles. Eventually, the U.S. Navy fielded the Tomahawk Land Attack Missile (TLAM) in the mid-1980s, followed in turn by the USAF "Secret Squirrel" program, which refitted a small number of Air Launched Cruise Missiles (ALCMs) with conventional warheads.

The Gulf War witnessed the first U.S. operational use of conventional cruise missiles to attack land targets—the Navy's TLAM and the Air Force's Conventional ALCM (CALCM). Since the weapons had not been employed in previous combat operations, many senior Desert Storm commanders had substantial doubts about relying on these new weapons during the opening phase of the air campaign. However, their well-publicized success in the Gulf War transformed the TLAM into the weapon of choice for punitive military raids in the 1990s, among them attacks on Iraq (1993, 1996, and 1998), Afghanistan (1998), and Sudan (1998). Why was this the case? Cruise missiles offered a unique capability: to strike rich target sets at long ranges with near precision, all without risking the lives of the aircrew. With this capability, cruise missiles vastly increased the striking power and range of surface ships and submarines. In the August 1998 strikes against Afghanistan and Sudan, the long reach of cruise missiles allowed a single Navy battle group to strike two separate continents simultaneously. Meanwhile, airlaunched cruise missiles allowed aircraft to strike from outside the range of enemy defenses and thus minimize potential risks.

Yet, owing to high production costs, cruise missiles represent a luxury item in U.S. munitions inventories. The TLAM program unit cost is approximately $3.0 million (in $FY03). Striking the same number of aimpoints attacked in the Gulf War (42,000) with TLAMs, for example, would cost over $120 billion in current dollars.

Unfortunately, reducing the cost of standoff weapons has proven difficult, as there appears to be an unbreakable correlation between range and cost. For this reason, projecting power with cruise missiles in a protracted compaign is simply unaffordable, particularly in light of the successful use of relatively inexpensive GPS-guided munitions. For example, the JDAM costs roughly $20,000 per unit in current dollars—substantially less than the cheapest standoff weapon. So for the price of a single TLAM, the U.S. could procure 150 JDAMs. Cruise missiles are, therefore, extremely valuable for striking a limited number of well-protected high-value targets, but are not cost-effective for sustained largescale operations.

Advances in Payload Fractionation

Within the past few years, considerable effort has been expended on increasing PGM delivery rates by fractionating aircraft payloads and introducing smaller precision weapons. Aside from lessening the logistical burden associated with transporting heavy munitions, developing smaller precision weapons offers the potential to substitute accuracy for explosive weight. Following Allied Force, the USAF accelerated a program to increase the number of JDAMs a B-2 could deliver by developing new racks and adding guidance kits to 500 lb. bombs. Thus, a B-2 that could previously deliver sixteen 2,000 lb. JDAMs will soon be able to deliver eighty 500 lb. weapons, vastly increasing the number of aim points that can be attacked per sortie. The USAF has also accelerated the development of the Small Diameter Bomb (SDB), a 250 lb. GPS-guided weapon offering even greater potential payload fractionation. Currently, the F/A-22 is designed to carry two 1,000 lb. bombs internally, as opposed to the F-35 (formerly known as the Joint Strike Fighter) and its designed capability to carry two 2,000 lbs.

internally. In contrast, the F/A-22 is designed to internally store and deliver eight SDBs, and the F-35 at least double that. Large payload aircraft like the B-1 or B-2 could carry several hundred such weapons. Ultimately, fielding these smaller precision weapons will result in impressive increases in their delivery rate. Already, the potential fruits of payload fractionation have been demonstrated in Afghanistan when the USAF and USN delivered 100 JDAMs in 20 minutes. During the Gulf War, in contrast, the average hourly rate of precision weapons delivery stood at about 16 per hour. In the future, similar delivery rates will not require an increase in overall force size, demonstrating that precision can substitute for mass and greatly increase lethality. The potential implications of mass precision are still not understood, but may portend a significant outgrowth of the precision revolution. In essence, the U.S. may soon develop the capability to conduct a decisive blow against adversaries with small precision weapons designed to strike thousands of targets within a few hours.

Enabling Network-Centric Warfare: More, Better, and Integrated Sensors and Sensor Networks

The rush for increased integration of sensors and networks—to enable what is known increasingly as "network-centric warfare"—is motivated by the promise of information dominance and battlefield situational awareness. Underpinning this promise are technologies to create networkcentric architectures consisting of high quality sensors and rapidly transmitted data streams that will be fused and integrated at command and control centres. The objective is to "successfully combine data from many intelligence-gathering sensors—while compensating accurately for all the different types of physics and time latencies involved—and use the product to present a single, unified picture of the battlefield."

While network-centric warfare remains an objective in defense policy circles, each of the three conflicts examined here provided ample demonstrations of new sensors for intelligence, surveillance, and reconnaissance activities. Many of these sensors were outfitted on existing airbreathing ISR platforms, such as the E-3A AWACS (for detecting enemy air activity and directing friendly fighters); the RC-135 and EP-3 aircraft (for detecting and locating enemy radar and radio emissions); and the U-2 (for providing strategic reconnaissance and wide-area surveillance). At the same time, new manned and unmanned

ISR platforms have appeared in the force structure, the most prominent of which is the E-8 Joint STARS.

Regarded as a highly capable ISR and battle management platform, Joint STARS is outfitted with a 24-foot "canoe" housing a synthetic aperture radar that can detect moving targets and provide high-resolution radar imagery of selected areas. It also possesses a ground moving target indicator (GMTI), capable of detecting moving targets over an area 10,000 times greater than the same radar attempting to provide a high resolution image. "The ability to target vehicles in a large area," as one air-to-ground (AGS) surveillance expert recently noted, "makes it possible to destroy an enemy's ability to fight effectively and do so much faster—using far fewer and lighter forces—and at less risk than traditional attritionoriented warfighting."

The capabilities provided by Joint STARS were illustrated in several incidents during the Gulf War. On the night of 29 January 1991, Joint STARS detected Iraqi armored forces moving toward Al Khafji, allowing coalition forces to locate and target them with devastating air attacks. Later, during the Coalition ground offensive, which took place during the worst weather of the war, GMTI surveillance quickly exposed Iraqi efforts to reposition their forces, providing advancing coalition forces with the information needed to defeat the Iraqi maneuver before it could create a serious threat. A Joint STARS image brought forward to the tactical command post of General Fred Franks, the commander of the Army's VII Corps that conducted the main attack around the Iraqi western flank, confirmed his decision to turn his force eastward and attack the Republican Guard divisions in their new positions. This decision placed the VII Corps at precisely the right position in relation to the enemy and facilitated the ensuing rout.

And, when Iraqi forces began withdrawing from Kuwait, GMTI provided timely information alerting the coalition that a large-scale withdrawal had begun. Conflicts since the Gulf War witnessed modest forms of C2ISR integration, links that facilitated data exchanges between a multitude of sensors, multiple-sensor platforms, and geographically disparate command and control centres. Enabling this were three technology sub-trends: advances in smaller, low-cost and high-quality sensors; outfitting multiple sensor suites on manned and unmanned ISR platforms; and exponential increases in data transmission rates. Fielding these new technologies led, in turn, to increased situational awareness. Over Kosovo, the Predator unmanned air vehicle (UAV) conducted surveillance missions with a SAR, offering resolution similar to the larger radar on the U-2. Later, over Afghanistan, Predator and Global Hawk UAVs— both with powerful SARs—expanded the coverage area that the U-2 and Joint STARS initially provided. The UAVs are also multi-sensor platforms. A Global Hawk can take a highresolution radar image and provide electro-optical and infrared pictures of the same area within seconds. During the Gulf War, in contrast, developing multiple images of a target site took days, even weeks.

Finally, increases in computational power and the availability of satellite data links have accelerated data transmission from sensors to users. For example, the computational power on-board Joint STARS increased 200 times from the Gulf War to Serbia. By enhancing on-board imagery processing and data compression, this power boost increased both data volume and quality to the user. Similarly, satellite links provided rapid transmission of data pre-processed by on-board sensor platforms. Whereas in 1991 sensor data transmitted over line-of-sight links encountered routine delays, by 1999 U-2 imagery was transmitted by satellite to the United States, analyzed, and promptly relayed electronically to the CAOC in Vincenza, Italy. Data from platforms could also be beamed directly into command centres.

UAVs were able to transmit near-real time imagery back to the CAOC, while the older systems were consigned to sending imagery back to control stations or over limited distances. These capabilities increasingly provided battle commanders access to data at a rate traditional intelligence distribution chains could not match. In sum, the increasing number of quality intelligence sensors, the availability of multi-sensor platforms, and the capability to process, analyze, and distribute data quickly over vast distances has led to at least an order of magnitude increase in situational awareness and the capability to conduct operations more flexibly and rapidly.

Overall integration of increasing data flows still remains a challenge, but technological solutions are being actively pursued. In the future, trends in sensor technology toward less expensive, more capable, and lighter sensors will support intelligence-quality sensors networked around the battlefield. Moreover, outfitting the F-35, F/A-22, and F/A-18E/F with active, electronically- scanned radar arrays will multiply the number of high-quality sensors on the battlefield. Assuming these data streams from multiple sources can be integrated in a timely fashion—a tall order—future commanders will enjoy even greater situational awareness to employ their forces more effectively.

The Increasing Importance of Stealth Aircraft and Electronic Countermeasures

Stealth—using technology and tactics to lower a platform's signature, thereby making it less detectable to sensors seeking its presence—is unarguably one of the most significant advancements in U.S. combat aircraft performance since the Cold War. From Iraq to Kosovo and, to a lesser degree, in Afghanistan, low observable aircraft were employed with remarkable success and revolutionary impact. Low observable technologies applied to combat aircraft have allowed them to operate with relative impunity against sophisticated air defense systems, enabling them to deliver paralyzing attacks on the first night of the war. The ability of stealth aircraft to operate independently has also reduced the requirement for devoting considerable resources to escorting attack aircraft. Non-stealthy fighters and bombers typically need more assistance from multiple additional aircraft providing defense suppression, dedicated support jamming, fighter cover and radar warning.

Stealth critics are fond of pointing out, however, that even low observable aircraft have benefited from supporting, if not direct, electronic countermeasures when transiting through hostile airspace. That is true to a limited extent, but the weight of electronic warfare during the conduct of three major air wars has been in support of the overwhelming majority of Air Force,

Navy, and Marine Corps attack aircraft that are not stealthy. Because these aircraft will form the bulk of the U.S. force structure for years to come, investments in electronic jamming, in addition to electronic and infrared self-protection systems and stealth, will continue to be required. Trends established in these areas during America's post- Cold War conflicts are therefore worthy of our attention.

Operation Desert Storm

Although the F-117 stealth "fighter"—in actuality, a single-seat bomber that attacks only ground targets—was employed in combat in Panama, it first encountered a sophisticated air defense system on the opening night of Desert Storm. On that and subsequent nights, airborne stealth worked exceptionally well, leading the authors of GWAPS to select "stealth/low observability" as one of the five technologies that worked best in the Gulf War. Indeed, the stealthy F-117 was regarded as "the single greatest technological advance fielded in Desert Storm," due in large part to a record 1,299 sorties without any battle damage, but also for its precision and combat efficiency. According to GWAPS, the F-117 flew only 2% of total attack sorties but struck almost 40% of the strategic targets. Moreover, the F-117s' deep strike capability enabled them to disrupt and destroy the Iraqi integrated air defense system. In post-conflict analysis, GWAPS concluded that Iraqi air defenses never recovered from those first attacks as the F-117 paved the way for the use of non-stealthy aircraft in follow-on strikes.

It is not clear from available evidence whether the EF-111 electronic warfare aircraft supporting the F-117s on the first night of the air war were more effective than stealth in protecting the aircraft. Although GWAPS sided with the latter, it can be assumed that even indirect support assisted in suppressing and distracting enemy radars. But it is also true that stealthy strikes were conducted autonomously, not only by F-117s in Desert Storm but later by B-2s in Kosovo and Afghanistan.

The need for stealth and the amount of electronic warfare support required for the nonstealthy fleet depends on the sophistication and integration of enemy air defenses, and on the skill with which they are employed. As concluded in the

GWAPS report: [E]lectronic countermeasure support contributed substantially to Coalition effectiveness by denying early warning and tracking data to enemy integrated air defense system (IADS) operators and by disrupting the firing solutions of enemy antiaircraft weapons. EA-6B support was considered essential for every Navy and Marine strike. During Desert Storm, 27 EA-6Bs operated from aircraft carriers in the Red Sea and the Persian Gulf, with an additional 12 Marine EA-6Bs based in Bahrain. Throughout the air war, EA-6Bs escorted USN and USMC tactical aircraft, jamming Iraqi radars during strike and refueling operations. In fact, the unavailability of electronic jamming aircraft was often considered sufficient reason to abort a mission. In all, the Prowlers flew 1,630 sorties and fired 150 antiradiation missiles during the war, forcing Iraqi radars to shut down or to operate in ineffective modes.

Meanwhile, the USAF relied on 24 EF-111 aircraft to meet its electronic countermeasure requirements, in standoff, penetration, and close-in jamming roles. The Ravens flew 1,105 sorties without a combat loss and were considered a major contributor to the general ineffectiveness of Iraqi air defenses and the subsequent low loss rate of allied aircraft. GWAPS cited an after-action report concluding that Iraqi air defense capabilities were seriously impaired or completely denied by EF-111 radar jamming.

Nevertheless, EW shortfalls in the Air Force, which had traditionally relied more on aircraft carrying self-protection pods rather than dedicated jamming aircraft, resulted in the frequent borrowing of EA-6Bs from its sister services to accompany Air Force attack aircraft.

Operation Allied Force

One reason the EA-6B proved so essential in Allied Force was that the Air Force, based on bureaucratic and budgetary arguments, retired the EF-111 in 1998. As a result, when NATO aircraft began bombing over the former Yugoslavia in late March 1999, the tactical jammers available consisted of about 90 EA-6Bs split among 19 USN and USMC squadrons. Ultimately, more than 10 of those squadrons were deployed to support Allied Force, including some aircraft redeployed from

Northern Watch operations over Iraq. In short, the performance of the EA-6B during Allied Force was described as "absolutely important to the air operation" in the U.S. Department of Defense's official after-action report.

During the conflict, the available EA-6B aircraft and their aircrews were stretched to the limit— the perennial low density, high demand problem. The Serbs had learned from the Iraqi experience in the opening days of the Gulf War and operated their integrated air defense system sporadically, thereby requiring a sustained tactical jamming effort far greater than that anticipated at the war's onset. As a result, NATO aircraft were forced to fly through active SAM engagement zones on a daily basis. The EA-6Bs flew 1,318 total sorties to support roughly 12,000 combat sorties which resulted in only two aircraft (including a stealthy F-117), and no aircrew, lost to enemy fire. Nearly the entire available EA-6B inventory was tasked to support a small contingency against a relatively unsophisticated adversary equipped with outmoded air defenses.

Rather than trending away from electronic jamming support, as the Air Force had hoped after the Gulf War, modern wars—even relatively small ones—suggest that additional EW assets will be in great demand in the future.

Penetrating the Serbian air defense network during Allied Force also underscored the comparative advantages of stealth aircraft. Only the B-2, in its combat debut, was able to evade the integrated air defenses on the first night of the war and strike highly defended targets with nearprecision and in spite of adverse weather. A pool of six available aircraft launched 45 sorties during the war—less than one percent of total strike sorties. Yet, astonishingly, these 45 sorties accounted for 11% of all precision munitions delivered. Based on this performance, the Pentagon's Operation Test and Evaluation (OT&E) report on the B-2 observed that the "B-2s damaged a higher percentage of their targets than any other aircraft participating in combat operations." With a payload of GPS-aided JDAMs, the B-2 afforded NATO air planners an unprecedented all-weather capability to acquire elusive targets, such as moveable air defense radars, and attack the most highly defended areas at night. Owing to their low observability and the lingering air defense threat, only the B-2s and F-117s were sent against targets in heavily defended Belgrade— a repeat of the decision made during the Gulf War to restrict air attacks over Baghdad to the F-117.

Operation Enduring Freedom

The war in Afghanistan against the Taliban was, like the war in Yugoslavia, one fought primarily in the air. But it was also waged against a far less capable adversary, in terms of air defense and tactics, than the Serbs or even the Iraqis. Therefore, the need for stealth and electronic jamming was considerably less in Enduring Freedom than the two previous conflicts. But it would be wrong to conclude that Afghanistan has reversed the trend. Although targets in Afghanistan remained out of range for short-range land-based fighters, the B-2 participated in the first strikes on the Taliban to destroy air defense assets and SAM sites. Moreover, the highly survivable B-2 enabled the U.S. to strike targets deep in the north prior to establishing the search and rescue infrastructure needed to support non-stealthy airborne operations.

The Taliban lacked weapons systems with the reliability, range, and guidance systems to threaten high-altitude bombers and, after the initial attacks on air defenses, waves of B-1s and B-52s were able to penetrate, loiter, and strike with impunity. At lower altitudes, however, the threat was not eradicated and non-stealthy aircraft such as carrier-based fighters and B-1Bs still required EA-6B jamming support. And, because the EA-6B's range was limited due to the extreme distance—about 700 miles—between Kabul and the carriers in the Arabian Sea, the B-1s were not sent to attack deep targets because they would be deprived of jamming support.

Not surprisingly, the demand for stealth and electronic jamming was significantly decreased after the first few days of the air war. The B-2 turned the long-range strike mission over to its nonstealthy ancestors and, with U.S. air supremacy over Afghanistan assured, the EA-6B shifted to jamming enemy land communications and assisting in the campaign against enemy ground forces. However, the relatively relaxed pace of deploying stealth and standoff jamming during Enduring Freedom does not undermine the low density, high demand status assigned them in the 1990s. During the Gulf War, only 4% of the total combat sorties flown were electronic warfare sorties (EA-6Bs and EF-111s). In Kosovo, U.S. forces flew a total of 12,000 combat sorties, of which 1,318 were electronic warfare sorties— almost triple the percentage in the Gulf War. Clearly the aging EA-6B force is too small to meet the nation's future electronic jamming requirements, particularly when advanced threats or simultaneous conflicts are considered. Nor has the nation, in producing only 59 F-117s and 21 B-2s, reaped sufficient benefits from the enormous investments made in airborne stealth. The performance of these platforms and systems across the three wars argues for their future importance and for providing the resources necessary to ensure that these capabilities are available when needed.

The Increasing Use and Roles for Unmanned Vehicles

The final trend considered here is the increased use of unmanned aerial vehicles for ISR and strike missions. Historically, interest in unmanned systems was motivated by the requirement for strategic reconnaissance flights over the Soviet Union, particularly after Soviet air defenses were successful in shooting down a U-2 in May 1960. U.S. intelligence agencies were most interested in developing these systems, such as the D-12 Oxcart drone, to obtain imagery to support their intelligence estimates. With the advent of space surveillance systems, however, intelligence interest flagged, but the military services continued their pursuit. Overall, since the 1950s, the U.S. has invested over $25 billion ($FY98) in developing and fielding unmanned aerial vehicles (UAVs), primarily for ISR missions.

Eventually, this sizeable investment resulted in unmanned systems which, when finally enabled by advances in satellite guidance and communications, computerized flight control systems, and sensor technologies, demonstrated their operational utility over the battlefield. Indeed, in each conflict examined, unmanned systems assumed new roles, due in large part to improvements in range, endurance, on-board sensors, and data transmission. Used primarily as decoys during the Gulf War, by 2001 UAVs had evolved into sophisticated air-breathing ISR platforms with an organic strike capability.

From the Gulf War to Kosovo

Because of their limitations, unmanned systems were used primarily to spoof Iraqi air defenses and serve as decoys. At the outset of the air campaign, the USAF and USN employed target drones to confuse and disrupt Iraqi air defenses. Following the initial F-117 and cruise missile strikes, Navy A-6s launched 25 Tactical Air Launched Decoys and USAF ground crews launched 44 BQM-34C target drones. Thinking the decoys and drones were incoming strike packages, Iraqi air defenses turned on their radars and engaged them, only to be attacked by radiationhoming missiles. The USN and USMC also used the Pioneer unmanned drone for limited reconnaissance missions. In all, the Pioneer conducted 313 sorties averaging about three hours each. A short-range, remotely piloted vehicle, the Pioneer provided television imagery through a data link back to its control station. Many of these sorties provided spotting and near real-time battle damage assessment for U.S. Navy battleships employing their 16-inch naval rifles; others provided surveillance when other sensors were not available.

In the buildup to Allied Force, U.S. forces employed the newly fielded Predator A, derived from the CIA-developed Gnat 750, to support peacekeeping operations in Bosnia from July to October 1995. The Predator offered slightly increased speed over the Pioneer (110 knots versus 95 knots), 450% greater payload (450 lbs. versus 100 lbs.), and eight times the endurance (40 hours versus five hours). Three Predators, equipped with a color video camera and an electro-optical/infrared camera, conducted 128 missions each totaling 850 hours (and with 6.6 hours average endurance—more than double what the Pioneers averaged in Desert Storm). One Predator was lost to enemy fire; another due to engine failure. In November 1995, the Predators, still in limited supply, were fitted with synthetic aperture radars and redeployed to Bosnia to provide detailed radar images in adverse weather. By May 1998, Predators had logged more than 600 sorties and 3800 flying hours over Bosnia.

During Allied Force, the U.S. deployed seven Predators, about 20 Hunters (an Army shortrange UAV), and a Navy Pioneer detachment. The allies also provided a mix of UAVs to support combat operations, such as the German CL-drone, the British Phoenix, and the French Crecerelle. Overall, U.S. and allied UAVs flew 469 missions, an average of six per day, many more than in the Gulf War and with more capable sensors and increased endurance.

While they were incapable of wide-area surveillance and were thus limited to providing real time views of small patches of terrain, the Hunters and Predators could transmit near-real time imagery back to command and control facilities, where it was used to provide a "second set of eyes" on targets.

This development stood in stark contrast to the Pioneer and Crecerelle, which could only send video back to a control station, and the CL-289 and Phoenix, which could only transmit infrared imagery over limited distances.

Commanders, moreover, were willing to expose UAVs to low-level air defenses to acquire time-sensitive intelligence. The near-real time capability of the Phoenix and Hunter proved extremely useful in this regard. As one British officer commented: "We in Britain have traditionally shied away from providing real-time video for senior commanders to prevent them from micro-managing things, but the lesson of Kosovo is unless you have real-time you will be sidelined."

Yet, UAVs were plagued with reliability problems, as evidenced by a per sortie loss rate that was 285 times higher than manned aircraft. The reported 27 UAVs lost during the 78-day air campaign equated to a per sortie loss rate of 5.7%, as compared with 0.02% for the fighter and bomber force.

Even then, there was no public outcry when one of the UAVs crashed. USAF Chief of Staff General Michael Ryan observed: "[UAVs] go out there and die for their country—and we don't mourn." Toward the end of the campaign, the Serbs had also become proficient in specialized anti-UAV tactics, which had been honed in encounters with UAVs over Bosnia earlier in the 1990s.

From Kosovo to Afghanistan

In the spring of 2000, U.S. interest in Osama bin Laden's activities in Taliban-controlled Afghanistan led to a plan to conduct Predator surveillance missions over the country to gather intelligence.

Basing rights were negotiated with Uzbekistan and surveillance missions began in September 2000. The Predators provided real time imagery of activities in terrorist training camps. On several occasions, Predators tracked what appeared to be the movements of bin Laden and his security entourage. But, in the end, bin Laden's movements were so unpredictable that Predators could not provide an exact location to enable a cruise missile strike. Added to this frustration were concerns about the political upheaval that would ensue. UAV operations ended by mid-October 2000.

CIA officials then considered whether it was possible to conduct armed surveillance missions with the Predators, to improve their chances of attacking bin Laden in the event his whereabouts could be determined. Learning that the USAF had successfully reconfigured the Predator for hunterkiller missions by equipping it with a laser designator and Hellfire missiles, the CIA moved to deploy the armed Predators in the hunt for bin Laden.

With this new capability, Predator controllers then conducted mock hunter-killer missions at a mud complex built in an American desert. "Because of that development," one U.S. official later acknowledged, "we were able to launch our Predator into Afghanistan."

Ultimately, inter-agency disagreements would delay their deployment over the issue of command and control. After the September 11, 2001 terrorist attacks, the issue was quickly resolved and the armed Predators deployed as part of Enduring Freedom.

On 7 October, an armed Predator located the Taliban leader, Mullah Omar, but military leaders were unable to receive approval in time to strike the building with the drone's two Hellfire missiles. Later, in mid-November, a Predator pinpointed the location of senior al Qaeda officials, including the organization's operations chief Muhammed Atef, and relayed real time imagery to military officials. U.S. Navy F/A-18s were quickly dispatched to strike the building, and the Predator used its Hellfire missiles to attack the occupants as they fled the building.

On another occasion, a Predator was cued by a Joint STARS aircraft to monitor a small convoy, which had stopped in front of a hotel for an apparent gathering of al Qaeda officials. U.S. Air Force F-15Es quickly moved into position and attacked the hotel; the Predator then tracked fleeing Taliban vehicles and destroyed them with its Hellfire missiles. In all, Predators are reported to have fired 40 Hellfires during Afghanistan operations.

Aside from imagery sent back to command and control facilities, Predators also beamed imagery directly to aircrew in attack aircraft. One battlefield innovation was to equip AC-130 gunships with on-board monitors for attacks on targets under surveillance.

The results exemplified the potential for increased kill chain compression. On one occasion, in mid-January 2002, a Predator viewed a gathering of suspected al Qaeda fighters near the Zawar Kili cave complex in eastern Afghanistan. An AC-130 gunship was provided with the UAV's television imagery as it approached the area, avoided ground fire, and struck the target. In another operation, a Predator alerted an AC-130 to a threat by providing the gunship with live color video of al Qaeda fighters armed with man-portable anti-aircraft missiles.

Although still in development, the Global Hawk UAV was also deployed to support Afghanistan operations. Global Hawk's wide area surveillance capabilities portend future trends in UAV development.

Compared with the Predator, the Global Hawk features an extended radius of action and deployment options due to a 300% increase in speed (342 knots versus 110 knots); a much larger payload (2,000 lbs. versus 450 pounds); and a more sophisticated sensor suite that includes a powerful synthetic aperture radar as well as high-resolution electro-optical and infrared sensors. The Global Hawk is also capable of orbiting at higher altitudes (65,000 versus 26,000 feet) for a similar period (36 hours versus 40 hours). Finally, the Global Hawk does not require remote piloting from a ground station; its computerized flight control system enables it to take off, orbit and land autonomously. Once in flight, ground controllers simply use satellite data links to alter its orbit.

What General Franks, CENTCOM commander, found particularly noteworthy about the performance of the Global Hawk was its ability to conduct persistent surveillance over a fluid battlefield: "[It] flew sorties approaching 30 hours in duration and imaged over 600 targets during a single mission over Afghanistan."

Together, the Predator and Global Hawk combined to form an extremely effective ISR capability: the highaltitude Global Hawk providing wide-area situational awareness while the low altitude Predator supplied tactical surveillance. Overall, four Predators and two Global Hawks were lost due to enemy action or system failures.

However, the military value of these systems more than compensated for the UAV loss rate. Secretary of Defense Donald Rumsfeld observed in February 2002: "We do not have enough of these aircraft [UAVs]. There isn't a week that goes by that General Myers and I are not confronted by a combatant commander in some part of the world who is asking for additional unmanned aerial vehicles and, in fact, we are forced to deny them because there are simply not enough to go around."

CONCLUSION

What can America's post-Cold War conflicts tell us about the future of war? First, we argued that we could identify, and perhaps learn from lessons from the three major post-Cold War military conflicts. We agree that these wars are sui generis but, based on our analysis, we disagree with those who conclude that the conflicts examined here were so unique that we cannot learn from the collective experience. The United States, at this writing, may be on the verge of launching a military strike against Iraq.

Although such a conflict will certainly not repeat the campaign and consequences of the 1991 war, many similar strategic calculations, military forces, and technological capabilities will exert powerful influences on how the U.S. will conduct military operations against its decade-long nemesis.

Moreover, a retrospective look at how those calculations, forces, and capabilities evolved and were showcased in prior military operations should provide useful insights into the vagaries of future conflicts, large and small, either against Iraq or other foreign enemies.

More to the point, we argued that while the wars examined here were quite different, we could nevertheless point to a combination of strategic, military, and technological thrusts that were manifested in operations Desert Storm, Allied Force, and Enduring Freedom.

On this basis, we proceeded to explore these thrusts, discern salient patterns, and present them here as trends most likely to persist and impact the conduct of future warfare in the early 21st century.

The ensuing analysis was informed by a methodology frequently used in the art of long-range planning and premised on the predictive value of scenario development to identify key factors that might exert powerful shaping influences over future actions. Yet, while most long-range planners ponder alternative futures to build their assessments of the emerging environment, our trend analysis is rooted in factual evidence from three relatively high-intensity post-Cold War conflicts.

With this in mind, our examination of the wars in the Persian Gulf, over Kosovo, and in Afghanistan leads to the following conclusions. Strategically, the U.S. way of warfare, as exhibited over the last decade, is no longer compatible with the clash of interstate armies that prevailed during the Cold War.

Indeed, as opposed to Cold War conceptions of warfare, involving large armies and superpower struggles over geopolitical interests, the strategic centre-of-gravity has shifted eastward toward the vast reaches of Asia.

That shift has been accompanied by a fundamental change in the way the U.S. relates to existing and potential allies: a tendency to favour temporary relationships and seek ad hoc coalition partners for U.S-led military campaigns, with coalition partners valued more for their political and diplomatic support than their participation in military operations.

Meanwhile, our future adversaries (to include rogue states, non-state actors, and possibly a rising peer competitor) are poised to seek ways to undermine the threat and use of U.S. force, with specific aims to exploit perceived U.S. sensitivities to casualties, manipulate international public opinion and, failing that, degrade U.S. military effectiveness on the battlefield.

In parallel, future adversaries can be expected to exploit the multifold dimensions of the access challenge by confounding U.S. abilities to project and sustain military power in the region of conflict. Most ominously, recent events indicate that future adversaries will likely possess, threaten to use, and possibly employ weapons of mass destruction, the mere probability of which will deter some courses of action, limit basing options in theatre, compel U.S. forces to focus first on WMD counterforce missions, and frustrate campaign-level force employment options.

Militarily, we have seen a dramatic shift away from the scripted operational plans that characterized rehearsals for Cold War conflicts, to a very fluid, nonlinear and dynamic battlespace in which targets are generated while attack platforms are en route. Yet the embrace of adaptive planning and dynamic military operations in defense policy circles must also account for factors that will complicate U.S. power projection in the future.

Among them is the extended reach required to strike targets in denied or remote regions of the globe. Added to this is the elusive character of enemy combat forces and, more specifically, ambiguous target sets populated by fleeting targets of opportunity and masked by deception. Offsetting these factors, to some extent, is the order of magnitude increase in situational awareness that enables commanders— local, regional and global—to view the battlespace and intervene in near-real time (particularly when ongoing operations have the potential for collateral damage and political fallout). Trends in battle management indicate that this tendency toward centralized execution is a growing reality.

Finally, the most prominent force employment trends include an increased role for air and naval forces to project power quickly from a distance, a diminished emphasis on slow-moving, heavy ground forces requiring a large regional footprint in favour of agile fixing forces, and continued measures to lower the risk of U.S. casualties.

Technologically, the dominant trend in military conflict has been the use of precision munitions. Using precise weapons not only guarantees striking targets with unprecedented accuracy, but also minimizes the potential for collateral damage and offers the promise of cost-effective force employment options. With that said, however, precision weapons are of little use without precision information.

Therefore, PGMs have been increasingly coupled with improved targeting guidance enabled by a growing number of high-quality sensors, leveraged by stealth and electronic jamming (permitting the penetration of hostile airspace), and facilitated by unmanned vehicles in both ISR and hunter-killer roles.

What policy implications and investment streams are suggested by these trends? While the Analysis Centre has long speculated on the direction and weight of strategic and budgetary vectors for internal Northrop Grumman audiences, we hesitate—lest we evoke images of advocacy—to do so in detail here. Our corporate responsibility is analysis and not business development.

We therefore offer this study as a framework for policy debates on military transformation and related discussions of the conduct of warfare in the early 21st century. A final word of caution, though: while the U.S. has fielded impressive capabilities to meet the military challenges of the immediate post-Cold War era, up to and including the war on terrorism, the road ahead appears ever more challenging, both in terms of the diversity of our future adversaries and their military capabilities. Our trend analysis suggests strongly that, in order to adequately prepare for what is becoming an increasingly hostile security environment, the U.S. must invest in concepts, capabilities, and enabling technologies to sustain its competitive advantages on the future battlefield, all of which were demonstrated to varying degrees in the Gulf War, over the former Yugoslavia, and most recently in Afghanistan.

We have enumerated the most critical force attributes here: access insensitive and persistent; highly survivable; networked and situationally aware; precisely targeted and informed; and increasingly unmanned. In conclusion, based on this trend analysis, the U.S. will be best served by the creation of an agile, access-insensitive military force that can project sustained, precise, and survivable military power across great distances with little preparation or reliance on external political or military support.

BIBLIOGRAPHY

Alger, John I: *The Quest For Victory*, Westport, Greenwood Press, 1982.

Arend, A.: *International Law and the Use of Force,* London, Routledge, 1993.

Arrighi, G.: *The Long Twentieth Century: Money, Power and the Origins of Our Times,* N.Y., Verso Press, 1994.

Bellamy, C.: *Knights in White Armour: The New Art of War and Peace,* London, Random House, 1997.

Bellamy, Christopher: *The future of land warfare,* London, Croom Helm 1987.

Bond, B.: *The Pursuit of Victory: From Napoleon to Saddem Hussein,* Oxford, Oxford Univ. Press, 1996.

Campen, Allen D.: *The first information war,* Fairfax, AFCEA Press, 1992.

Chilcoat, Richard A: *Strategic art: the new discipline for 21st century leaders*, Carlisle Barracks, Strategic Studies Institute, 1995.

Collins, John M.: *Military space forces: the next 50 years,* Washington, Pergamon-Brassey's, 1989.

Damrosch, L.F.: *Law and Force in the New International Order,* Boulder, Westview Press, 1991.

Delanda, M.: *War in the Age of Intelligent Machines,* N.Y., M.I.T. Press, 1991.

DuBois, Edmund L., Wayne P. Hughes, and Lawrence J. Low: *A Concise Theory of Combat,* Institute for Joint Warfare Analysis, Monterey, 1997.

Fitzgerald, Mary C.: *The new revolution in Russian military affairs*, London, Royal United Services Institute for Defence Studies, 1994.

Friedman, G.: *The Future of War: Power, Technology and American World Dominance in the 21st Century,* N.Y., Random House, 1996.

Gray, C.H.: *Postmodern War: The New Politics of Conflict,* N.Y., The Guilford Press, 1997.

Gray, Colin S.: *The American revolution in military affairs : an interim assessment,* Camberley, Eng., Strategic and Combat Studies Institute, 1997.

Holsti, K.: *The State, War, and the State of War,* Cambridge, Cambridge Univ. Press, 1996.

Huntington, S.P.: *The Soldier and the State,* N.Y., Vintage Books, 1964.

Jablonsky, David: *The owl of Minerva flies at twilight : doctrinal change and continuity and the revolution in military affairs,* Carlisle Barracks, US Army War College, 1994.

Janowitz, M.: *The Professional Soldier: A Social and Political Portrait,* N.Y., The Free Press, 1960.

Kipp, Jacob W.: *The Russian military and the revolution in military affairs : a case of the oracle of Delphi or Cassandra?,* Fort Leavenworth, U.S. Army Foreign Military Studies Office, 1995.

Luttwak, E.N.: *Strategy: The Logic of War and Peace,* Cambridge, 1987, Harvard Univ. Press.

McInnes, Colin: *Hot war, Cold War: the British Army's way in warfare 1945-95,* London, Brassey's, 1996.

Metz, Steven and James Kievit: *The revolution in military affairs and conflict short of war,* Carlisle Barracks, U.S. Army War College, 1994.

Metz, Steven: *Armed Conflict in the 21st Century: The information revolution and Post-Modern Warfare,* Carlisle Barracks, Strategic Studies Institute, 2000.

Morton, D.: *A Military History of Canada,* Edmonton, 1985, Hurtig Publishers.

Murray, W.: *The Making of Strategy,* Cambridge, 1994, Cambridge Univ. Press.

O'Connell, Robert L.: *Of Arms and men: a history of war, weapons, and aggression*. New York, Oxford University Press, 1989.

Posen, B.R.: *The Sources of Military Doctrine,* Ithaca, 1984, Cornell Univ. Press.

Rodal, B.: *The Somalia Experience in Strategic Perspective,* Ottawa, 1997, Minister of Public Works.

Rosen, Stephen Peter: *Winning the next war : innovation and the modern military*, Ithaca, Cornell University Press, 1991.

Roseneau, J.: *Along The Domestic-Foreign Frontier,* Cambridge, 1997, Cambridge Univ Press.

Ruggie, J.G.: *Winning the Peace,* N.Y., 1996, Columbia Univ. Press.

Schneider, Barry and Lawrance Grinter: *Battlefield of the future : 21st century warfare issues*, Maxwell AFB, U.S. Air War College, 1995.

Simpkin, Richard E.: *Race to the swift: thoughts on twenty-first century warfare*, London, Brassey's Defence, 1986.

Sloan, Elinor C.: *The Revolution in Military Affairs : implications for Canada and NATO*, Montreal : McGill-Queen's University Press, 2002.

Sloan, Elinor C.: *The United States and the revolution in military affairs,* Ottawa, Directorate of Strategic Analysis, Dept. of National Defence, 1998.

Stanley, G.F.G.: *Canada's Soldiers,* Toronto, 1960, MacMillan Co. Ltd.

Tilford, Earl H.: *The Revolution in Military Affairs: prospects and cautions*, Carlisle Barracks, Strategic Studies Institute, 1995.

Van Creveld, M.: *Technology and War,* N.Y., 1991, The Free Press.

INDEX

A

Air Pollution, 10.
Air Superiority, 264, 267.
Air Warfare, 293.
Airborne Operations, 303.
American Military, 28, 45, 47, 50, 57, 58, 88, 89, 150, 168, 172, 178, 180, 224, 240.
Amplification, 225, 238, 239, 245.
Annihilation, 65, 90.
Application, 56, 62, 90, 94, 134, 135, 138, 148, 175, 187, 192, 196, 268.
Armed Forces, 30, 31, 43, 75, 79, 82, 87, 93, 138, 140, 141, 146, 149, 151, 167, 169, 173, 176, 187, 195, 196, 199, 201, 203, 206, 223, 230, 232.

B

Battleship, 31, 50, 94, 95, 96, 97, 98, 99, 100, 101, 102, 103, 105, 106, 107, 108, 109, 110, 111, 112, 113, 114, 115, 116, 117, 118, 119, 120, 124, 125, 126, 129, 131, 133, 142, 291.
Biological Warfare, 83, 155, 173.

C

Capacity, 9, 19, 24, 143, 186, 187, 188, 189, 203, 212, 216.
Civil Authorities, 177.
Cold War, 9, 28, 29, 32, 34, 39, 46, 49, 52, 53, 54, 56, 69, 72, 79, 80, 81, 83, 84, 93, 134, 137, 140, 151, 153, 154, 157, 158, 159, 160, 161, 162, 163, 164, 165, 172, 176, 178, 183, 184, 187, 190, 192, 194, 195, 196, 197, 199, 201, 202, 206, 207, 223, 224, 226, 229, 230, 232, 233, 237, 238, 239, 241, 242, 245, 264, 269, 271, 278, 279, 287, 291, 299, 300, 309, 310, 311, 312.
Combat Power, 150, 246, 280, 290.
Communication, 7, 14, 30, 45, 148, 166, 167, 170, 263, 275.
Composition, 158, 176.
Concentration, 11, 91.
Cooperation, 10, 65, 93, 155, 213, 244, 253.

D

Democracy, 69, 73, 80.

Destruction, 10, 29, 39, 43, 47, 52, 63, 78, 80, 81, 84, 88, 92, 124, 134, 137, 158, 161, 164, 168, 173, 175, 176, 177, 179, 180, 182, 184, 195, 225, 239, 246, 251, 253, 268, 269, 274, 287, 311.
Dimension, 45, 48, 138, 142, 161, 173, 183, 191, 247, 250, 251.
Dissemination, 2, 6, 14.
Dynamics, 6, 11, 14, 15, 86, 235.

E

Economy, 29, 36, 37, 38, 40, 48, 51, 175, 182, 240.
Employment, 142, 143, 178, 222, 230, 237, 238, 248, 250, 253, 269, 270, 277, 278, 292, 293, 311, 312.
Evolution, 8, 9, 60, 63, 64, 66, 71, 103, 109, 134.

F

Flexibility, 31, 54, 96, 176, 177, 186, 305.
Freedom, 55, 63, 92, 134, 185, 191, 226, 230, 231, 237, 248, 249, 258, 259, 270, 274, 275, 281, 282, 288, 292, 303, 304, 307, 310.
Future War, 8, 28, 31, 32, 33, 60, 66, 68, 71, 74, 82, 83, 130, 224, 240, 245.

G

Guidance, 47, 178, 226, 228, 231, 262, 271, 274, 276, 278, 282, 284, 286, 292, 294, 295, 303, 304, 312.
Gulf War, 39, 45, 52, 58, 75, 79, 81, 82, 86, 109, 113, 116, 119, 120, 125, 129, 133, 142, 144, 145, 150, 168, 172, 182, 188, 191, 193, 203, 226, 227, 228, 229, 231, 235, 236, 237, 244, 245, 247, 252, 260, 263, 264, 265, 266, 268, 269, 271, 273, 275, 276, 278, 279, 282, 283, 287, 290, 291, 292, 293, 294, 295, 296, 297, 298, 300, 302, 303, 304, 305, 306, 313.

H

Helicopters, 123, 265, 267.

I

Infrastructure, 15, 48, 140, 167, 180, 190, 215, 225, 229, 240, 245, 246, 247, 250, 251, 257, 303.
Initiative, 157, 176.
Investment, 5, 24, 38, 228, 233, 240, 245, 251, 304, 312.

J

Joint Operations, 91, 150.

K

Kingfisher, 107, 122, 123.

L

Language, 64, 196.
Leadership, 5, 16, 23, 27, 34, 44, 47, 49, 156, 168, 189, 190, 232, 261, 269, 277, 285.
Logistics, 5, 17, 78, 120, 123, 148, 214, 246.

M

Management, 3, 4, 15, 27, 93, 131, 132, 148, 149, 176, 177, 207, 225, 236, 271, 276, 297, 312.
Methodology, 62, 150, 223, 232, 233, 234, 310.
Missions, 8, 9, 10, 12, 20, 22, 23, 27, 33, 70, 87, 88, 93, 113, 149, 228, 247, 266, 274, 278, 281, 284, 287, 288, 298, 304, 305, 306, 307, 311.

N

Network, 15, 30, 40, 77, 94, 143, 206, 227, 250, 252, 263, 269, 278, 290, 296, 302.
Nuclear Future, 209, 214.
Nuclear Weapons, 35, 37, 46, 135, 136, 137, 140, 141, 142, 151, 152, 154, 158, 159, 160, 162, 163, 172, 177, 178, 179, 180, 183, 184, 185, 187, 188, 195, 209, 210, 212, 216, 217, 218, 220, 221, 222, 264, 268, 269.

O

Observation, 62, 104, 125, 231, 236, 279.
Organisation, 206.

P

Peace, 8, 9, 10, 31, 65, 66, 79, 80, 85, 89, 147, 148, 153, 162, 193, 196, 199, 201, 202, 203, 204, 206, 207, 208, 229, 242.
Perspectives, 60, 62.
Politics, 37, 54, 79, 80, 82, 89, 90, 94, 154, 158, 163, 207, 215, 246, 276.
Principles, 61, 63, 65, 68, 139, 288.
Protection, 13, 42, 47, 85, 93, 95, 97, 98, 102, 103, 117, 121, 122, 131, 132, 176, 188, 191, 262, 287, 300, 301.

R

Radar, 124, 126, 127, 128, 132, 265, 266, 267, 268, 273, 277, 281, 291, 296, 297, 298, 299, 301, 305, 308.
Relationship, 39, 61, 66, 67, 145, 177, 180, 183, 186, 188, 241.
Research, 15, 21, 22, 23, 26, 27, 69, 141, 154, 165, 178, 179, 209, 214, 221, 222, 230, 234, 252, 269.

S

Seahawk, 123.
Security, 12, 18, 28, 30, 31, 32, 33, 34, 37, 38, 39, 41, 42, 43, 44, 46, 47, 50, 52, 55, 56, 57, 58, 59, 68, 69, 75, 77, 78, 79, 80, 83, 84, 85, 87, 93, 94, 134, 136, 141, 147, 151, 155, 156, 157, 158, 162, 163, 171, 174, 175, 177, 179, 183, 187, 190, 192, 193, 194, 195, 196, 197, 198, 207, 209, 210, 213, 214, 215, 218, 219, 224, 229, 234, 237, 238, 242, 307, 313.
Socialism, 65.

Society, 11, 51, 62, 65, 76, 77, 80, 81, 86, 92, 93, 271.
Special Forces, 31, 56, 245, 247, 284.
Structure, 2, 5, 8, 16, 17, 22, 25, 27, 32, 45, 50, 68, 77, 84, 122, 149, 159, 196, 206, 228, 251, 278, 297, 300.

T

Technology, 3, 4, 5, 6, 7, 8, 11, 12, 17, 19, 20, 22, 24, 25, 28, 29, 30, 32, 42, 45, 47, 54, 57, 67, 70, 71, 72, 75, 77, 78, 79, 80, 82, 88, 90, 92, 99, 121, 127, 134, 137, 138, 139, 140, 141, 142, 143, 144, 146, 147, 149, 150, 158, 164, 165, 166, 167, 169, 170, 171, 181, 182, 183, 201, 211, 218, 219, 228, 230, 235, 238, 244, 272, 274, 276, 277, 284, 286, 290, 294, 298, 299.
Troops, 79, 85, 91, 113, 123, 133, 136, 143, 147, 148, 167, 201, 235, 242, 253, 286.

W

Warfare, 8, 11, 12, 18, 28, 30, 31, 34, 35, 39, 44, 47, 48, 50, 61, 62, 63, 66, 70, 71, 72, 75, 76, 78, 79, 80, 81, 82, 83, 84, 85, 86, 88, 89, 90, 91, 92, 109, 113, 118, 126, 128, 131, 134, 136, 137, 138, 139, 140, 141, 142, 143, 144, 145, 146, 147, 148, 151, 155, 164, 168, 169, 173, 174, 183, 187, 191, 192, 193, 195, 196, 197, 203, 205, 206, 223, 224, 225, 227, 228, 230, 232, 233, 234, 235, 237, 238, 242, 246, 266, 269, 270, 271, 279, 284, 286, 290, 293, 296, 299, 300, 304, 310, 312.
Warfighting, 6, 12, 31, 50, 85, 130, 235, 241, 252, 297.
Weapons, 7, 8, 10, 11, 29, 35, 37, 39, 43, 46, 47, 52, 68, 71, 78, 80, 81, 87, 88, 91, 92, 106, 118, 120, 122, 128, 130, 134, 135, 136, 137, 140, 141, 142, 143, 144, 146, 151, 152, 153, 154, 155, 156, 158, 159, 160, 161, 162, 163, 164, 166, 167, 168, 169, 170, 171, 172, 173, 174, 175, 176, 177, 178, 179, 180, 181, 182, 183, 184, 185, 187, 188, 192, 193, 194, 195, 196, 197, 201, 204, 209, 210, 212, 216, 217, 218, 220, 221, 222, 225, 227, 231, 232, 235, 238, 239, 243, 244, 246, 248, 250, 251, 252, 253, 255, 256, 258, 261, 262, 263, 264, 268, 269, 271, 281, 283, 284, 287, 288, 289, 290, 291, 292, 293, 294, 295, 296, 301, 303, 311, 312.

❑❑❑